MAGDALEN COLLEGE, OXFORD.

# THE WORKS

OF

# JOSEPH ADDISON,

INCLUDING

THE WHOLE CONTENTS OF BP. HURD'S EDITION, WITH LETTERS AND OTHER PIECES NOT FOUND IN ANY PREVIOUS COLLECTION; AND MACAULAY'S ESSAY ON HIS LIFE AND WORKS.

EDITED,

WITH CRITICAL AND EXPLANATORY NOTES

BY GEORGE WASHINGTON GREENE.

"No whiter page than Addison remains,
He from the taste obscene reclaims our youth,
And sets the passions on the side of truth;
Forms the soft bosom with the gentlest art,
And pours each human virtue thro' the heart."—POPE

IN SIX VOLUMES.

VOL. III.

PHILADELPHIA:
J. B. LIPPINCOTT & CO.
1870.

# TABLE OF CONTENTS.

## INTRODUCTORY REMARKS.

Queen Anne died on the first of August, 1714, and was succeeded by George Ist, whose accession was the signal for the fall of the Tory administration. The Whigs returned to power, and Addison with them. In the following year an insurrection in favor of the Pretender broke out, first in Scotland under the Earl of Mar, and then in England itself. Its fatal results and the vindictive cruelty of the new king are well known to every reader of history. It was on this occasion that Addison wrote the 'Freeholder,' the most elaborate of his political writings, and one of the noblest monuments of his genius.

Of this work Johnson says: "This was undertaken in defence of the established government, sometimes with argument and sometimes with mirth. In argument he had many equals: but his humour was singular and matchless. Bigotry itself must be delighted with the Tory Fox Hunter.

"There are, however, some strokes less elegant and less decent: such as the Pretender's journal, in which one topic of ridicule is his poverty This mode of abuse had been employed by Milton against Charles II.

> ————" *Jacobaei*
> Centum, exulantis viscera marsupii regis."

And Oldmixon delights to tell of some alderman of London, that he had more money than the exiled princes: but that which might be expected from Milton's savageness or Oldmixon's meanness was not suitable to the delicacy of Addison.

"Steele thought the humour of the *Freeholder* too nice and gentle for such noisy times; and is reported to have said that the ministry made use of a lute, when they should have called for a trumpet."—V. Johnson's Lives of the Poets.—Addison.

Johnson, who was a Jacobite at heart, and could illy bear a sarcasm upon the exiled family, has confounded the 'annals of the Pretender's reign' in No. 83, with the 'journal of a rebel' in No. 3.

Swift's remarks upon the Freeholder are so characteristic, that I give them separately from Scott's edition.

Drake, an enthusiastic admirer of Addison, speaks of the "Freeholder" in still higher terms than Johnson:—

"The *Freeholder*, which has been justly termed a *political Spectator*, stands at the head of its class, and was written by our author to evince the enormity of rebellion, and to repel the prejudices of ignorance and faction. It commenced December 23d, 1715; was published every Friday and Monday, and, having reached fifty-five numbers, closed on the 29th of June, 1716."

"Though in this work Addison was entirely unassisted, every page indicates an unwearied spirit. The same elegance and sweetness of style, the same humour and allegoric vein of description, which distinguished his former periodical writings, are discoverable in these essays. Political periodical papers, which have been extremely numerous in this country, have seldom survived the occasion which gave them birth. Who now enquires for the productions of Welwood or L'Estrange? Even the *Freeholder*, owing to the polemical nature of its subject, and notwithstanding its beauty of style and fecundity of illustration, is seldom read through. It possesses, however, some delineations, which, being exact copies from nature, are independent of local circumstances, and will live for ever. Of these the portrait of the *Tory Fox-hunter*, with which, as Johnson observes, 'Bigotry itself must be delighted,' is so exquisitely drawn, that I purpose introducing it with a few observations in the Essay on the *Humour* of Addison.

"If the literary merit of the *Freeholder* be great, its political moderation is entitled to no inferior encomium. At a period when scurrility and abuse were thought more efficient, in proportion as they were keen and bitter, this work presented a specimen of what urbanity combined with wit and argument might effect. Though Steele is said to have declared, that the ministry in employing Addison had chosen a lute, when they should have selected a trumpet, the *Freeholder*, it is acknowledged, proved of essential service to the government, and contributed much towards the promotion of its tranquillity and establishment."—G.

# THE FREEHOLDER.[a]

No. 1. FRIDAY, DECEMBER, 23, 1715.

Rara temporum felicitas, ubi sentire quæ velis, et quæ sentias dicere licet.—Tacit.

The arguments of an author lose a great deal of their weight, when we are persuaded that he only writes for argument's sake, and has no real concern in the cause which he espouses. This is the case of one, who draws his pen in the defence of property without having any; except, perhaps, in the copy of a libel, or a ballad. One is apt to suspect, that the passion for liberty, which appears in a Grub-street patriot, arises only from his apprehen-

[a] It is but justice to a great writer, to distinguish between his hasty, and his deliberate compositions; between such of his works, as he had planned at his leisure, and finished with care, and such as he was called upon to furnish, on the sudden, not with a view to his own fame, but to the discharge of some occasional duty, which, a present emergency, or his character and station in life, imposed upon him. Such was apparently the case of the *Freeholder;* a set of periodical essays, undertaken in the heat of the rebellion in 1715, and with the best purpose of reconciling an abused people to the new succession; at a time when the writer was deeply engaged in public business, and had scarce the leisure to produce these papers so fast, as they were demanded from him. For it was important, in that conjuncture, that the minds of men should be calmed and softened by some immediate applications; and the general good taste of that age, made it expedient that such applications should be administered, not by an ordinary hand, but by the most polite and popular of our writers.

If these considerations be allowed their just weight, *The Freeholder* will be read with pleasure, and must even be thought to do no small credit to its author, though it be not always written with that force, or polished every where up to that perfect grace, which we admire so much in the *Tatler*, *Spectator*, and *Guardian.*

sions of a gaol; and that, whatever he may pretend, he does not write to secure, but to get something of his own. Should the government be overturned, he has nothing to lose but an old standish.

I question not but the reader will conceive a respect for the author of this paper, from the title of it; since he may be sure, I am so considerable a man, that I cannot have less than forty shillings a year.

I have rather chosen this title than any other, because it is what I most glory in, and what most effectually calls to my mind the happiness of that government under which I live. As a British freeholder, I should not scruple taking place of a French marquis; and when I see one of my countrymen amusing himself in his little cabbage-garden, I naturally look upon him as a greater person than the owner of the richest vineyard in Champagne.

The House of Commons is the representative of men in my condition. I consider myself as one who[a] give my consent to every law which passes: a freeholder in our government being of the nature of a citizen of Rome in that famous commonwealth; who, by the election of a tribune, had a kind of remote voice in every law that was enacted. So that a freeholder is but one remove from a legislator, and for that reason ought to stand up in the defence of those laws, which are in some degree of his own making. For such is the nature of our happy constitution, that the bulk of the people virtually give their approbation to every thing they are bound to obey, and prescribe to themselves those rules by which they are to walk.

At the same that I declare I am a freeholder, I do not exclude myself from any other title. A freeholder may be either a

[a] *Who* refers to, *one*, and not to *I*. He should then have said—*who gives his* consent.

voter, or a knight of the shire; a wit, or a fox-hunter; a scholar, or a soldier; an alderman, or a courtier; a patriot, or a stock-jobber. But I chuse to be distinguished by this denomination, as the freeholder is the basis of all other titles. Dignities may be grafted upon it; but this is the substantial stock, that conveys to them their life, taste, and beauty; and, without which, they are no more than blossoms, that would fall away with every shake of wind.[b]

And here I cannot but take occasion to congratulate my country upon the increase of this happy tribe of men, since, by the wisdom of the present parliament, I find the race of freeholders spreading into the remotest corners of the island. I mean that act which passed in the late session for the encouragement of loyalty in Scotland: by which it is provided, 'That all and every vassal and vassals in Scotland, who shall continue peaceable, and in dutiful allegiance to his majesty, his heirs, and successors, holding lands or tenements of any offender (guilty of high-treason) who holds such lands or tenements immediately of the crown, shall be vested and seized, and are hereby enacted and ordained to hold the said lands or tenements of his majesty, his heirs, and successors, in fee and heritage for ever, by such manner of holding, as any such offender held such lands or tenements of the crown,' &c.

By this means it will be in the power of a Highlander to be at all times a good tenant, without being a rebel; and to deserve the character of a faithful servant, without thinking himself obliged to follow his master to the gallows.

How can we sufficiently extol the goodness of his present majesty, who is not willing to have a single slave in his dominions! or enough to rejoice in the exercise of that loyalty, which, in-

[b] *Shake of wind* Better, *blast*, or, *breath*.—We say, a *shake* in music, but in nothing else

stead of betraying a man into the most ignominious servitude, (as it does in some of our neighbouring kingdoms) entitles him to the highest privileges of freedom and property! It is now to be hoped, that we shall have few vassals, but to the laws of our country.

When these men have a taste of property, they will naturally love that constitution from which they derive so great a blessing. There is an unspeakable pleasure in calling any thing one's own. A freehold, though it be but in ice and snow, will make the owner pleased in the possession, and stout in the defence of it; and is a very proper reward of our allegiance to our present king, who (by an unparalleled instance of goodness in a sovereign and infatuation in subjects) contends for the freedom of his people against themselves; and will not suffer many of them to fall into a state of slavery, which they are bent upon with so much eagerness and obstinacy.

A freeholder of Great Britain is bred with an aversion to every thing that tends to bring him under a subjection to the arbitrary will of another. Of this we find frequent instances in all our histories; where the persons, whose characters are the most amiable, and strike us with the highest veneration, are those who stood up manfully against the invasions of civil liberty, and the complicated tyranny which popery imposes upon our bodies, our fortunes, and our minds. What a despicable figure then must the present mock-patriots make in the eyes of posterity, who venture to be hanged, drawn, and quartered, for the ruin of those civil rights which their ancestors rather than part with, chose to be cut to pieces in the field of battle? And what an opinion will after-ages entertain of their religion who bid fair for a gibbet, by endeavouring to bring in a superstition, which their forefathers perished in flames to keep out?

But how instructive soever the folly of these men may prove

to future times, it will be my business more immediately to consult the happiness of the age in which I live. And since so many profligate writers have endeavoured to varnish over a bad cause, I shall do all in my power to recommend a good one, which indeed requires no more than barely to explain what it is. While many of my gallant countrymen are employed in pursuing rebels half discomfited through the consciousness of their guilt, I shall labour to improve those victories to the good of my fellow-subjects; by carrying on our successes over the minds of men, and by reconciling them to the cause of their king, their country, and their religion.

To this end, I shall in the course of this paper (to be published every Monday and Friday) endeavour to open the eyes of my countrymen to their own interest, to shew them the privileges of an English freeholder, which they enjoy in common with myself, and to make them sensible how these blessings are secured to us by his majesty's title, his administration, and his personal character.

I have only one request to make to my readers, that they will peruse these papers with the same candour and impartiality in which they are written; and shall hope for no other prepossession in favour of them, than what one would think should be natural to every man, a desire to be happy, and a good will towards those, who are the instruments of making them so.

## No. 2. MONDAY, DECEMBER 26.

Non de domino, sed de parente loquimur. Intelligamus ergo bona nostra, dignosque nos illius usu probemus; atque identidem cogitemus, si majus principibus præstemus obsequium, qui servitute civium, quam qui libertate lætantur. PLIN.

HAVING in my first paper set forth the happiness of my station as a freeholder of Great Britain, and the nature of that property which is secured to me by the laws of my country; I cannot forbear considering, in the next place, that person who is intrusted with the guardianship and execution of those laws. I have lived in one reign, when the prince, instead of invigorating the laws of our country, or giving them their proper course, assumed a power of dispensing with them: and in another, when the sovereign was flattered by a set of men into a persuasion, that the regal authority was unlimited and uncircumscribed. In either of these cases good laws are at best but a dead letter; and by showing the people how happy they ought to be, only serve to aggravate the sense of their oppressions.

We have the pleasure at this time to see a king upon the throne who hath too much goodness to wish for any power, that does not enable him to promote the welfare of his subjects; and too much wisdom to look upon those as his friends, who would make their court to him by the profession of an obedience, which they never practised, and which has always proved fatal to those princes, who have put it to the trial. His majesty gave a proof of his sovereign virtues, before he came to the exercise of them in this kingdom. His inclination to justice led him to rule his German subjects in the same manner, that our constitution directs him to govern the English. He regarded those which are our civil liberties, as the natural rights of mankind; and therefore indulged them to a people, who pleaded no other claim to them than from his known goodness and humanity. This experience of a good prince, before we had the happiness to enjoy him, must give great satisfaction to every thinking man, who considers how apt sovereignty is to deprave human nature; and how many of our own princes made very ill figures upon the throne, who, before they ascended it, were the favourites of the people.

What gives us the greatest security in the conduct of so excellent a prince is, that consistency of behaviour, whereby he inflexibly pursues those measures which appear the most just and equitable. As he hath the character of being the most prudent in laying proper schemes; he is no less remarkable for being steady in accomplishing what he has once concerted. Indeed, if we look into the history of his present majesty, and reflect upon that wonderful series of successes which have attended him, I think they cannot be ascribed to any thing so much as to his uniformity and firmness of mind, which has always discovered itself in his proceedings. It was by this that he surmounted those many difficulties which lay in the way to his succession; and by which, we have reason to hope, he will daily make all opposition fall before him. The fickle and unsteady politics of our late British monarchs, have been the perpetual source of those dissensions and animosities which have made the nation unhappy: whereas the constant and unshaken temper of his present majesty, must have a natural tendency to the peace of his government, and the unanimity of his people.

Whilst I am enumerating the public virtues of our sovereign, which are so conducive to the advantage of those who are to obey him, I cannot but take notice, that his majesty was bred up from his infancy with a love to this our nation, under a princess, who was the most accomplished woman of her age, and particularly famous for her affection to the English. Our countrymen were dear to him, before there was any prospect of their being his subjects; and every one knows, that nothing recommended a man so much to the distinguishing civilities of his court, as the being born in Great Britain.

To the fame of his majesty's civil virtues, we may add the reputation he has acquired by his martial achievements. It is observed by Sir William Temple, that the English are particu larly fond of a king who is valiant; upon which account his ma jesty has a title to all the esteem that can be paid the most warlike prince ; though at the same time, for the good of his subjects, he studies to decline all occasions of military glory : and chuses rather to be distinguished as the father, than as the captain of his people. I am glad his rebellious subjects are too inconsiderable to put him upon exerting that courage and conduct, which raised him so great a reputation in Hungary and the Morea, when he fought against the enemies of Christianity ; and in Germany and Flanders, where he commanded against the great disturber of the peace of Europe. One would think there was reason for the opinion of those, who make personal courage to be an hereditary virtue, when we see so many instances of it in the line of Brunswick.

To go no farther back than the time of our present king, where can we find among the sovereign houses of Europe, any other family that has furnished so many persons of distinguished fortitude? Three of his majesty's brothers have fallen gloriously in the field, fighting against the enemies of their native country : and the bravery of his royal highness, the Prince of Wales, is still fresh in our memory, who fought, with the spirit of his father, at the battle of Audenarde, when the children of France, and the Pretender, fled before him.

I might here take notice of his majesty's more private virtues, but have rather chosen to remind my countrymen of the public parts of his character, which are supported by such incontestable facts as are universally known and acknowledged

Having thus far considered our happiness in his majesty's civil and military character, I cannot forbear pleasing myself with regarding him in the view of one, who has been always fortunate. Cicero recommends Pompey under this particular head to the Romans, with whom the character of being fortunate was so popular, that several of their emperors gave it a place among their titles. Good fortune is often the reward of virtue, and as often the effect of prudence. And whether it proceeds from either of these, or from both together, or whatever may be the cause of it, every one is naturally pleased to see his interests conducted by a person who is used to good success. The establishment of the electoral dignity in his majesty's family, was a work reserved for him finally to accomplish. A large accession of dominion fell to him, by his succeeding to the dukedom of Zell, whereby he became one of the greatest princes of Germany; and one of the most powerful persons, that ever stood next heirs to the throne of Great Britain. The duchy of Bremen, and the bishopric of Osnaburg, have considerably strengthened his interests in the empire, and given a great additional weight to the Protestant cause. But the most remarkable interpositions of Providence, in favor of him, have appeared in removing those seemingly invincible obstacles to his succession; in taking away, at so critical a juncture, the person who might have proved a dangerous enemy; in con founding the dangerous and open attempts of his traitorous subjects; and in giving him the delightful prospect of transmitting his power through a numerous and still increasing progeny.

Upon the whole, it is not to be doubted but every wise and honest subject will concur with Providence, in promoting the glory and happiness of his present majesty, who is endowed with all those royal virtues, that will naturally secure to us the national blessings, which ought to be dear and valuable to a free people.

## No. 3. FRIDAY, DECEMBER 30.

Quibus otio vel magnifice, vel molliter vivere copia erat, incerta pro certis, bellum quam pacem, malebant. SALL.

EVERY one knows, that it is usual for a French officer, who can write and read, to set down all the occurrences of a campaign, in which he pretends to have been personally concerned; and to publish them under the title of his 'Memoirs,' when most of his fellow-soldiers are dead that might have contradicted any of his matters of fact. Many a gallant young fellow has been killed in battle, before he came to the third page of his secret history; when several, who have taken more care of their persons, have lived to fill a whole volume with their military performances, and to astonish the world with such instances of their bravery, as had escaped the notice of every body else. One of our late Preston heroes had, it seems, resolved upon this method of doing himself justice: and, had he not been nipped in the bud, might have made a very formidable figure in his own works, among posterity. A friend of mine, who had the pillage of his pockets, has made me a present of the following memoirs, which he desires me to accept as a part of the spoils of the rebels. I have omitted the introduction, as more proper for the inspection of a secretary of state; and shall only set down so much of the memoirs, as seem to be a faithful narrative of that wonderful expedition, which drew upon it the eyes of all Europe.

"Having thus concerted measures for a rising, we had a general meeting over a bowl of punch. It was here proposed, by one of the wisest among us, to draw up a manifesto, setting forth the grounds and motives of our taking arms: for, as he observed, there had never yet been an insurrection in England, where the leaders had not thought themselves obliged to give some reasons for it. To this end, we laid our heads together to consider what grievances the nation had suffered under the reign of King George. After having spent some hours upon this subject, without being able to discover any, we unanimously agreed to rebel first, and to find out reasons for it afterwards. It was, indeed, easy to guess at several grievances of a private nature, which influenced particular persons. One of us had spent his fortune: another was a younger brother: a third had the incumbrance of a father upon his estate. But that which principally disposed us in favor of the Chevalier was, that most of the company had been obliged to take the abjuration oath against their will. Being at length thoroughly inflamed with zeal and punch, we resolved to take horse the next morning, which we did accordingly, having been joined by a considerable reinforcement of Roman Catholics, whom we could rely upon, as knowing them to be the best tories in the nation, and avowed enemies to Presbyterianism. We were, likewise, joined by a very useful associate, who was a fiddler by profession, and brought in with him a body of lusty young fellows whom he had tweedled into the service. About the third day of our march, I was made a colonel; though I must needs say I gained my commission by my horse's virtues, not my own; having leaped over a six-bar gate at the head of the cavalry. My general, who is a discerning man, hereupon gave me a regiment; telling me, 'He did not question but I would do the like when I came to the enemy's pallisadoes.' We pursued our march, with much intrepidity, through two or three open towns, to the great terror of the market-people, and the miscarriage of half a dozen big-bellied women. Notwithstanding the magistracy was generally against us, we could discover many friends among our spectators; particularly in two or three balconies, which were filled with several tawdry females, who are known by the ancient name of Harlots. This sort of ladies received us every where with great demonstrations of joy, and promised to assist us with their prayers. After these signal successes in the north of England, it was thought advisable, by our general, to proceed towards our Scotch confederates. During our first day's march, I amused myself with considering what post I should accept of under James the third, when we had put him in possession of the British dominions. Being a great lover of country sports, I absolutely determined not to be a minister of state, nor to be fobbed off with a garter; until at length, passing by a noble country-seat, which belongs to a whig, I resolved to beg it; and pleased myself, the remainder of the day, with several alterations I intended to make in it. For though the situation was very delightful, I neither liked the front of the house, nor the avenues that led to it. We were, indeed, so confident of success, that I found most of my fellow-soldiers were taken up with imaginations of the same nature. There had like to have been a duel between two of our subalterns upon a dispute, which of them should be governor of Portsmouth. A popish priest, about the same time gave great offence to a Northumberland squire, whom he threatened to excommunicate, if he did not give up to him the church-lands, which his family had usurped ever since the reformation. In short, every man had cut out a place for himself in his own thoughts; so that I could reckon up in our little army, two or three lord-treasurers, half a dozen secretaries of state, and at least a score of lords-justices in Eyre, for each side of Trent. We pursued our march through several villages, which we drank dry, making proclamation at our entrance, in the name of James the third, against all concealments of ale and brandy. Being very much fatigued with the action of a whole week, it was agreed to rest on Sunday, when we heard a most excellent sermon. Our chaplain insisted principally upon two heads. Under the first he proved to us that the breach of public oaths is no perjury; and nuder the second, expounded to us the nature of non-resistance; which might be interpreted from the Hebrew, to signify either loyalty or rebellion, according as his sovereign bestowed his favours and preferments. He concluded with exhorting us, in a most pathetic manner, to purge the land by wholesome severities, and to propagate sound principles by fire and sword. We set forward the next day towards our friends at Kelso; but by the way had like to have lost our general, and some of our most active officers. For a fox unluckily crossing the road, drew off a considerable detachment, who clapped spurs to their horses, and pursued him with whoops and halloos, till we had lost sight of them. A covey of partridges springing in our front, put our infantry into disorder on the same day. It was not long after this, that we were joined by our friends from the other side of the Frith. Upon the junction of the two corps, our spies brought us word that they discovered a great cloud of dust at some distance; upon which we sent out a party to reconnoitre. They returned to us with intelligence, that the dust was raised by a great drove of black cattle. This news was not a little welcome to us, the army of both nations being very hungry. We quickly formed ourselves, and received orders for the attack, with positive instructions to give no quarter. Every thing was executed with so much good order, that we made a very plentiful supper. We had, three days after, the same success against a flock of sheep, which we were forced to eat with great precipitation, having received advice of General Carpenter's march as we were at dinner. Upon this alarm, we made incredible stretches towards the south, with a design to gain the fastnesses of Preston. We did little remarkable in our way, except setting fire to a few houses, and frighting an old woman into fits. We had now got a long day's march of the enemy; and meeting with a considerable refreshment of October, all the officers assembled over it, among whom were several Popish lords and gentlemen, who toasted many loyal healths and confusions, and wept very plentifully for the danger of the church. We sat till midnight, and at our parting resolved to give the enemy battle; but the next morning changed our resolutions, and prosecuted our march with indefatigable speed. We were no sooner arrived upon the frontiers of Cumberland, but we saw a great body of militia drawn up in array against us. Orders were given to halt: and a council of war was immediately called, wherein we agreed, with that great unanimity which was so remarkable among us on these occasions, to make a retreat. But before we could give the word, the train bands, taking advantage of our delay, fled first. We arrived at Preston without any memorable adventure; where, after having formed many barricades, and prepared for a vigorous resistance, upon the approach of the king's troops under General Wills, who was used to the outlandish way of making war, we thought it high time to put in practice that passive-obedience, in which our party so much glories, and which I would advise them to stick to for the future."

Such was the end of this rebellion; which, in all probability, will not only tend to the safety of our constitution, but the preservation of the game

---

## NO. 4. MONDAY, JANUARY 2, 1716.

Ne se mulier extra virtutum cogitationes, extraque bellorum casus putet, ipsis incipientis matrimonii auspiciis admonetur, venire se laborum periculorumque sociam, idem in pace, idem in prælio passuram ausuramque. Sic vivendum, sic pereundum. Tacit.

It is with great satisfaction I observe, that the women of our island, who are the most eminent for virtue and good sense, are in the interest of the present government. As the fair sex very much recommend the cause they are engaged in, it would be no small misfortune to a sovereign, though he had all the male part of the nation on his side, if he did not find himself king of the most beautiful half of his subjects. Ladies are always of great use to the party they espouse, and never fail to win over numbers to it. Lovers, according to Sir William Petty's computation, make at least the third part of the sensible men of the British nation; and it has been an uncontroverted maxim in all ages, that though a husband is sometimes a stubborn sort of a creature, a lover is always at the devotion of his mistress. By this means, it lies in the power of every fine woman, to secure at least half a dozen able-bodied men men to his majesty's service. The female world are, likewise, indispensably necessary in the best causes, to manage the controversial part of them, in which no man of tolerable breeding is ever able to refute them. Arguments out of a pretty mouth are unanswerable.

It is, indeed, remarkable, that the inferior tribe of common women, who are a dishonour to their sex, have, in most reigns, been the professed sticklers for such as have acted in opposition to the true interest of the nation. The most numerous converts in King James's reign, were particularly noted to be of this kind. I can give no other reason for such a behaviour, unless it be, that it is not for the advantage of these female adventurers, the laws of the land should take place, and that they know Bridewell is a part of our constitution.

There are many reasons why the women of Great Britain should be on the side of the Freeholder, and enemies to the person who would bring in arbitrary government and popery. As there are several of our ladies, who amuse themselves in the reading of travels, they cannot but take notice, what uncomfortable lives those of their own sex lead, where passive-obedience is professed and practised in its utmost perfection. In those coun tries, the men have no property but in their wives, who are the slaves to slaves: every married woman being subject to a domestic tyrant, that requires from her the same vassalage which he pays to his sultan. If the ladies would seriously consider the evil consequences of arbitrary power, they would find, that it spoils the shape of the foot in China, where the barbarous politics of the men so diminish the basis of the female figure, as to unqualify a woman for an evening walk or country-dance. In the East-Indies, a widow, who has any regard to her character, throws herself into the flames of her husband's funeral pile, to shew, forsooth, that she is faithful and loyal to the memory of her deceased lord. In Persia, the daughters of Eve, as they call them, are reckoned in the inventory of their goods and chattels: and it is a usual thing, when a man sells a bale of silk, or a drove of camels, to toss half a dozen women into the bargain Through all the dominions of the Great Turk, a woman thinks herself happy, if she can get but the twelfth share of a husband, and is thought of no manner of use in the creation, but to keep up a proper number of slaves for the commander of the faithful. I need not set forth the ill usage which the fair ones meet with, in those despotic governments that lie nearer us. Every one hath heard of the several ways of locking up women in Spain and Italy; where, if there is any power lodged in any of the sex, it is not among the young and the beautiful, whom nature seems to have formed for it, but among the old and withered matrons, known by the frightful name of *gouvernantes* and *duennas*. If any should alledge the freedoms indulged to the French ladies, he must own that these are owing to the natural gallantry of the people, not to their form of government, which excludes, by its very constitution, every female from power, as naturally unfit to hold the sceptre of that kingdom.

Women ought, in reason, to be no less averse to popery than

to arbitrary power. Some merry authors have pretended to demonstrate, that the Roman Catholic religion could never spread in a nation where women would have more modesty than to expose their innocent liberties to a confessor. Others of the same turn have assured us, that the fine British complexion, which is so peculiar to our ladies, would suffer very much from a fish-diet: and that a whole Lent would give such a sallowness to the celebrated beauties of this island, as would scarce make them distinguishable from those of France. I shall only leave to the serious consideration of my country-women, the danger any of them might have been in, (had popery been our national religion,) of being forced by their relations to a state of perpetual virginity. The most blooming toast in the island might have been a nun; and many a lady, who is now a mother of fine children, condemned to a condition of life, disagreeable to herself, and unprofitable to the world. To this I might add, the melancholy objects they would be daily entertained with, of several sightly men delivered over to an inviolable celibacy. Let a young lady imagine to herself the brisk embroidered officer, who now makes love to her with so agreeable an air, converted into a monk; or the beau, who now addresses himself to her in a full-bottomed wig, distinguished by a little bald pate covered with a black leather skull-cap. I forbear to mention many other objections, which the ladies, who are no strangers to the doctrines of popery, will easily recollect: though I do not in the least doubt but those I have already suggested, will be sufficient to persuade my fair readers to be zealous in the Protestant cause.

The freedom and happiness of our British ladies is so singular, that it is a common saying in foreign countries, 'If a bridge were built across the seas, all the women in Europe would flock into England.' It has been observed, that the laws relating to them are so favourable, that one would think they themselves had given votes in enacting them. All the honours and indulgences of society are due to them by our customs; and by our constitution, they have all the privileges of English-born subjects, without the burdens. I need not acquaint my fair fellow-freeholders, that every man who is anxious for our sacred and civil rights, is a champion in their cause; since we enjoy in common a religion agreeable to that reasonable nature, of which we equally partake; and since in point of property, our law makes no distinction of sexes.

We may, therefore, justly expect from them, that they will act in concert with us for the preservation of our laws and religion, which cannot subsist, but under the government of his present majesty; and would necessarily be subverted, under that of a person bred up in the most violent principles of popery and arbitrary power. Thus may the fair sex contribute to fix the peace of a brave and generous people, who, for many ages, have disdained to bear any tyranny, but theirs; and be as famous in history, as those illustrious matrons, who, in the infancy of Rome, reconciled the Romans and the Sabines, and united the two contending parties under their new king.

---

## No. 5, FRIDAY, JANUARY 6.

Omnium Societatum nulla est gravior, nulla carior, quam ea quæ cum republica est unicuique nostrum: cari sunt parentes, cari liberi, propinqui, familiares: sed omnes omnium caritates patria una complexa est: pro qua quis bonus dubitet mortem oppetere, si ei sit profuturus? Cic.

There is no greater sign of a general decay of virtue in a nation, than a want of zeal in its inhabitants for the good of their country. This generous and public-spirited passion has been observed of late years to languish and grow cold in this our island; where a party of men have made it their business to represent it as chimerical and romantic, to destroy in the minds of the people, the sense of national glory, and to turn into ridicule our natural and ancient allies, who are united to us by the common interests both of religion and policy. It may not, therefore, be unseasonable to recommend to this present generation, the practice of that virtue, for which their ancestors were particularly famous, and which is called, 'The love of one's country.' This love to our country, as a moral virtue, is a fixed disposition of mind to promote the safety, welfare, and reputation of the community in which we are born, and of the constitution under which we are protected. Our obligation to this great duty, may appear to us from several considerations.

In the first place, we may observe, that we are directed to it by one of those secret suggestions of nature, which go under the name of Instinct, and which are never given in vain. As self-love is an instinct planted in us, for the good and safety of each particular person, the love of our country is impressed on our minds for the happiness and preservation of the community. This instinct is so remarkable, that we find examples of it in those who are born in the most uncomfortable climates, or the worst of governments. We read of an inhabitant of Nova Zembla, who after having lived some time in Denmark, where he was clothed and treated with the utmost indulgence, took the first opportunity of making his escape, though with the hazard of his life, into his native regions of cold, poverty, and nakedness. We have an instance of the same nature among the very Hottentots. One of these savages was brought into England, taught our language, and, in a great measure, polished out of his natural barbarity: but, upon being carried back to the Cape of Good Hope, (where it was thought he might have been of advantage to our English traders) he mixed, in a kind of transport, with his countrymen, brutalized with them in their habits and manners, and would never again return to his foreign acquaintance. I need not mention the common opinion of the negroes in our plantations, who have no other notion of a future state of happiness, than that, after death, they shall be conveyed back to their native country. The Swiss are so remarkable for this passion, that it often turns to a disease among them; for which there is a particular name in the German language, and which the French call 'The distemper of the country:' for nothing is more usual, than for several of their common soldiers, who are listed into a foreign service, to have such violent hankerings after their home, as to pine away, even to death, unless they have a permission to return; which. on such an occasion, is generally granted them. I shall only add under this head, that since the love of one's country is natural to every man, any particular nation, who, by false politics, shall endeavour to stifle or restrain it, will not be upon a level with others.

As this love of our country is natural to every man, so it is likewise very reasonable; and that, in the first place, because it inclines us to be beneficial to those, who are and ought to be dearer to us than any others. It takes in our families, relations, friends, and acquaintance, and in short, all whose welfare and security we are obliged to consult, more than that of those who are strangers to us. For this reason, it is the most sublime and extensive of all social virtues: especially, if we consider that it does not only promote the well-being of those who are our contemporaries, but likewise of their children and their posterity. Hence it is, that all casuists are unanimous in determining, that when the good of their country interferes even with the life of the most beloved relation, dearest friend, or greatest benefactor, it is to be preferred without exception.

Farther, though there is a benevolence due to all mankind, none can question but a superior degree of it is to be paid to a father, a wife, or child. In the same manner, though our love should reach to the whole species, a greater proportion of it should exert itself towards that community in which Providence has placed us. This is our proper sphere of action, the province allotted to us for the exercise of our civil virtues, and in which alone we have opportunities of expressing our good-will to mankind. I could not but be pleased, in the accounts of the late Persian embassy into France, with a particular ceremony of the ambassador; who, every morning, before he went abroad, religiously saluted a turf of earth dug out of his own native soil, to remind him, that in all the transactions of the day, he was to think of his country, and pursue its advantages. If, in the several districts and divisions of the world, men would thus study the welfare of those respective communities, to which their power of doing good is limited, the whole race of reasonable creatures would be happy, as far as the benefits of society can make them so. At least, we find so many blessings naturally flowing from this noble principle, that in proportion as it prevails, every nation becomes a prosperous and flourishing people.

It may be yet a farther recommendation of this particular virtue, if we consider, that no nation was ever famous for its morals, which was not, at the same time, remarkable for its public spirit; patriots naturally rise out of a Spartan or Roman virtue: and there is no remark more common among the ancient historians, than that, when the state was corrupted with avarice and luxury, it was in danger of being betrayed, or sold.

To the foregoing reasons for the love which every good man owes to his country, we may add, that the actions, which are most celebrated in history, and which are read with the greatest admiration, are such as proceed from this principle. The establishing of good laws, the detecting of conspiracies, the crushing of seditions and rebellions, the falling in battle, or the devoting of a man's self to certain death for the safety of his fellow-citizens, are actions that always warm the reader, and endear to him persons of the remotest ages, and the most distant countries.

And as actions, that proceed from the love of one's country, are more illustrious than any others in the records of time; so we find, that those persons who have been eminent in other virtues, have been particularly distinguished by this. It would be endless to produce examples of this kind out of Greek and Roman authors. To confine myself, therefore, in so wide and beaten a field, I shall chuse some instances from holy writ, which abounds in accounts of this nature, as much as any other history whatsoever. And this I do the more willingly, because, in some books lately written, I find it objected against revealed religion, that it does not inspire the love of one's country. Here I must premise, that as the sacred author of our religion chiefly inculcated to the Jews those parts of their duty wherein they were most defective, so there was no need of insisting upon this; the Jews being remarkable for an attachment to their own country, even to the exclusion of all common humanity to strangers. We see, in the behaviour of this divine person, the practice of this virtue in conjunction with all others. He deferred working a miracle in the behalf of a Syro-Phœnician woman, until he had declared his superior good-will to his own nation; and was prevailed upon to heal the daughter of a Roman centurion, by hearing from the Jews, that he was one who loved their nation, and had built them a synagogue. But, to look out for no other instance, what was ever more moving, than his lamentation over Jerusalem, at his first approach to it, notwithstanding he had foretold the cruel and unjust treatment he was to meet with in that city! for he foresaw the destruction, which, in a few years, was to fall upon that people; a destruction not to be paralleled in any nation, from the beginning of the world to this day; and in the view of it melted into tears. His followers have, in many places, expressed the like sentiments of affection for their countrymen, among which, none is more extraordinary, than that of the great convert, who wished he himself might be made a curse, provided it might turn to the happiness of his nation; or, as he words it, 'of his brethren and kinsmen who are Israelites.' This instance naturally brings to mind the same heroic temper of soul in the great Jewish law-giver, who would have devoted himself in the same manner, rather than see his people perish. It would, indeed, be difficult, to find out any man of extraordinary piety, in the sacred writings, in whom this virtue is not highly conspicuous. The reader, however, will excuse me, if I take notice of one passage, because it is a very fine one, and wants only a place in some polite author of Greece or Rome, to have been admired and celebrated. The king of Syria lying sick upon his bed, sent Hasael, one of his great officers, to the prophet Elisha, to inquire of him, whether he should recover. The prophet looked so attentively on this messenger, that it put him into some confusion; or, to quote this beautiful circumstance, and the whole narrative, in the pathetic language of scripture, 'Elisha settled his countenance stedfastly upon him, until he was ashamed: and Hasael said, why weepeth my lord? And he said, because I know the evil that thou wilt do unto the children of Israel: their strong holds wilt thou set on fire, and their men wilt thou slay with the sword, and wilt dash their children, and rip up their women with child. And Hasael said, But what, is thy servant a dog, that he should do this great thing? And Elisha answered, The Lord hath shewed me, that thou shalt be king over Syria.'

I might enforce these reasons for the love of our country, by considerations adapted to my readers as they are Englishmen, and as by that means they enjoy a purer religion, and a more excellent form of government, than any other nation under heaven.

But, being persuaded that every one must look upon himself as indispensably obliged to the practice of a duty, which is recommended to him by so many arguments and examples, I shall only desire the honest, well-meaning reader, when he turns his thoughts towards the public, rather to consider what opportunities he has of doing good to his native country, than to throw away his time in deciding the rights of princes, or the like speculations, which are so far beyond his reach. Let us leave these great points to the wisdom of our legislature, and to the determination of those, who are the proper judges of our constitution. We shall otherwise be liable to the just reproach, which is cast upon such Christians as waste their lives in the subtle and intricate disputes of religion, when they should be practising the doctrine which it teaches. If there be any right upon earth, any relying on the judgment of our most eminent lawyers and divines, or, indeed, any certainty, in human reason, our present sovereign has an undoubted title to our duty and obedience. But supposing, for argument's sake, that this right were doubtful, and that an Englishman could be divided in his opinion, as to the person to whom he should pay his allegiance: in this case, there is no question, but the love of his country ought to cast the balance, and to determine him on that side, which is most conducive to the welfare of his community. To bring this to our present case. A man must be destitute of common sense, who is capable of imagining that the Protestant religion could flourish under the government of a bigoted Roman Catholic, or that our civil rights could be protected by one who has been trained up in the politics of the most arbitrary prince in Europe, and who could not acknowledge his gratitude to his benefactor, by any remarkable instance, which would not be detrimental to the British nation. And are these such desirable blessings, that an honest man would endeavour to arrive at them, through the confusions of a civil war, and the blood of many thousands of his fellow-subjects? On the contrary, the arguments for our steady, loyal, and affectionate adherence to King George, are so evident from this single topic, that if every Briton, instead of aspiring after private wealth or power, would sincerely desire to make his country happy, his present majesty would not have a single malecontent in his whole dominions.

---

## No. 6. MONDAY, JANUARY 9.

Fraus enim astringit, non dissolvit perjurium.
CICERO.

At a time when so many of the king's subjects present themselves before their respective magistrates to take the oaths required by law, it may not be improper to awaken in the minds of my readers a due sense of the engagement under which they lay themselves. It is a melancholy consideration, that there should be several among us so hardened and deluded, as to think an oath a proper subject for a jest; and to make this, which is one of the most solemn acts of religion, an occasion of mirth. Yet such is the depravation of our manners at present, that nothing is more frequent than to hear profligate men ridiculing, to the best of their abilities, these sacred pledges of their duty and allegiance; and endeavouring to be witty upon themselves, for daring to prevaricate with God and man. A poor conceit of their own, or a quotation out of Hudibras, shall make them treat with levity an obligation wherein their safety and welfare are concerned both as to this world and the next. Raillery of this nature is enough to make the hearer tremble. As these miscreants seem to glory in the profession of their impiety, there is no man, who has any regard to his duty, or even to his reputation, that can appear in their defence. But if there are others of a more serious turn, who join with us deliberately in these religious professions of loyalty to our sovereign, with any private salvos or evasions, they would do well to consider those maxims, in which all casuists are agreed, who have gained any esteem for their learning, judgment, or morality. These have unanimously determined that an oath is always to be taken in the sense of that authority which imposes it: and that those, whose hearts do not concur with their lips in the form of these public protestations; or who have any mental reserves, or who take an oath against their consciences, upon any motive whatsoever; or with a design to break it, or repent of it, are guilty of perjury. Any of these, or the like circumstances, instead of alleviating the crime, make it more heinous, as they are premeditated frauds (which it is the chief design of an oath to prevent) and the most flagrant instances of insincerity to men, and irreverence to their Maker. For this reason, the perjury of a man, who takes an oath, with an intention to keep it, and is afterwards seduced to the violation of it, (though a crime not to be thought of, without the greatest horror) is yet, in some respects, not quite so black as the perjury abovementioned. It is, indeed, a very unhappy token of the great corruption of our manners, that there should be any so inconsiderate among us, as to sacrifice the standing and essential duties of morality, to the views of politics; and that, as in my last paper, it was not unseasonable to prove the love of our country to be a virtue, so in this there should be any occasion to shew that perjury is a sin. But it is our misfortune to live in an age when such wild and unnatural doctrines have prevailed among some of our fellow-subjects, that if one looks into their schemes of government, they seem, according as they are in the humour, to believe that a sovereign is not to be restrained by his coronation oath, or his people by their oaths of allegiance: or to represent them in a plainer light, in some reigns they are for a power and an obedience that is unlimited, and in others, are for retrenching within the narrowest bounds, both the authority of the prince, and the allegiance of the subject.

Now the guilt of perjury is so self-evident, that it was always reckoned among the greatest crimes, by those who were only governed by the light of reason: the inviolable observing of an oath, like the other practical duties of Christianity, is a part of natural religion. As reason is common to all mankind, the dictates of it are the same through the whole species: and since every man's own heart will tell him, that there can be no greater affront to the Deity, whom he worships, than to appeal to him with an intention to deceive; nor a greater injustice to men than to betray them by false assurances; it is no wonder that pagans and Christians, infidels and believers, should concur in a point wherein the honour of a Supreme Being, and the welfare of society, are so highly concerned. For this reason, Pythagoras to his first precept of honouring the immortal gods, immediately subjoins that of paying veneration to an oath. We may see the reverence which the heathens showed to these sacred and solemn engagements from the inconveniences which they often suffered, rather than break through them. We have frequent instances of this kind in the Roman commonwealth; which, as it has been observed by several eminent pagan writers, very much excelled all other pagan governments in the practice of virtue. How far they exceeded, in this particular, those great corrupters of Christianity, and, indeed, of natural religion, the Jesuits, may appear from their abhorrence of every thing that looked like a fraudulent or mental evasion. Of this I shall only produce the following instance. Several Romans, who had been taken prisoners by Hannibal, were released, upon obliging themselves by an oath to return again to his camp. Among these there was one, who, thinking to elude the oath, went the same day back to the camp on pretence of having forgot something. But this prevarication was so shocking to the Roman senate, that they ordered him to be apprehended, and delivered up to Hannibal.

We may farther see the just sense the heathens had of the crime of perjury, from the penalties which they inflicted on the persons guilty of it. Perjury among the Scythians was a capital crime; and among the Egyptians also was punished with death, as Diodorus Siculus relates, who observes, that an offender of this kind is guilty of those two crimes (wherein the malignity of perjury truly consists), a failing in his respect to the Divinity, and in his faith towards men. 'Tis unnecessary to multiply instances of this nature, which may be found in almost every author who has written on this subject.

If men, who had no other guide but their reason, considered an oath to be of such a tremendous nature, and the violation of it to be so great a crime; it ought to make a much deeper impression upon minds enlightened by revealed religion, as they have more exalted notions of the Divinity. A supposed heathen deity might be so poor in his attributes, so stinted in his knowledge, goodness, or power, that a pagan might hope to conceal his perjury from his notice, or not to provoke him, should he be discovered; or should he provoke him, not to be punished by him. Nay, he might have produced examples of falsehood and perjury in the gods themselves, to whom he appealed. But as revealed religion has given us a more just and clear idea of the divine nature, He, whom we appeal to, is Truth itself, the great Searcher of Hearts, who will not let fraud and falsehood go unpunished, or, 'hold him guiltless that taketh his name in vain.' And as with regard to the Deity, so likewise with regard to man, the obligation of an oath is stronger upon Christians than upon any other part of mankind; and that because charity, truth, mutual confidence, and all other social duties, are carried to greater heights, and enforced with stronger motives, by the principles of our religion.

Perjury, with relation to the oaths which are at present required by us, has in it all the aggravating circumstances, which can attend that crime. We take them before the magistrates of public justice; are reminded by the ceremony, that it is a part of that obedience which we learn from the gospel; expressly disavow all evasions and mental reservations whatsoever; appeal to Almighty God for the integrity of our hearts, and only desire him to be our helper, as we fulfil the oath we there take in his presence. I mention these circumstances, to which several other might be added, because it is a received doctrine among those, who have treated of the nature of an oath, that the greater the solemnities are which attend it, the more they aggravate the violation of it. And here what must be the success that a man can hope for who turns a rebel, after having disclaimed the divine assistance, but upon condition of being a faithful and loyal subject? He first of all desires that God may help him, as he shall keep his oath, and afterwards hopes to prosper in an enterprise, which is the direct breach of it.

Since, therefore, perjury, by the common sense of mankind, the reason of the thing, and from the whole tenor of Christianity, is a crime of so flagitious a nature, we cannot be too careful in avoiding every approach towards it.

The virtue of the ancient Athenians is very remarkable in the case of Euripides. This great tragic poet, though famous for the morality of his plays, had introduced a person, who being reminded of an oath he had taken, replied, 'I swore with my mouth, but not with my heart.' The impiety of this sentiment set the audience in an uproar; made Socrates (though an intimate friend of the poet) go out of the theatre with indignation; and gave so great offence, that he was publicly accused, and brought upon his trial, as one who suggested an evasion of what they thought the most holy and indissoluble bond of human society. So jealous were these virtuous heathens of any the smallest hint, that might open a way to perjury.

And here it highly imports us to consider, that we do not only break our oath of allegiance by actual rebellion, but by all those other methods which have a natural and manifest tendency to it. The guilt may lie upon a man, where the penalty cannot take hold of him. Those who speak irreverently of the person to whom they have sworn allegiance; who endeavour to alienate from him the hearts of his subjects; or to inspire the people with disaffection to his government, cannot be thought to be true to the oath they have taken. And as for those, who by concerted falsehoods and defamations, endeavour to blemish his character, or weaken his authority; they incur the complicated guilt both of slander and perjury. The moral crime is completed in such offenders, and there are only accidental circumstances wanting, to work it up for the cognizance of the law.

Nor is it sufficient for a man, who has given these solemn assurances to his prince, to forbear the doing him any evil, unless, at the same time, he do him all the good he can in his proper station of life.

Loyalty is of an active nature, and ought to discover itself in all the instances of zeal and affection to our sovereign: and if we carefully examine the duty of that allegiance which we pledge to his majesty, by the oaths that are tendered to us, we shall find that 'We do not only renounce, refuse, and abjure any allegiance or obedience to the pretender,' but 'swear to defend King George to the utmost of our power, against all traitorous conspiracies and attempts whatsoever, and to disclose and make known to his majesty, all treasons and traitorous conspiracies, which we shall know to be against him.'

To conclude, as among those who have bound themselves by these sacred obligations, the actual traitor or rebel is guilty of perjury in the eye of the law; the secret promoter, or well-wisher of the cause, is so before the tribunal of conscience. And though I should be unwilling to pronounce the man who is indolent, or indifferent in the cause of his prince, to be absolutely perjured; I may venture to affirm, that he falls very short of that allegiance, to which he is obliged by oath. Upon the whole we may be assured, that, in a nation which is tied down by such religious and solemn engagements, the people's loyalty will keep pace with their morality; and that, in proportion as they are sincere Christians, they will be faithful subjects.

---

## NO 7. FRIDAY, JANUARY 13.

Veritas pluribus modiis infracta: primum inscitiâ reipublicæ, ut alienæ; mox libidine assentandi, aut rursus odio adversus dominantes. Obtrectatio & livor pronis auribus accipiuntur: quippe adulationi fœdum crimen servitutis, malignitati falsa species libertatis inest.

TAC.

THERE is no greater sign of a bad cause, than when the patrons of it are reduced to the necessity of making use of the most wicked artifices to support it. Of this kind are the falsehoods and calumnies, which are invented and spread abroad by the enemies to our king and country. This spirit of malice and slander does not discover itself in any instances so ridiculous, as in those, by which seditious men endeavour to depreciate his majesty's person and family; without considering, that his court at Hanover was always allowed to be one of the politest in Europe, and that before he became our king, he was reckoned among the greatest princes of Christendom.

But the most glorious of his majesty's predecessors was treated after the same manner. Upon that prince's first arrival, the inconsiderable party, who then laboured to make him odious to the people, gave out, that he brought with him twenty thousand Laplanders, clothed in the skins of bears, all of their own killing; and that they mutinied, because they had not been regaled with a bloody battle within two days after their landing. He was no sooner on the throne than those, who had contributed to place him there, finding that he had made some changes at court which were not to their humour, endeavoured to render him unpopular by misrepresentations of his person, his character, and his actions. They found that his nose had a resemblance to that of Oliver Cromwell, and clapt him on a huge pair of mustachoes to frighten his people with: his mercy was fear; his justice was cruelty; his temperance, economy, prudent behaviour, and application to business, were Dutch virtues; and such as we had not been used to in our English kings. He did not fight a battle in which the tories did not slay double the number of what he had lost in the field; nor ever raised a siege or gained a victory, which did not cost more than it was worth. In short he was contriving the ruin of his kingdom; and, in order to it, advanced Dr. Tillotson to the highest station of the church, my Lord Somers of the law, Mr. Montague of the treasury, and the admiral at La Hogue of the fleet. Such were the calumnies of the party in those times, which we see so faithfully copied out by men of the same principles under the reign of his present majesty.

As the schemes of these gentlemen are the most absurd and contradictory to common sense, the means by which they are promoted must be of the same nature. Nothing but weakness and folly can dispose Englishmen and Protestants to the interest of a popish pretender: and the same abilities of mind will naturally qualify his adherents to swallow the most palpable and notorious falsehoods. Their self-interested and designing leaders cannot desire a more ductile and easy people to work upon. How long was it before many of this simple, deluded tribe were brought to believe that the Highlanders were a generation of men that could be conquered! The rabble of the party were instructed to look upon them as so many giants and Saracens; and were very much surprised to find, that every one of them had not with his broad sword mowed down at least a squadron of the king's forces. There were not only public rejoicings in the camp at Perth, but likewise many private congratulations nearer us, among these well-wishers to their country, upon the victories of their friends at Preston; which continued till the rebels made their solemn cavalcade from Highgate. Nay, there were then some of these wise partisans, who concluded, the government had hired two or three hundred hale men, who looked like fox-hunters, to be bound and pinioned, if not to be executed, as representatives of the pretended captives. Their victories in Scotland have been innumerable; and no longer ago than last week, they gained a very remarkable one, in which the Highlanders cut off all the Dutch forces to a man; and afterwards, disguising themselves in their habits, came up as friends to the king's troops, and put them all to the sword. This story had a great run for a day or two; and I believe one might still find out a whisper among their secret intelligence, that the Duke of Mar is actually upon the road to London, if not within two days' march of the town. I need not take notice, that their successes in the battle of Dumblain are magnified among some of them to this day; though a tory may very well say, with king Pyrrhus, 'That such another victory would undo them.'

But the most fruitful source of falsehood and calumny, is that which, one would think, should be the least apt to produce them ; I mean a pretended concern for the safety of our established religion. Were these people as anxious for the doctrines, which are essential to the church of England, as they are for the nominal distinction of adhering to its interests, they would know, that the sincere observation of public oaths, allegiance to their king, submission to their bishops, zeal against popery, and abhorrence of rebellion, are the great points that adorn the character of the church of England, and in which the authors of the reformed religion in this nation have always gloried. We justly reproach the Jesuits, who have adapted all Christianity to temporal and political views, for maintaining a position so repugnant to the laws of nature, morality, and religion, that an evil may be committed for the sake of good, which may arise from it. But we cannot suppose even this principle, (as bad a one as it is) should influence those persons, who, by so many absurd and monstrous falsehoods, endeavour to delude men into a belief of the danger of the church. If there be any relying on the solemn declarations of a prince, famed for keeping his word, constant in the public exercises of our religion, and determined in the maintenance of our laws, we have all the assurances that can be given us, for the security of the established church under his government. When a leading man, therefore, begins to grow apprehensive for the church, you may be sure, that he is either in danger of losing a place, or in despair of getting one. It is pleasant on these occasions, to see a notorious profligate seized with a concern for his religion, and converting his spleen into zeal. These narrow and selfish views have so great an influence in this city, that, among those who call themselves the landed interest, there are several of my fellow freeholders, who always fancy the church in danger upon the rising of bank-stock. But the standing absurdities, without the belief of which no man is reckoned a staunch churchman, are, that there is a calve's-head club; for which, (by the way,) some pious tory has made suitable hymns and devotions: that there is a confederacy among the greatest part of the prelates to destroy Episcopacy; and that all, who talk against Popery, are Presbyterians in their hearts. The emissaries of the party are so diligent in spreading ridiculous fictions of this kind, that at present, if we may credit common report, there are several remote parts of the nation in which it is firmly believed, that all the churches in London are shut up; and that, if any clergyman walks the streets in his habits, it is ten to one but he is knocked down by some sturdy schismatic.

We may observe upon this occasion, that there are many particular falsehoods suited to the particular climates and latitudes in which they are published, according as the situation of the place makes them less liable to discovery: there is many a lie that will not thrive within a hundred miles of London: nay, we often find a lie born in Southwark, that dies the same day on this side the water: and several produced in the loyal ward of Portsoken of so feeble a make, as not to bear carriage to the Royal-Exchange. However, as the mints of calumny are perpetually at work, there are a great number of curious inventions issued out from time to time, which grow current among the party, and circulate through the whole kingdom.

As the design of this paper is not to exasperate, but to undeceive my countrymen, let me desire them to consider the many inconveniences they bring upon themselves by these mutual intercourses of credulity and falsehood. I shall only remind the credulous of the strong delusion they have by this means been led into, the greatest part of their lives. Their hopes have been kept up by a succession of lies for near thirty years. How many persons have starved in expectation of those profitable employ ments, which were promised them by the author of these forgeries! how many of them have died with great regret, when they thought they were within a month of enjoying the inestimable blessings of a popish and arbitrary reign!

I would, therefore, advise this blinded set of men, not to give credit to those persons, by whom they have been so often fooled and imposed upon; but, on the contrary, to think it an affront to their parts, when they hear from any of them such accounts as they would not dare to tell them, but on the presumption that they are ideots. Or if their zeal for the cause shall dispose them to be credulous in any points that are favourable to it, I would beg of them not to venture wagers upon the truth of them: and in this present conjuncture, by no means to sell out of the stocks upon any news they shall hear from their good friends at Perth. As these party fictions are the proper subjects of mirth and laughter, their deluded believers are only to be treated with pity or contempt. But as for those incendiaries of figure and distinction, who are the inventors and publishers of such gross falsehoods and calumnies, they cannot be regarded by others, but with the utmost detestation and abhorrence; nor, one would think, by themselves, without the greatest remorse and compunction of heart; when they consider, that in order to give a spirit to a desperate cause, they have, by their false and treacherous insinuations and reports, betrayed so many of their friends into their destruction.

## No. 8. MONDAY, JANUARY 16.

Adveniet qui vestra dies muliebribus armis
Verba redarguerit. VIRG.

I HAVE heard that several ladies of distinction, upon the reading of my fourth paper, are studying methods how to make themselves useful to the public. One has a design of keeping an open tea-table, where every man shall be welcome that is a friend to King George. Another is for setting up an assembly for basset, where none shall be admitted to punt that have not taken the oaths. The third is upon an invention of a dress, which will put every tory lady out of countenance: I am not informed of the particulars, but am told in general, that she has contrived to shew her principles by the setting of her commode; so that it will be impossible for any woman, that is disaffected, to be in the fashion. Some of them are of opinion that the Fan may be made use of, with good success, against popery, by exhibiting the corruptions of the church of Rome in various figures; and that their abhorrence of the superstitious use of beads, may be very aptly expressed in the make of a pearl necklace. As for the civil part of our constitution, it is unanimously agreed, among the leaders of the sex, that there is no glory in making a man their slave, who has not naturally a passion for liberty; and to disallow of all professions of passive-obedience, but from a lover to his mistress.

It happens very luckily for the interest of the whigs, that their very enemies acknowledge the finest women of Great Britain to be of that party. The tories are forced to borrow their toasts from their antagonists; and can scarce find beauties enough of their own side, to supply a single round of October. One may, indeed, sometimes discover among the malignants of the sex, a face that seems to have been naturally designed for a whig lady:

but then it is so often flushed with rage, or soured with disappointments, that one cannot but be troubled to see it thrown away upon the owner. Would the pretty malecontent be persuaded to love her king and country, it would diffuse a cheerfulness through all her features, and give her quite another air. I would, therefore, advise these, my gentle readers, as they consult the good of their faces, to forbear frowning upon loyalists, and pouting at the government. In the mean time, what may we not hope, from a cause which is recommended by all the allurement of beauty, and the force of truth! It is, therefore, to be hoped, that every fine woman will make this laudable use of her charms; and that she may not want to be frequently reminded of this great duty, I will only desire her to think of her country every time she looks in her glass.

But because it is impossible to prescribe such rules as shall be suitable to the sex in general, I shall consider them under their several divisions of maids, wives, and widows.

As for virgins, who are unexperienced in the wiles of men, they would do well to consider, how little they are to rely on the faith of lovers who, in less than a year, have broken their allegiance to their lawful sovereign; and what credit is to be given to the vows and protestations of such as shew themselves so little afraid of perjury. Besides, what would an innocent young lady think, should she marry a man without examining his principles, and afterwards find herself got with child by a rebel?

In the next place, every wife ought to answer for her man. If the husband be engaged in a seditious club, or drinks[a] mysterious healths, or be frugal of his candles on a rejoicing night, let her look to him, and keep him out of harm's way; or the world will be apt to say, she has a mind to be a widow before her time.

The uniformity of the sentence requires—*drink*—that is, the subjunctive mood—*be* engaged—*drink*—*be* frugal.

She ought, in such cases, to exert the authority of the curtain lecture; and if she finds him of a rebellious disposition, to tame him, as they do birds of prey, by dinning him in the ears all night long.

Widows may be supposed women of too good sense not to discountenance all practices that have a tendency to the destruction of mankind. Besides, they have a greater interest in property, than either maids or wives, and do not hold their jointures by the precarious tenure of portions or pin-money. So that it is as unnatural for a dowager, as a free-holder, to be an enemy to our constitution.

As nothing is more instructive than examples, I would recommend to the perusal of our British virgins, the story of Clelia, a Roman spinster, whose behaviour is represented by all their historians, as one of the chief motives that discouraged the Tarquins from prosecuting their attempt to regain the throne, from whence they had been expelled. Let the married women reflect upon the glory acquired by the wife of Coriolanus, who, when her husband, after long exile, was returning into his country with fire and sword, diverted him from so cruel and unnatural an enterprise. And let those who have out-lived their husbands, never forget their countrywoman Boadicea, who headed her troops in person, against the invasion of a Roman army, and encouraged them with this memorable saying, 'I, who am a woman, am resolved upon victory or death: but as for you, who are men, you may, if you please, chuse life and slavery.'

But I do not propose to our British ladies, that they should turn Amazons in the service of their sovereign, nor so much as let their nails grow for the defence of their country. The men will take the work of the field off their hands, and shew the world, that English valour cannot be matched, when it is animated by English beauty. I do not, however, disapprove the project which is now on foot for a 'Female Association;' and since I hear the fair confederates cannot agree among themselves upon a form, shall presume to lay before them the following rough draft, to be corrected or improved, as they in their wisdom shall think fit.

"We, the consorts, relicts, and spinsters, of the isle of Great Britain, whose names are under-written, being most passionately offended at the falsehood and perfidiousness of certain faithless men, and at the lukewarmth and indifference of others, have entered into a voluntary association for the good and safety of our constitution. And we do hereby engage ourselves to raise and arm our vassals for the service of his majesty King George, and him to defend, with our tongues and hearts, our eyes, eye-lashes, favourites, lips, dimples, and every other feature, whether natural or acquired. We promise publicly and openly to avow the loyalty of our principles in every word we shall utter, and every patch we shall stick on. We do farther promise, to annoy the enemy with all the flames, darts, and arrows, with which nature has armed us; never to correspond with them by sigh, ogle, or billet-doux; not to have any intercourse with them, either in snuff or tea; nor to accept the civility of any man's hand, who is not ready to use it in the defence of his country. We are determined, in so good a cause, to endure the greatest hardships and severities, if there should be occasion; and even to wear the manufacture of our country, rather than appear the friends of a foreign interest in the richest French brocade. And forgetting all private feuds, jealousies, and animosities, we do unanimously oblige ourselves, by this our association, to stand and fall by one another, as loyal and faithful sisters and fellow subjects."

*N.B.* This association will be lodged at Mr. Motteux's where attendance will be given to the subscribers, who are to be ranged in their respective columns, as maids, wives, and widows

## No. 9. FRIDAY, JANUARY 20.

Consilia qui dant prava cautis hominibus,
Et perdunt operam, et deridentur turpiter.—PHAEDR.

THOUGH I have already seen, in 'The Town-talk,' a letter from a celebrated Englishman to the Pretender, which is, indeed an excellent answer to his declaration, the title of this paper obliges me to publish the following piece, which considers it in different lights.

The Declaration of the Freeholders of Great Britain, in answer to that of the Pretender.

WE, by the mercy of God, freeholders of Great Britain, to the Popish Pretender, who styles himself King of Scotland and England, and defender of our faith, DEFIANCE. Having seen a libel, which you have lately published against the king and people of these realms, under the title of a DECLARATION, We, in justice to the sentiments of our own hearts, have thought fit to return you the following answer; wherein we shall endeavour to reduce to method the several particulars, which you have contrived to throw together with much malice, and no less confusion.

We believe you sincere in the first part of your declaration, where you own it would be a great satisfaction to you, to be placed upon the throne by our endeavours: but you discourage us from making use of them, by declaring it to be your right, 'both by the laws of God and man.' As for the laws of God, we should think ourselves great transgressors of them, should we, for your sake, rebel against a prince, who, under God, is the most powerful defender of that religion which we think the most pleasing to him: and as for the laws of man, we conceive those to be of that kind, which have been enacted from time to time, for near thirty years past, against you and your pretensions, by the legislature of this kingdom.

You afterwards proceed to invectives against the royal family: which, we do assure you, is a very unpopular topic, except to your few deluded friends among the rabble.

You call them 'aliens to our country,' not considering that King George has lived above a year longer in England than ever you did. You say they are 'distant in blood,' whereas nobody ever doubted that King George is great grandson to King James the first, though many believe that you are not son to King James the second. Besides, all the world acknowledge he is the nearest to our crown of the Protestant blood, of which you cannot have one drop in your veins, unless you derive it from such parents as you do not care for owning.

Your next argument against the royal family, is, that they are 'strangers to our language:' but they must be strangers to the British court who told you so. However, you must know, that we plain men should prefer a king who was a stranger to our language, before one who is a stranger to our laws and religion: for we could never endure French sentiments, though delivered in our native dialect; and should abhor an arbitrary prince, though he tyrannised over us in the finest English that ever was spoken. For these reasons, sir, we cannot bear the thought of hearing a man, that has been bred up in the politics of Louis the fourteenth, talk intelligibly from the British throne; especially, when we consider, however he may boast of his speaking English, he says his prayers in an unknown tongue.

We come now to the grievances for which, in your opinion, we ought to take up arms against our present sovereign. The greatest you seem to insist upon, and which is most in the mouths of your party, is the union of the two kingdoms; for which his majesty ought most certainly to be deposed, because it was made under the reign of her, whom you call your 'dear sister of glorious memory.' Other grievances which you hint at under his majesty's administration, are, the murder of King Charles the first, who was beheaded before King George was born; and the sufferings of King Charles the second, which, perhaps, his present majesty cannot wholly clear himself of, because he came into the world a day before his restoration.

As on the one side you arraign his present majesty by this most extraordinary retrospect, on the other hand, you condemn his government by what we may call the spirit of second sight. You are not content to draw into his reign those mischiefs that were done a hundred years ago, unless we anticipate those that may happen a hundred years hence. So that the keenest of your arrows either fall short of him, or fly over his head. We take it for a certain sign that you are at a loss for present grievances, when you are thus forced to have recourse to your 'future prospects and future miseries.' Now, sir, you must know, that we freeholders have a natural aversion to hanging, and do not know how to answer it to our wives and families, if we should venture our necks upon the truth of your prophecies. In our ordinary way of judging, we guess at the king's future conduct by what we have seen already; and therefore beg you will excuse us, if, for the present, we defer entering into a rebellion, to which you so graciously invite us. When we have as bad a prospect of our King George's reign, as we should have of your's, then will be your time to date another declaration from your court at Commerci: which, if we may be allowed to prophecy in our turn, cannot possibly happen before the hundred and fiftieth year of your reign.

Having considered the past and future grievances mentioned in your declaration, we come now to the present; all of which are founded upon this supposition, that whatever is done by his majesty or his ministers to keep you out of the British throne, is a grievance. These, sir, may be grievances to you, but they are none to us. On the contrary, we look upon them, as the greatest instances of his majesty's care and tenderness for his people. To take them in order: the first relates to the ministry, who are chosen, as you observe very rightly, out of the worst, and not the best of 'your' subjects. Now, sir, can you in conscience think us to be such fools as to rebel against the king, for having employed those who are his most eminent friends, and were the greatest sufferers in his cause, before he came to the crown; and for having removed a general, who is now actually in arms against him, and two secretaries of state, both of whom have listed themselves in your service; or because he chose to substitute in their places, such men who had distinguished themselves by their zeal against you, in the most famous battles, negociations, and debates.

The second grievance you mention, is, that the glory of the late queen has suffered, who, you insinuate, 'had secured to you the enjoyment of that inheritance, out of which you had been so long kept.' This may, indeed, be a reason why her memory should be precious with you; but you may be sure we shall think never the better of her, for her having your good word. For the same reason, it makes us stare, when we hear it objected to his present majesty, 'that he is not kind to her faithful servants;' since, if we can believe what you yourself say, it is impossible they should be 'his faithful servants.' And by the way, many of your private friends here, wish you would forbear babbling at that rate: for to tell you a secret, we are very apt to suspect that any Englishman who deserves your praise deserves to be hanged.

The next grievance, which you have a mighty mind to redress among us, is the parliament of Great Britain, against whom you bring a stale accusation, which has been used by every minority in the memory of man; namely, that it was procured by unwarrantable influences and corruptions. We cannot, indeed, blame you for being angry at those, who have set such a round price upon your head. Your accusation of our high court of parliament, puts us in mind of a story, often told among us freeholders, concerning a rattle-brained young fellow, who being indicted for two or three pranks upon the highway, told the judge he would swear the peace against him, for putting him in fear of his life.

The next grievance is such a one, that we are amazed how it could come into your head. Your words are as follows. 'Whilst the principal powers engaged in the late wars, do enjoy the blessings of peace, and are attentive to discharge their debts, and ease their people, Great Britain, in the midst of peace, feels all the load of war. New debts are contracted, new armies are raised at home, Dutch forces are brought into these kingdoms.' What in the name of wonder do you mean? Are you in earnest, or do you design to banter us? Whom is the nation obliged to, for all this load of war that it feels? Had you been wise enough to have slept at Bar-le-duc in a whole skin, we should not have contracted new debts, raised new armies, or brought over Dutch forces to make an example of you.

The most pleasant grievance is still behind, and, indeed, a most proper one to close up this. 'King George has taken possession of the duchy of Bremen, whereby a door is opened to let in an inundation of foreigners from abroad, and to reduce these nations to the state of a province to one of the most inconsiderable provinces of the empire.' And do you then really believe the mob-story, that King George designs to make a bridge of boats from Hanover to Wapping? We would have you know, that some of us read Baker's Chronicle, and do not find that

William the Conqueror ever thought of making England a province to his native duchy of Normandy, notwithstanding it lay so much more convenient for that purpose: nor that King James the first had ever any thoughts of reducing this nation to the state of a province to his ancient kingdom of Scotland, though it lies upon the same continent. But pray how comes it to pass that the Electorate of Hanover has become all of a sudden one of the most inconsiderable provinces of the empire? If you undervalue it upon the account of its religion, you have some reason for what you say; though you should not think we are such strangers to maps, and live so much out of the world, as to be ignorant that it is for power and extent the second Protestant state in Germany; and whether you know it or no, the Protestant religion in the empire is looked upon as a sufficient balance against popery. Besides, you should have considered, that in your declaration upon the king's coming to the throne of Great Britain, you endeavoured to terrify us from receiving him, by representing him 'as a powerful foreign prince, supported by a numerous army of his own subjects.' Be that as it will; we are no more afraid of being a province to Hanover, than the Hanoverians are apprehensive of being a province to Bremen.

We have now taken notice of those great evils which you have come to rescue us from: but as they are such as we have neither felt or seen, we desire you will put yourself to no farther trouble for our sakes.

You afterwards begin a kind of Te Deum, before the time, in that remarkable sentence, 'We adore the wisdom of the Divine Providence, which has opened a way to our restoration, by the success of those very measures that were laid to disappoint us for ever.' We are at a loss to know what you mean by this devout jargon: but by what goes before and follows, we suppose it to be this: that the coming of King George to the crown has made many malecontents, and by that means opened a way to your restoration; whereas, you should consider, that, if he had not come to the crown, the way had been open of itself. In the same pious paragraph, 'You most earnestly conjure us to pursue those methods for your restoration, which the finger of God seems to point out to us." Now the only methods which we can make use of for that end, are civil war, rapine, bloodshed, treason, and perjury; methods which we Protestants do humbly conceive, can never be pointed out to us by the finger of God.

The rest of your declaration contains the encouragements you give us to rebel. First, you promise to share with us 'all dangers and difficulties' which we shall meet with in this worthy enterprise. You are very much in the right of it: you have nothing to lose, and hope to get a crown: we do not hope for any new freeholds, and only desire to keep what we have. As, therefore, you are in the right to undergo dangers and difficulties to make yourself our master, we shall think ourselves as much in the right to undergo dangers and difficulties to hinder you from being so.[a]

Secondly, You promise to 'refer your and our interest to a Scotch parliament,' which you are resolved to call immediately. We suppose you mean if the frost holds. But, sir, we are certainly informed there is a parliament now sitting at Westminster, that are busy at present in taking care both of the Scotch and English interest, and have actually done every thing which you would 'let' be done by our representatives in the Highlands.

Thirdly, 'You promise that if we will rebel for you against our present sovereign, you will remit and discharge all crimes of high-treason, misprision, and all other crimes and offences whatso-

[a] The honest freeholders conclude too fast, in this place. The inference from their own premises is only this.—*We shall think ourselves as much in the right to undergo nod angers and difficulties to assist you in being so.*

ever, done or committed against you or your father.' But will you answer in this case, that King George will forgive us? Otherwise we beseech you to consider what poor comfort it would be for a British freeholder to be conveyed up Holborn with your pardon in his pocket. And here we cannot but remark, that the conditions of your general pardon are so stinted, as to shew that you are very cautious lest your good nature should carry you too far. You exclude from the benefit of it, all those who do not 'from the time of your landing lay hold on mercy, and return to their duty and allegiance.' By this means all neuters and lookers-on are to be executed of course: and by the studied ambiguity in which you couch the terms of your gracious pardon, you still leave room to gratify yourself in all the pleasures of tyranny and revenge.

Upon the whole, we have so bad an opinion of rebellion, as well as of your motives to it, and rewards for it, that you may rest satisfied, there are few freeholders on this side the Forth who will engage in it: and we verily believe that you will suddenly take a resolution in your cabinet of Highlanders to scamper off with your new crown, which we are told the ladies of those parts have so generously clubbed for. And you may assure yourself that it is the only one you are like to get by this notable expedition. And so we bid you heartily farewel.

Dated Jan. 19, in the second year of
our public happiness.

## No. 10. MONDAY, JANUARY 23.

Potior visa est periculosa libertas quieto servitio.

SALL.

ONE may venture to affirm, that all honest and disinterested Britons of what party soever, if they understood one another, are of the same opinion in points of government: and that the gross of the people, who are imposed upon by terms which they do not comprehend, are whigs in their hearts. They are made to believe, that passive obedience and non-resistance, unlimited power and indefeasible right, have something of a venerable and religious meaning in them; whereas in reality they only imply, that a king of Great Britain has a right to be a tyrant, and that his subjects are obliged in conscience to be slaves. Were the case truly and fairly laid before them, they would know, that when they make a profession of such principles, they renounce their legal claim to liberty and property, and unwarily submit to what they really abhor.

It is our happiness, under the present reign, to hear our king from the throne exhorting us to be 'zealous assertors of the liberties of our country;' which exclude all pretensions to an arbitrary, tyrannic, despotic power. Those, who have the misfortune to live under such a power, have no other law but the will of their prince, and consequently no privileges, but what are precarious. For though in some arbitrary governments there may be a body of laws observed in the ordinary forms of justice, they are not sufficient to secure any rights to the people; because they may be dispensed with, or laid aside, at the pleasure of the sovereign.

And here it very much imports us to consider, that arbitrary power naturally tends to make a man a bad sovereign, who might possibly have been a good one, had he been invested with an authority limited and circumscribed by laws. None can doubt of this tendency in arbitrary power, who consider, that it fills the mind of man with great and unreasonable conceits of himself; raises him into a belief, that he is of a superior species to his subjects; extinguishes in him the principle of fear, which is one of the greatest motives to all duties; and creates an ambition of magnifying himself, by the exertion of such a power in all its instances. So great is the danger, that when a sovereign can do what he will, he will do what he can.

One of the most arbitrary princes in our age was Muley Ishmael, Emperor of Morocco, who, after a long reign, died about a twelve-month ago. This prince was a man of much wit and natural sense, of an active temper, undaunted courage, and great application. He was a descendant of Mahomet; and so exemplary for his adherence to the law of his prophet, that he abstained all his life from the taste of wine; began the annual fast, or Lent of Ramadan, two months before his subjects; was frequent in his prayers; and that he might not want opportunities of kneeling, had fixed in all the spacious courts of his palace large consecrated stones pointing towards the east, for any occasional exercise of his devotion. What might not have been hoped from a prince of these endowments, had they not been all rendered useless and ineffectual to the good of his people by the notion of that power which they ascribed to him! This will appear, if we consider how he exercised it towards his subjects in those three great points which are the chief ends of government, the preservation of their lives, the security of their fortunes, and the determinations of justice between man and man.

Foreign envoys, who have given an account of their audiences, describe this holy man mounted on horseback in an open court, with several of his Alcaydes, or governors of provinces about him standing bare-foot, trembling, bowing to the earth, and at every word he spoke, breaking out into passionate exclamations of praise, as, 'Great is the wisdom of our lord the king; our lord the king speaks as an angel from heaven.' Happy was the man among them, who was so much a favourite as to be sent on an errand to the most remote street in his capital; which he performed with the greatest alacrity, ran through every puddle that lay in the way, and took care to return out of breath and covered with dirt, that he might shew himself a diligent and faithful minister. His majesty at the same time, to exhibit the greatness of his power, and shew his horsemanship, seldom dismissed the foreigner from his presence, 'till he had entertained him with the slaughter of two or three of his liege subjects, whom he very dexterously put to death with the tilt of his lance. St. Olon, the French envoy, tells us, that when he had his last audience of him, he received him in robes just stained with an execution; and that he was blooded up to his elbows by a couple of Moors, whom he had been butchering with his own imperial hands. By the calculation of that author, and many others, who have since given an account of his exploits, we may reckon that by his own arm he killed above forty thousand of his people. To render himself the more awful, he chose to wear a garb of a particular colour when he was bent upon executions; so that when he appeared in yellow, his great men hid themselves in corners, and durst not pay their court to him, till he had satiated his thirst of blood by the death of some of his loyal commoners, or of such unwary officers of state as chanced to come in his way. Upon this account we are told, that the first news inquired after every morning at Mequinez, was, Whether the emperor were stirring, and in a good or bad humour? As this prince was a great admirer of architecture, and employed many thousands in works of that kind, if he did not approve the plan or the performance, it was usual for him to shew the delicacy of his taste by demolishing the building, and putting to death all that had a hand in it. I have heard but of one instance of his mercy; which was shewn to the master of an English vessel. This our countryman presented him with a curious hatchet, which he received very graciously; and asking him whether it had a good edge, tried it upon the donor, who slipping aside from the blow, escaped with the loss only of his right ear; for old Muley, upon second thoughts, considering that it was not one of his own subjects, stopped his hand, and would not send him to Paradise. I cannot quit this article of his tenderness for the lives of his people, without mentioning one of his queens, whom he was remarkably fond of; as also a favorite prime minister, who was very dear to him. The first died by a kick of her lord the king, when she was big with child, for having gathered a flower as she was walking with him in his pleasure garden. The other was bastinadoed to death by his majesty; who, repenting of the drubs he had given him when it was too late, to manifest his esteem for the memory of so worthy a man, executed the surgeon that could not cure him.

This absolute monarch was as notable a guardian of the fortunes, as of the lives of his subjects. When any man among his people grew rich, in order to keep him from being dangerous to the state, he used to send for all his goods and chattels. His governors of towns and provinces, who formed themselves upon the example of their *Grand Monarque*, practised rapine, violence, extortion, and all the arts of despotic government in their respective districts, that they might be the better enabled to make him their yearly presents. For the greatest of his viceroys could only propose to himself a comfortable subsistence out of the plunder of his province, and was in certain danger of being recalled or hanged, if he did not remit the bulk of it to his dread sovereign. That he might make a right use of these prodigious treasures, which flowed in to him from all the parts of his wide empire, he took care to bury them under ground, by the hands of his most trusty slaves, and then cut their throats, as the most effectual method to keep them from making discoveries. These were his Ways and Means for raising money, by which he weakened the hands of the factious, and in any case of emergency, could employ the whole wealth of his empire, which he had thus amassed together in his subterraneous exchequer.

As there is no such thing as property under an arbitrary government, you may learn what was Muley Ishmael's notion of it from the following story. Being upon the road, amidst his life-guards, a little before the time of the Ram-feast, he met one of his Alcaydes at the head of his servants, who were driving a great flock of sheep to market. The emperor asked whose they were: the Alcayde answered with profound submission, 'They are mine, O Ishmael, son of Elcherif, of the line of Hassan.' 'Thine! thou son of a cuckold,' said this servant of the Lord, 'I thought I had been the only proprietor in this country;' upon which he run him through the body with his lance, and very piously distributed the sheep among his guards, for the celebration of the feast.

His determinations of justice between man and man, were indeed very summary and decisive, and generally put an end to the vexations of a law-suit, by the ruin both of plaintiff and defendant. Travellers have recorded some samples of this kind, which may give us an idea of the blessings of his administration. One of his Alcaydes complaining to him of a wife, whom he had received from his majesty's hands, and therefore could not divorce her, that she used to pull him by the beard; the emperor, to redress this grievance, ordered his beard to be plucked up by the roots, that he might not be liable to any more such affronts. A country farmer having accused some of his negro guards for robbing him of a drove of oxen, the emperor readily shot the offenders: but afterwards demanding reparation of the accuser, for the loss of so many brave fellows, and finding him insolvent, compounded the matter with him by taking away his life. There are many other instances, of the same kind. I must observe, however, under this head, that the only good thing he is celebrated for, during his whole reign, was the clearing of the roads and highways of robbers, with which they used to be very much infested. But his method was to slay man, woman, and child, who lived within a certain distance from the place, where the robbery was committed. This extraordinary piece of justice could not but have its effect, by making every road in his empire unsafe for the profession of a free-booter.

I must not omit this emperor's reply to Sir Cloudesly Shovel, who had taken several of his subjects by way of reprisal, for the English captives that were detained in his dominions. Upon the admiral's offering to exchange them on very advantageous terms, this good emperor sent him word, The subjects he had taken were poor men, not worth the ransoming; and that he might throw them overboard, or destroy them otherwise as he pleased.

Such was the government of Muley Ishmael, 'the servant of God, the emperor of the faithful, who was courageous in the way of the Lord, the noble, the good.'

To conclude this account, which is extracted from the best authorities, I shall only observe, that he was a great admirer of his late most Christian majesty. In a letter to him, he compliments him with the title of 'sovereign arbiter of the actions and wills of his people.' And in a book published by a Frenchman, who was sent to him as an ambassador, is the following passage, 'He is absolute in his states, and often compares himself to the emperor of France, who he says is the only person that knows how to reign like himself, and to make his will the law.'

This was that emperor of France to whom the person who has a great mind to be king of these realms owed his education, and from whom he learned his notions of government. What should hinder one, whose mind is so well seasoned with such prepossessions, from attempting to copy after his patron, in the exercise of such a power; especially considering that the party who espouse his interest, never fail to compliment a prince that distributes all his places among them, with unlimited power on his part, and unconditional obedience on that of his subjects.

---

## No. 11. FRIDAY, JANUARY 27.

Honi soit qui mal y pense.

By our latest advices, both from town and country, it appears, that the ladies of Great Britain, who are able to bear arms, that is, to smile or frown to any purpose, have already begun to commit hostilities upon the men of each opposite party. To this end we are assured, that many of them on both sides exercise before their glasses every morning; that they have already cashiered several of their followers as mutineers, who have contradicted them in some political conversations; and that the whig ladies in particular, design very soon to have a general review of their forces at a play bespoken by one of their leaders. This set of ladies, indeed, as they daily do duty at court, are much more expert in the use of their airs and graces than their female antagonists, who are most of them bred in the country: so that the sisterhood of loyalists, in respect of the fair malecontents, are like an army of regular forces, compared with a raw undisciplined militia.

It is to this misfortune in their education that we may ascribe the rude and opprobrious language with which the disaffected part of the sex treat the present royal family. A little lively rustic, who hath been trained up in ignorance and prejudice, will prattle treason a whole winter's evening, and string together a parcel of silly seditious stories, that are equally void of decency and truth. Nay, you sometimes meet with a zealous matron, who sets up for the pattern of a parish, uttering such invectives as are highly mis-becoming her, both as a woman and a subject. In answer, therefore, to such disloyal termagants, I shall repeat to them a speech of the honest and blunt duke du Sully, to an assembly of popish ladies, who were railing very bitterly against Henry the fourth, at his accession to the French throne; "Ladies," said he, "you have a very good king, if you know when you are well. However, set your hearts at rest, for he is not a man to be scolded or scratched out of his kingdom."

But as I never care to speak of the fair sex, unless I have an occasion to praise them, I shall take my leave of these ungentle damsels; and only beg of them, not to make themselves less amiable than nature designed them, by being rebels to the best of their abilities, and endeavouring to bring their country into bloodshed and confusion. Let me, therefore, recommend to them the example of those beautiful associates, whom I mentioned in my eighth paper, as I have received the particulars of their behaviour from the person with whom I lodged their association.

This association being written at length in a large roll of the finest vellum, with three distinct columns for the maids, wives, and widows, was opened for the subscribers near a fortnight ago. Never was a subscription for a raffling or an opera more crowded. There is scarce a celebrated beauty about town that you may not find in one of the three lists; insomuch, that if a man, who did not know the design, should read only the names of the subscribers, he would fancy every column to be a catalogue of toasts Mr. Motteux has been heard to say more than once, that if he had the portraits of all the associates, they would make a finer auction of pictures, than he or any body else had exhibited.

Several of these ladies, indeed, criticised upon the form of the association. One of them, after the perusal of it, wondered that among the features to be used in defence of their country, there was no mention made of *teeth;* upon which she smiled very charmingly, and discovered as fine a set as ever eye beheld. Another, who was a tall lovely prude, holding up her head in a most majestic manner, said, with some disdain, she thought a *good neck* might have done his majesty as much service as smiles or dimples. A third looked upon the association as defective, because so necessary a word as *hands* was omitted; and by her manner of taking up the pen, it was easy to guess the reason of her objection.

Most of the persons who associated, have done much more than by the letter of the association they were obliged to; having not only set their names to it, but subscribed their several aids and subsidies for the carrying on so good a cause. In the virgin column is one who subscribes fifteen lovers, all of them good men and true. There is another who subscribes five admirers, with one tall handsome black man fit to be a colonel. In short, there is scarce one in this list who does not engage herself to supply a quota of brisk young fellows, many of them already equipt with hats and feathers. Among the rest, was a pretty sprightly coquette, with sparkling eyes, who subscribed two quivers of arrows.

In the column of wives, the first that took pen in hand, writ her own name and one vassal, meaning her husband. Another subscribes her husband and three sons. Another her husband and six coach-horses. Most in this catalogue paired themselves with their respective mates, answering for them as men of honest principles, and fit for the service.

N. B. There were two in this column that wore association ribbons; the first of them subscribed her husband, and her husband's friend; the second a husband and five lovers; but upon inquiry into their characters, they are both of them found to be tories, who hung out false colours to be spies upon the association, or to insinuate to the world by their subscriptions, as if a lady of whig principles could love any man besides her husband.

The widow's column is headed by a fine woman who calls herself Boadicea, and subscribes six hundred tenants. It was, indeed, observed that the strength of the association lay most in this column; every widow, in proportion to her jointure, having a great number of admirers, and most of them distinguished as able men. Those who have examined this list, compute that there may be three regiments raised out of it, in which there shall not be one man under six foot high.

I must not conclude this account, without taking notice of the association ribbon, by which these beautiful confederates have agreed to distinguish themselves. It is, indeed, so very pretty an ornament, that I wonder any English woman will be without it. A lady of the association who bears this badge of allegiance upon her breast, naturally produces a desire in every male beholder, of gaining a place in a heart which carries on it such a visible mark of its fidelity. When the beauties of our island are thus industrious to shew their principles as well as their charms, they raise the sentiments of their countrymen, and inspire them at the same time both with loyalty and love. What numbers of proselytes may we not expect, when the most amiable of the Britons thus exhibit to their admirers the only terms upon which they are to hope for any correspondence or alliance with them! It is well known that the greatest blow the French nation ever received, was the dropping of a fine lady's garter, in the reign of King Edward the third. The most remarkable battles which have been since gained over that nation, were fought under the auspices of a blue ribbon. As our British ladies have still the same faces, and our men the same hearts, why may we not hope for the same glorious achievements from the influence of this beautiful breast-knot?

---

## No. 12. MONDAY, JANUARY 30.

Quapropter, de summâ salute vestrâ, P. C. de vestris conjugibus ac liberis, de aris ac focis, de fanis ac templis, de totius urbis tectis ac sedibus, de imperio, de libertate, de salute patriæ, deque universâ republicâ decernite diligenter, ut instituistis, ac fortiter.

CICERO.

THIS day having been set apart by public authority to raise in us an abhorrence of the great rebellion, which involved this nation in so many calamities, and ended in the murder of their sovereign; it may not be unseasonable to shew the guilt of rebellion in general, and of that rebellion in particular which is stirred up against his present majesty.

That rebellion is one of the most heinous crimes which it is in the power of man to commit, may appear from several considerations. First, As it destroys the end of all government, and the benefits of civil society. Government was instituted for maintaining the peace, safety, and happiness of a people. These great ends are brought about by a general conformity and submission to that frame of laws which is established in every community, for the protection of the innocent, and the punishment of the guilty. As on the one side men are secured in the quiet possession of their lives, properties, and every thing they have a right to: so on the other side, those who offer them any injury in these particulars, are subject to penalties proportioned to their respective offences. Government, therefore, mitigates the in equality of power among particular persons, and makes an innocent man, though of the lowest rank, a match for the mightiest of his fellow-subjects; since he has the force of the whole community on his side, which is able to control the insolence or injustice of any private oppressor. Now rebellion disappoints all these ends and benefits of government, by raising a power in opposition to that authority which has been established among a people for their mutual welfare and defence. So that rebellion is as great an evil to society, as government itself is a blessing.

In the next place, rebellion is the violation of those engagements, which every government exacts from such persons as live under it; and consequently, the most base and pernicious instance of treachery and perfidiousness. The guilt of rebellion increases in proportion as these engagements are more solemn and obligatory. Thus if a man makes his way to rebellion through perjury, he gives additional horrors to that crime, which is in itself of the blackest nature.

We may likewise consider rebellion as a greater complication of wickedness than any other crime we can commit. It is big with rapine, sacrilege, and murder. It is dreadful in its mildest effects, as it impoverishes the public; ruins particular families; begets and perpetuates hatreds among fellow-subjects, friends, and relations; makes a country the seat of war and desolation, and exposes it to the attempts of its foreign enemies. In short, as it is impossible for it to take effect, or to make the smallest progress, but through a continued course of violence and bloodshed; a robber or a murderer looks like an innocent man, when we compare him with a rebel.

I shall only add, that as in the subordination of a government the king is offended by any insults or oppositions to an inferior magistrate; so the sovereign ruler of the universe is affronted by a breach of allegiance to those whom he has set over us: Providence having delegated to the supreme magistrate in every country the same power for the good of men, which that supreme magistrate transfers to those several officers and substitutes who act under him, for the preserving of order and justice.

Now if we take a view of the present rebellion which is formed against his majesty, we shall find in it all the guilt that is naturally inherent in this crime, without any single circumstance to alleviate it. Insurrections among a people to rescue themselves from the most violent and illegal oppressions; to throw off a tyranny that makes property precarious, and life painful; to preserve their laws and their religion to themselves and their posterity; are excused from the necessity of such an undertaking, when no other means are left for the security of every thing that is dear and valuable to reasonable creatures. By the frame of our constitution, the duties of protection and allegiance are reciprocal; and as the safety of a community is the ultimate end and design of government, when this, instead of being preserved, is manifestly destroyed, civil societies are excusable before God and man, if they endeavour to recover themselves out of so miserable a condition. For in such a case government becomes an evil instead of a blessing, and is not at all preferable to a state of anarchy and mutual independence. For these reasons, we have scarce ever yet heard of an insurrection that was not either coloured with grievances of the highest kind, or countenanced by one or more branches of the legislature. But the present rebellion is formed against a king, whose right has been established by frequent parliaments of all parties, and recognised by the most solemn oaths; who has not been charged with one illegal proceeding; who acts in perfect concert with the lords and commons of the realm; who is famed for his equity and goodness, and has already very much advanced the reputation and interest of our country. The guilt, therefore, of this rebellion, has in it all the most aggravating circumstances; which will still appear more plainly, if we consider, in the first place, the real motives to it.

The rebellion, which was one of the most flagitious in itself, and described with the most horror by historians, is that of Cataline and his associates. The motives to it are displayed at large by the Roman writers, in order to inspire the reader with the utmost detestation of it. Cataline, the chief of the rebellion, had been disappointed in his competition for one of the first offices in the government, and had involved himself in such private debts and difficulties, as nothing could extricate him out of, but the ruin of an administration that would not intrust him with posts of honour or profit. His principal accomplices were men of the same character, and animated by the same incentives. They complained that power was lodged in the hands of the worst, to the oppression of the best: and that places were conferred on unworthy men, to the exclusion of themselves and their friends. Many of them were afraid of public justice for past crimes, and some of them stood actually condemned as traitors to their country. These were joined by men of desperate fortunes, who hoped to find their account in the confusions of their country, were applauded by the meanest of the rabble, who always delighted in change, and privately abetted by persons of a considerable figure, who aimed at those honours and preferments which were in the possession of their rivals. These are the motives with which Cataline's rebellion is branded in history, and which are expressly mentioned by Sallust. I shall leave it to every unprejudiced reader to compare them with the motives which have kindled the present rebellion in his majesty's dominions.

As this rebellion is of the most criminal nature from its motives, so it is likewise if we consider its consequences. Should it succeed, (a supposition which, God be thanked, is very extravagant) what must be the natural effects of it upon our religion! what could we expect from an army, blest by the pope, headed by a zealous Roman Catholic, encouraged by the most bigotted princes of the church of Rome, supported by contributions not only from these several potentates, but from the wealthiest of their convents, and officered by Irish papists and out-laws! Can we imagine that the Roman Catholics of our own nation would so heartily embark in an enterprise, to the visible hazard of their lives and fortunes, did they only hope to enjoy their religion under those laws which are now in force? In short, the danger to the Protestant cause is so manifest, that it would be an affront to the understanding of the reader to endeavour farther to prove it.

Arbitrary power is so interwoven with popery, and so necessary to introduce it, so agreeable to the education of the Pretender, so conformable to the principles of his adherents, and so natural to the insolence of conquerors, that should our invader gain the sovereign power by violence, there is no doubt but he would preserve it by tyranny. I shall leave to the reader's own consideration, the change of property in general, and the utter extinction of it in our national funds, the inundation of nobles without estates, prelates without bishoprics, officers civil and military without places; and in short, the several occasions of rapine and revenge, which would necessarily ensue upon such a fatal revolution. But by the blessing of Providence, and the wisdom of his majesty's administration, this melancholy prospect is as distant as it is dreadful.

These are the consequences which would necessarily attend the success of the present rebellion. But we will now suppose that the event of it should for some time remain doubtful. In this case we are to expect all the miseries of a civil war: nay, the armies of the greatest foreign princes would be subsisted,[a] and all the battles of Europe fought in England. The rebels have already shewn us, that they want no inclination to promote their cause by fire and sword, where they have an opportunity of practising their barbarities. Should such a fierce and rapacious host of men, as that which is now in the highlands, fall down into our country, that is so well peopled, adorned, and cultivated, how would their march be distinguished by ravage and devastation! might not we say of them in the sublime and beautiful words of the prophet, describing the progress of an enraged army from the north; 'Before them is as the garden of Eden, and behind them as the desolate wilderness; yea, and nothing shall escape them.'

What then can we think of a party, who would plunge their native country into such evils as these; when the only avowed motive for their proceedings is a point of theory, that has been already determined by those who are proper judges, and in whose determination we have so many years acquiesced. If the calamities of the nation in general can make no impression on them, let them at least, in pity to themselves, their friends and dependants, forbear all open and secret methods of encouraging a rebellion, so destructive, and so unprovoked. All human probabilities are against them; and they cannot expect success, but from a miraculous interposition of the Almighty. And this we may with all christian humility hope, will not turn against us, who observe those oaths which we have made in his presence; who are zealous for the safety of that religion, which we think most acceptable in his sight; and who endeavour to preserve that constitution which is most conducive to the happiness of our country.

[a] *Subsisted*—the proper word is *maintained*, or *supported*. To *subsist*, is a neutral verb, and cannot be used, as here, in a passive sense.

## No. 13. FRIDAY, FEBRUARY 3.

Ignavum fucos pecus à præsepibus arcent.—VIRG.

THE most common, and indeed the most natural division of all offences, is into those of omission and commission. We may make the same division of that particular set of crimes which regard human society. The greatest crime which can be committed against it is rebellion; as was shewn in my last paper. The greatest crime of omission, is an indifference in the particular members of a society, when a rebellion is actually begun among them. In such a juncture, though a man may be innocent of the great breach which is made upon government, he is highly culpable, if he does not use all the means that are suitable to his station, for reducing the community into its former state of peace and good order.

Our obligation to be active on such an occasion appears from the nature of civil government, which is an institution, whereby we are all confederated together for our mutual defence and security. Men who profess a state of neutrality in times of public danger, desert the common interest of their fellow-subjects; and act with independence to[a] that constitution into which they are incorporated. The safety of the whole requires our joint endeavours. When this is at stake, the indifferent are not properly a part of the community; or rather are like dead limbs, which are an encumbrance to the body, instead of being of use to it. Besides that, the protection which all receive from the same government, justly calls upon the gratitude of all to strengthen it, as well as upon their self-interest to preserve it.

But farther; if men, who in their hearts are friends to a government, forbear giving it their utmost assistance against its

[a] *To.* Rather *on.* But the expression is hardly English. It should be—*and act, as if they had no dependance on.*

enemies, they put it in the power of a few desperate men to ruin the welfare of those who are much superior to them in strength, number, and interest. It was a remarkable law of Solon, the great legislator of the Athenians, that any person who in the civil tumults and commotions of the republic remained neuter, or an indifferent spectator of the contending parties, should, after the re establishment of the public peace, forfeit all his possessions and be condemned to perpetual banishment. This law made it necessary for every citizen to take his party, because it was highly probable the majority would be so wise as to espouse that cause which was most agreeable to the public weal, and by that means hinder a sedition from making a successful progress. At least, as every prudent and honest man, who might otherwise favour any indolence in his own temper, was hereby engaged to be active, such a one would be sure to join himself to that side which had the good of their country most at heart. For this reason their famous law-giver condemned the persons who sat idle in divisions so dangerous to the government, as aliens to the community, and therefore to be cut off from it as unprofitable members.

Further; Indifference cannot but be criminal, when it is conversant about objects which are so far from being of an indifferent nature, that they are of the highest importance to ourselves and our country. If it be indifferent to us whether we are free subjects or slaves; whether our prince be of our own religion, or of one that obliges him to extirpate it; we are in the right to give ourselves no trouble in the present juncture. A man governs himself by the dictates of virtue and good sense, who acts without zeal or passion in points that are of no consequence: but when the whole community is shaken, and the safety of the public endangered, the appearance of a philosophical or an affected indolence must arise either from stupidity, or perfidiousness.

When in the division of parties among us, men only strove for the first place in the prince's favour; when all were attached to the same form of government, and contended only for the highest offices in it; a prudent and an honest man might look upon the struggle with indifference, and be in no great pain for the success of either side. But at present the contest is not in reality between Whigs and Tories, but between Loyalists and Rebels. Our country is not now divided into two parties, who propose the same end by different means; but into such as would preserve and such as would destroy it. Whatever denominations we might range ourselves under in former times, men who have any natural love to their country, or sense of their duty, should exert their united strength in a cause that is common to all parties, as they are Protestants and Britons. In such a case, an avowed indifference is treachery to our fellow-subjects; and a lukewarm allegiance may prove as pernicious in its consequences as treason.

I need not repeat here what I have proved at large in a former paper, that we are obliged to an active obedience by the solemn oaths we have taken to his majesty; and that the neutral kind of indifference, which is the subject of this paper, falls short of that obligation they lie under, who have taken such oaths; as will easily appear to any one who considers the form of those sacred and religious engagements.

How then can any man answer it to himself, if, for the sake of managing his interest or character among a party, or out of any personal pique to those who are the most conspicuous for their zeal in his majesty's service, or from any other private and self-interested motive, he stands as a looker-on when the government is attacked by an open rebellion? especially when those engaged in it, cannot have the least prospect of success, but by the assistance of the ancient and hereditary enemies to the British nation. It is strange that these lukewarm friends to the government, whose zeal for their sovereign rises and falls with their credit at court, do not consider, before it be too late, that as they strengthen the rebels by their present indifference, they at the same time establish the interest of those who are their rivals and competitors for public posts of honour. When there is an end put to this rebellion, these gentlemen cannot pretend to have had any merit in so good a work: and they may well believe the nation will never care to see those men in the highest offices of trust, who when they are out of them, will not stir a finger in its defence.

---

## No. 14. MONDAY, FEBRUARY 6.

Periculosum est credere, et non credere:
Utriusque exemplum breviter exponam rei,
Hippolytus obiit, quia novercæ creditum est:
Cassandræ quia non creditum, ruit Ilium.
Ergo exploranda est veritas multùm priùs,
Quàm stulta pravè judicet sententia.

PHÆDR.

Having in the seventh paper considered many of those falsehoods, by which the cause of our malecontents is supported; I shall here speak of that extravagant credulity, which disposes each particular member of their party to believe them. This strange alacrity in believing absurdity and inconsistence may be called the political faith of a tory.

A person who is thoroughly endowed with this political faith like a man in a dream, is entertained from one end of his life to the other with objects that have no reality or existence. He is daily nourished and kept in humour by fiction and delusion; and may be compared to the old obstinate knight in Rabelais, that every morning swallowed a chimera for his breakfast.

This political faith of a malecontent is altogether founded on hope. He does not give credit to any thing because it is probable, but because it is pleasing. His wishes serve him instead of reasons, to confirm the truth of what he hears. There is no report so incredible or contradictory in itself which he doth not cheerfully believe, if it tends to the advancement of the cause. In short, a malecontent, who is a good believer, has generally reason to repeat the celebrated rant of an ancient father, 'Credo quia impossibile est:' which is as much as to say, 'It must be true, because it is impossible.'

It has been very well observed, that the most credulous man in the world is the atheist, who believes the universe to be the production of chance. In the same manner a tory, who is the greatest believer in what is improbable, is the greatest infidel in what is certain. Let a friend to the government relate to him a matter of fact, he turns away his ear from him, and gives him the lie in every look. But if one of his own stamp should tell him that the king of Sweden would be suddenly at Perth, and that his army is now actually marching thither upon the ice; he hugs himself at the good news, and gets drunk upon it before he goes to bed. This sort of people puts one in mind of several towns in Europe that are inaccessible on the one side, while they lie open and unguarded on the other. The minds of our malecontents are indeed so depraved with those falsehoods which they are perpetually imbibing, that they have a natural relish for error, and have quite lost the taste of truth in political matters. I shall therefore dismiss this head with a saying of King Charles the second. This monarch, when he was at Windsor, used to amuse himself with the conversation of the famous Vossius, who was full of stories relating to the antiquity, learning, and manners, of the Chinese; and at the same time a free-thinker in points of religion. The king, upon hearing him repeat some incredible accounts of these eastern people, turning to those who were about him, 'This learned divine,' said he, 'is a very strange man: he believes every thing but the bible.'

Having thus far considered the political faith of the party as it regards matters of fact, let us, in the next place, take a view of it with respect to those doctrines which it embraces, and which are the fundamental points whereby they are distinguished from those, whom they used to represent as enemies to the constitution in church and state. . How far their great articles of political faith, with respect to our ecclesiastical and civil government, are consistent with themselves, and agreeable to reason and truth, may be seen in the following paradoxes, which are the essentials of a tory's creed, with relation to political matters. Under the name of tories, I do not here comprehend multitudes of well-designing men, who were formerly included under that denomination, but are now in the interest of his majesty and the present government. These have already seen the evil tendency of such principles, which are the Credenda of the party, as it is opposite to that of the whigs.

ARTICLE I.

That the church of England will be always in danger, till it has a popish king for its defender.

That, for the safety of the church, no subject should be tolerated in any religion different from the established; but that the head of our church may be of that religion which is most repugnant to it.

III.

That the Protestant interest in this nation, and in all Europe, could not but flourish under the protection of one, who thinks himself obliged, on pain of damnation, to do all that lies in his power for the extirpation of it.

IV.

That we may safely rely upon the promises of one, whose religion allows him to make them, and at the same time obliges him to break them.

V.

That a good man should have a greater abhorrence of Presbyterianism which is perverseness, than of Popery which is but idolatry.

VI.

That a person who hopes to be King of England by the assistance of France, would naturally adhere to the British interest, which is always opposite to that of the French.

VII.

That a man has no opportunities of learning how to govern the people of England in any foreign country, so well as in France.

VIII.

That ten millions of people should rather chuse to fall into slavery, than not acknowledge their prince to be invested with an hereditary and indefeasible right of oppression.

IX.

That we are obliged in conscience to become subjects of a duke of Savoy, or of a French king, rather than enjoy for our sovereign, a prince who is the first of the royal blood in the Protestant line.

X.

That non-resistance is the duty of every Christian, whilst he is in a good place.

XI.

That we ought to profess the doctrine of passive obedience until such time as nature rebels against principle, that is, until we are put to the necessity of practising it.

XII.

That the Papists have taken up arms to defend the church of England with the utmost hazard of their lives and fortunes.

XIII.

That there is an unwarrantable faction in this island, consisting of King, Lords, and Commons.

XIV.

That the legislature, when there is a majority of whigs in it, has not power to make laws.

XV.

That an act of parliament to impower the king to secure suspected persons in times of rebellion, is the means to establish the sovereign on the throne, and consequently a great infringement of the liberties of the throne.

## No. 15. FRIDAY, FEBRUARY 10, 1710.

——————Auxilium, quoniam sic cogitis ipsi,
Dixit, ab hoste petam: vultus avertite vestros,
Si quis amicus adest: et Gorgonis extulit ora.
OVID.

It is with great pleasure that I see a race of female patriots springing up in this island. The fairest among the daughters of Great Britain no longer confine their cares to a domestic life, but are grown anxious for the welfare of their country, and shew themselves good stateswomen as well as good housewives.

Our she-confederates keep pace with us in quashing that rebellion which had begun to spread itself among part of the fair sex. If the men who are true to their king and country have taken Preston and Perth, the ladies have possessed themselves of the opera and the play-house with as little opposition of bloodshed. The non-resisting women, like their brothers in the Highlands, think no post tenable against an army that makes so fine an appearance; and dare not look them in the face, when they are drawn up in battle-array.

As an instance of this cheerfulness in our fair fellow-subjects to oppose the designs of the pretender, I did but suggest in one of my former papers, 'That the fan might be made use of with good success against Popery, by exhibiting the corruptions of the church of Rome in various figures;' when immediately they took the hint, and have since had frequent consultations upon several ways and methods 'to make the fan useful.' They have unanimously agreed upon the following resolutions, which are indeed very suitable to ladies who are at the same time the most beautiful and the most loyal of their sex. To hide their faces behind the fan, when they observe a tory gazing upon them. Never to peep through it, but in order to pick out men, whose principles make them worth the conquest. To return no other answer to a tory's addresses, than by counting the sticks of it all the while he is talking to them. To avoid dropping it in the neighbourhood of a malecontent, that he may not have an opportunity of taking it up. To shew their disbelief of any Jacobite story by a flirt of it. To fall a fanning themselves, when a tory comes into one of their assemblies, as being disordered at the sight of him.

These are the uses by which every fan may in the hands of a fine woman become serviceable to the public. But they have at present under consideration, certain fans of a Protestant make, that they may have a more extensive influence, and raise an abhorrence of Popery in a whole crowd of beholders: for they intend to let the world see what party they are of, by figures and designs upon these fans; as the knights-errant used to distinguish themselves by devices on their shields.

There are several sketches of pictures which have been already presented to the ladies for their approbation, and out of which several have made their choice. A pretty young lady will very soon appear with a fan, which has on it a nunnery of lively black-eyed vestals, who are endeavouring to creep out at the grates. Another has a fan mounted with a fine paper, on which is represented a group of people upon their knees very devoutly worshipping an old ten-penny nail. A certain lady of great learning has chosen for her device the council of Trent; and another, who has a good satirical turn, has filled her fan with the figure of a huge tawdry woman, representing the whore of Babylon; which sne is resolved to spread full in the face of any sister-disputant, whose arguments have a tendency to Popery. The following designs are already executed on several mountings. The ceremony of the holy Pontiff opening the mouth of a cardinal in a full consistory. An old gentleman with a triple crown upon his head, and big with child, being the portrait of Pope Joan. Bishop Bonner purchasing great quantities of faggots and brushwood, fl r the conversion of heretics. A figure reaching at a sceptre with one hand, and holding a chaplet of beads in the other; with a distant view of Smithfield.

When our ladies make their zeal thus visible upon their fans, and every time they open them, display an error of the church of Rome, it cannot but have a good effect, by shewing the enemies of our present establishment the folly of what they are contending for. At least, every one must allow that fans are much more innocent engines for propagating the Protestant religion, than racks, wheels, gibbets, and the like machines, which are made use of for the advancement of the Roman Catholic. Besides, as every lady will of course study her fan, she will be a perfect mistress of the controversy, at least in one point of Popery; and as her curiosity will put her upon the perusal of every other fan that is fashionable, I doubt not but in a very little time there will scarce be a woman of quality in Great Britain, who would not be an over-match for an Irish priest.

The beautiful part of this island, whom I am proud to number among the most candid of my readers, will likewise do well to reflect, that our dispute at present concerns our civil as well as religious rights. I shall therefore only offer it to their thoughts as a point that highly deserves their consideration, whether the fan may not also be made use of with regard to our political constitution. As a Freeholder, I would not have them confine their cares for us as we are Protestants, but at the same time have an eye to our happiness as we are Britons. In this case they would give a new turn to the minds of their country men, if they would exhibit on their fans the several grievances of a tyrannical government. Why might not an audience of Muley Ishmael, or a Turk dropping his handkerchief in his Seraglio, be proper subjects to express their abhorrence both of despotic power, and of male tyranny? or if they have a fancy for burlesque, what would they think of a French cobbler cutting shoes for several of his fellow-subjects out of an old apple-tree? on the contrary, a fine woman, who would maintain the dignity of her sex, might bear a string of galley slaves, dragging their chains the whole breadth of her fan; and at the same time, to celebrate her own triumphs, might order every slave to be drawn with the face of one of her admirers.

I only propose these as hints to my gentle readers, which they may alter or improve as they shall think fit: but cannot conclude without congratulating our country upon this disposition among the most amiable of its inhabitants, to consider in their ornaments the advantage of the public as well as of their persons It was with the same spirit, though not with the same politeness, that the ancient British women had the figures of monsters painted on their naked bodies, in order (as our historians tell us) to make themselves beautiful in the eyes of their countrymen, and terrible to their enemies. If this project goes on, we may boast that our sister whigs have the finest fans, as well as the most beautiful faces, of any ladies in the world. At least, we may venture to foretel, that the figures in their fans will lessen the tory interest, much more than those in tbe Oxford Almanacs will advance it.

---

## No. 16, MONDAY, FEBRUARY 13.

Itaque quod plerumque in atroci negotio solet, Senatus decrevit, darent operam consules nè quid Respublica detrimenti caperet. Ea potestas per Senatum more Romano magistratui maxuma permittitur, exercitum parare, bellum gerere, coercere omnibus modis socios atque cives, domi militiæque imperium atque judicium summum habere. Aliter, sine populi jussu nulli earum rerum Consuli jus est. SALL.

It being the design of these papers to reconcile men to their own happiness, by removing those wrong notions and prejudices which hinder them from seeing the advantage of themselves and their posterity in the present establishment, I cannot but take notice of every thing that by the artifice of our enemies is made a matter of complaint.

Of this nature is the suspension of the Habeas Corpus act, by which his Majesty has been enabled, in these times of danger, to seize and detain the persons of such, who he had reason to believe were conspiring against his person and government. The expediency and reasonableness of such a temporary suspension in the present juncture may appear to every considerate man, who will turn his thoughts impartially on this subject.

I have chosen in points of this nature to draw my arguments from the first principles of government, which, as they are of no party, but assented to by every reasonable man, carry the greater weight with them, and are accommodated to the notions of all my readers. Every one knows, who has considered the nature of government, that there must be in each particular form of it an absolute and unlimited power ; and that this power is lodged in the hands of those, who have the making of its laws, whether by the nature of the constitution it be in one or more persons, in a single order of men, or in a mixt body of different ranks and degrees. It is an absurdity to imagine that those, who have the authority of making laws, cannot suspend any particular law, when they think it expedient for the public. Without such a power all government would be defective, and not armed with a sufficient force for its own security. As self-preservation by all honest methods is the first duty of every community as well as of every private person, so the public safety is the general view of all laws. When, therefore, any law does not conduce to this great end, but on the contrary in some extraordinary and unnatural junctures, the very observation of it would endanger the community, that law ought to be laid asleep for such a time, by the proper authority. Thus the very intention of our Habeas Corpus act, namely, the preservation of the liberties of the subject, absolutely requires that act to be now suspended, since the confinement of dangerous and suspected persons, who might strengthen this rebellion, and spread a civil war through all parts of this kingdom, secures to us our civil rights, and every thing that can be valuable to a free people.

As every government must in its nature be armed with such an authority, we may observe that those governments which have been the most famous for public spirit, and the most jealous of their liberty, have never failed to exert it upon proper occasions. There cannot be a greater instance of this, than in the old commonwealth of Rome, who flattered themselves with an opinion, that their government had in it a due temper of the regal, noble, and popular power represented by the consuls, the senators, and the tribunes. The regal part was, however, in several points, notoriously defective, and particularly because the consuls had not a negative in the passing of a law, as the other two branches had. Nevertheless, in this government, when the republic was threatened with any great and imminent danger, they thought it for the common safety to appoint a temporary dictator, invested with the whole power of the three branches; who, when the danger was over, retired again into the community, and left the government in its natural situation. But what is more to our case, the consular power itself, though infinitely short of the regal power in Great Britain, was intrusted with the whole authority which the legislature has put into the hands of his Majesty. We have an eminent instance of this in the motto of my paper, which I shall translate for the benefit of the English reader, after having advertised him, that the power there given to the consul, was in the time of a conspiracy. 'The senate, therefore, made a decree, as usual, when they have matters before them of so horrid a nature, That the consuls should take care the commonwealth did not suffer any prejudice. By virtue of this very great power which the senate allows to the magistrate, according to the ancient customs of Rome, he may raise an army, wage war, make use of all kinds of methods to restrain the associates and citizens of Rome, and exercise the supreme authority both at home and abroad in matters civil and military; whereas otherwise the consul is not invested with any of these powers without the express command of the people.

There now only remains to shew, that his Majesty is legally possessed of this power; and that the necessity of the present affairs requires he should be so. He is intrusted with it by the legislature of the nation; and in the very notion of a legislature is implied a power to change, repeal, and suspend, what laws are in being, as well as to make what new laws they shall think fit for the good of the people. This is so uncontroverted a maxim, that I believe never any body attempted to refute it. Our legislature have, however, had that just regard for their fellow-subjects, as not to entertain a thought of abrogating this law, but only to hinder it from operating at a time when it would endanger the constitution. The king is empowered to act but for a few months by virtue of this suspension; and by that means differs from a king of France, or any other tyrannical prince, who in times of peace and tranquillity, and upon what occasion he pleases, sends any of his subjects out of the knowledge of their friends into such castles, dungeons, or imprisonments, as he thinks fit. Nor did the legislature do any thing in this that was unprecedented. The Habeas Corpus act was made but about five and thirty years ago, and since that time has been suspended four times before his present Majesty's accession to the throne: twice under the reign of King William and Queen Mary; once under the reign of King William; and once under the reign of Queen Anne.

The necessity of this law at this time arose from the prospect of an invasion, which has since broke out into an actual rebellion; and from informations of secret and dangerous practices among men of considerable figure, who could not have been prevented from doing mischief to their country but by such a suspension of this act of parliament.

I cannot, however, but observe, that notwithstanding the lawfulness and necessity of such a suspension, had not the rebellion broke out after the passing of this act of parliament, I do not know how those who had been the most instrumental in procuring it, could have escaped that popular odium, which their malicious and artful enemies have now in vain endeavoured to stir up against them. Had it been possible for the vigilance and endeavours of a ministry to have hindered even the attempts of an invasion, their very endeavours might have proved prejudicial to them. Their prudent and resolute precautions would have turned to their disadvantage, had they not been justified by those events, which they did all that was in their power to obviate. This naturally brings to mind the reflection of Tully in the like circumstances, 'That amidst the divisions of Rome, a man was in an unhappy condition who had a share in the administration, nay even in the preservation of the commonwealth. *O conditionem miseram non modo administrandæ, verùm etiam conservandæ Reipublicæ!*'

Besides, every unprejudiced man will consider how mildly and equitably this power has been used. The persons confined have been treated with all possible humanity, and abridged of nothing but the liberty of hurting their country, and very probably of ruining both themselves and their families. And as to the numbers of those who are under this short restraint, it is very observable, that people do not seem so much surprised at the confinement of some, as at the liberty of many others. But we may from hence conclude, what every Englishman must observe with great pleasure, that his Majesty does not in this great point regulate himself by any private jealousies or suspicions, but by those evidences and informations he has received.

We have already found the good consequences of this suspension, in that it has hindered the rebellion from gathering the strength it would otherwise have gained; not to mention those numbers it has kept from engaging in so desperate an enterprise, with the many lives it has preserved, and the desolations it has prevented.

For these and many other reasons, the representatives of Great Britain in parliament could never have answered it to the people they represent, who have found such great benefits from the suspension of the Habeas Corpus act, and without it must have felt such fatal consequences, had they not, in a case of such great necessity, made use of this customary, legal, and reasonable method for securing his Majesty on the throne, and their country from misery or ruin.

---

## No. 17. FRIDAY, FEBRUARY 17.

———Hic niger est: hunc tu, Romane, caveto. HOR.

WE are told that in Turkey, when any man is the author of notorious falsehoods, it is usual to blacken the whole front of his house: nay, we have sometimes heard, that an ambassador whose 'business it is' (if I may quote his character in Sir Henry Wotton s words) 'to lie for the good of his country,' has sometimes had this mark set upon his house; when he has been detected in any piece of feigned intelligence, that has prejudiced the government, and misled the minds of the people. One could almost wish that the habitations of such of our countrymen as deal in forgeries detrimental to the public, were distinguished in the same manner; that their fellow-subjects might be cautioned not to be too easy in giving credit to them. Were such a method put in practice, this metropolis would be strangely checquered; some entire parishes would be in mourning, and several streets darkened from one end to the other.

But I have given my thoughts in two preceding papers, both on the inventors and the believers of these public falsehoods and calumnies, and shall here speak of that contempt with which they are and ought to be received by those in high stations, at whom they are levelled. Any person, indeed, who is zealous for promoting the interest of his country, must conquer all that tenderness and delicacy which may make him afraid of being ill spoken of; or his endeavours will often produce no less uneasiness to himself, than benefit to the public. Among a people who indulge themselves in the utmost freedoms of thought and speech, a man must either be insignificant, or able to bear an undeserved reproach. A true patriot may comfort himself under the attacks of falsehood and obloquy, from several motives and reflections.

In the first place he should consider, that the chief of his antagonists are generally acted by a spirit of envy; which would not rise against him, if it were not provoked by his desert. A statesman, who is possessed of real merit, should look upon his political censurers with the same neglect, that a good writer regards his critics; who are generally a race of men that are not able to discover the beauties of a work they examine, and deny that approbation to others which they never met with themselves. Patriots, therefore, should rather rejoice in the success of their honest designs, than be mortified by those who misrepresent them.

They should likewise consider, that not only envy, but vanity, has a share in the detraction of their adversaries. Such aspersions, therefore, do them honour at the same time that they are intended to lessen their reputation. They should reflect, That those who endeavour to stir up the multitude against them, do it to be thought considerable; and not a little applaud themselves in a talent that can raise clamours out of nothing, and throw a ferment among the people, by murmurs or complaints, which they know in their own hearts are altogether groundless. There is a pleasant instance of this nature recorded at length in the first book of the annals of Tacitus. When a great part of the Roman legions were in a disposition to mutiny, an impudent varlet, who was a private sentinel, being mounted upon the shoulders of his fellow-soldiers, and resolved to try the power of his eloquence, addressed himself to the army, in all the postures of an orator, after the following manner: 'You have given liberty to these miserable men,' said he, (pointing to some criminals whom they had rescued) 'but which of you can restore life to my brother? who can give me back my brother? he was murdered no longer ago than last night, by the hands of those ruffians, who are entertained by the general to butcher the poor soldiery. Tell me, Blæsus, (for that was the name of the general, who was then sitting on the tribunal) tell me, where hast thou cast his dead body? An enemy does not grudge the rites of burial. When I have tired myself with kissing his cold corpse, and weeping over it, order me to be slain upon it. All I ask of my fellow-soldiers, since we both die in their cause, is, that they would lay me in the same grave with my brother.' The whole army was in an uproar at this moving speech, and resolved to do the speaker justice, when, upon inquiry, they found that he never had a brother in his life; and that he had stirred up the sedition only to shew his parts.

Public ministers would likewise do well to consider, that the principal authors of such reproaches as are cast upon them, are those who have a mind to get their places: and as for a censure arising from this motive, it is in their power to escape it when they please, and turn it upon their competitors. Malecontents of an inferior character are acted by the same principle; for so long as there are employments of all sizes there will be murmurers of all degrees. I have heard of a country gentleman, who made a very long and melancholy complaint to the late Duke of Buckingham, when he was in great power at court, of several public grievances. The duke, after having given him a very patient hearing, 'My dear friend (says he) this is but too true; but I have thought of an expedient which will set all things right, and that very soon.' His country friend asked him what it was. 'You must know, (says the duke,) there's a place of five hundred pounds a year fallen this very morning, which I intend to put you in possession of." The gentleman thanked his grace, went away satisfied, and thought the nation the happiest under heaven, during that whole ministry.

But farther, every man in a public station ought to consider, that when there are two different parties in a nation, they will see things in different lights. An action, however conducive to the good of their country, will be represented by the artful and appear to the ignorant as prejudicial to it. Since I have here, according to the usual liberty of essay-writers, rambled into several stories, I shall fetch one to my present purpose out of the Persian history. We there read of a virtuous young emperor, who was very much afflicted to find his actions misconstrued and defamed by a party among his subjects that favoured another interest As he was one day sitting among the ministers of his Divan, and amusing himself after the eastern manner, with the solution of difficult problems and enigmas, he proposed to them in his turn the following one. 'What is the tree that bears three hundred and sixty-five leaves, which are all black on the one side, and white on the other?' His Grand vizier immediately replied, it was the year, which consisted of three hundred and sixty-five days and nights: 'But sir, (says he,) permit me at the same time to take notice, that these leaves represent your actions, which carry different faces to your friends and enemies, and will always appear black to those who are resolved only to look upon the wrong side of them.

A virtuous man, therefore, who lays out his endeavours for the good of his country, should never be troubled at the reports which are made of him, so long as he is conscious of his own integrity. He should rather be pleased to find people descanting upon his actions, because when they are thoroughly canvassed and examined, they are sure in the end to turn to his honour and advantage. The reasonable and unprejudiced part of mankind will be of his side, and rejoice to see their common interest lodged in such honest hands. A strict examination of a great man's character, is like the trial of a suspected chastity, which was made among the Jews by the waters of jealousy. Moses assures us, that the criminal burst upon the drinking of them; but if she was accused wrongfully, the Rabbins tell us, they heightened her charms, and made her much more amiable than before: so that they destroyed the guilty, but beautified the innocent.

## No. 18. FRIDAY, FEBRUARY 20.

———Inopem me copia fecit.—Ovid.

Every Englishman will be a good subject to King George, in proportion as he is a good Englishman, and a lover of the constitution of his country. In order to awaken in my readers the love of this their constitution, it may be necessary to set forth its superior excellency to that form of government, which many wicked and ignorant men have of late years endeavoured to introduce among us. I shall not, therefore, think it improper, to take notice from time to time of any particular act of power, exerted by those among whom the pretender to his Majesty's crown has been educated; which would prove fatal to this nation, should it be conquered and governed by a person, who, in all probability, would put in practice the politics in which he has been so long instructed.

There has been nothing more observable in the reign of his present Gallic Majesty, than the method he has taken for supplying his exchequer with a necessary sum of money. The ways and means for raising it has been an edict, or a command in writing signed by himself, to increase the value of louis d'ors from fourteen to sixteen livres, by virtue of a new stamp which shall be struck upon them. As this method will bring all the gold of the kingdom into his hands, it is provided by the same edict that they shall be paid out again to the people at twenty livres each; so that four livres in the score by this means accrue to his Majesty out of all the money in the kingdom of France.

This method of raising money is consistent with that form of government, and with the repeated practice of their late *Grand Monarque;* so that I shall not here consider the many evil consequences which it must have upon their trade, their exchange, and public credit: I shall only take notice of the whimsical circumstances a people must lie under, who can be thus made poor or rich by an edict, which can throw an alloy into a louis d'or, and debase it into half its former value, or, if his Majesty pleases, raise the price of it, not by the accession of metal, but of a mark. By the present edict, many a man in France will swell into a plumb, who fell several thousand pounds short of it the day before its publication. This conveys a kind of fairy treasure into their chests, even whilst they are under lock and key; and is a secret of multiplication without addition. It is natural enough, however, for the vanity of the French nation to grow insolent upon this imaginary wealth, not considering that their neighbours think them no more rich by virtue of an edict to make fourteen twenty, than they would think them more formidable should there be another edict to make every man in the kingdom seven foot high.

It was usual for his late most Christian Majesty to sink the value of their louis d'ors about the time he was to receive the taxes of his good people, and to raise them when he had got them safe into his coffers. And there is no question but the present government in that kingdom will so far observe this kind of conduct, as to reduce the twenty livres to their old number of fourteen, when they have paid them out of their hands; which will immediately sink the present timpany of wealth, and re-establish the natural poverty of the Gallic nation.

One cannot but pity the melancholy condition of a miser in this country, who is perpetually telling his livres, without being able to know how rich he is. He is as ridiculously puzzled and perplexed as a man that counts the stones on Salisbury plain, which can never be settled to any certain number, but are more or fewer every time he reckons them.

I have heard of a young French lady, a subject of Louis the fourteenth, who was contracted to a marquis upon the foot of a five thousand pound fortune, which she had by her in specie; but one of these unlucky edicts coming out a week before the intended marriage, she lost a thousand pound, and her bridegroom into the bargain.

The uncertainty of riches is a subject much discoursed of in all countries, but may be insisted on more emphatically in France than any other. A man is here under such a kind of situation, as one who is managed by a juggler. He fancies he has so many pieces of money in his hand; but let him grasp them never so carefully, upon a word or two of the artist they increase or dwindle to what number the doctor is pleased to name.

This method of lowering or advancing money, we, who have the happiness to be in another form of government, should look upon as unwarrantable kind of clipping and coining. However, as it is an expedient that is often practised, and may be justified in that constitution which has been so thoroughly studied by the pretender to his Majesty's crown, I do not see what should have hindered him from making use of so expeditious a method for raising a supply, if he had succeeded in his late attempt to dethrone his Majesty, and subvert our constitution. I shall leave it to the consideration of the reader, if in such a case the following edict, or something very like it, might not have been expected.

"Whereas these our kingdoms have long groaned under an expensive and consuming land-war, which has very much exhausted the treasure of the nation, we, being willing to increase the wealth of our people, and not thinking it advisable for this purpose to make use of the tedious methods of merchandise and commerce, which have been always promoted by a faction among the worst of our subjects, and were so wisely discountenanced by the best of them in the late reign, do hereby enact by our sole will and pleasure, that every shilling in Great Britain shall pass in all payments for the sum of fourteen pence, till the first of September next, and that every other piece of money shall rise and pass in current payment in the same proportion. The advantage which will accrue to these nations by this our royal donative, will visibly appear to all men of sound principles, who are so justly famous for their antipathy to strangers, and would not see the landed interest of their country weakened by the importations of foreign gold and silver. But since by reason of the great debts which we have contracted abroad, during our fifteen years reign, as well as of our present exigencies, it will be necessary to fill our exchequer by the most prudent and expeditious methods, we do also hereby order every one of our subjects to bring in these his fourteen-penny pieces, and all the other current cash of this kingdom, by what new titles soever dignified or distinguished, to the master of our mint, who, after having set a mark upon them, shall deliver out to them, on or after the first of September aforesaid, their respective sums, taking only four pence for ourself for such his mark on every fourteen penny piece, which from henceforth shall pass in payment for eighteenpence, and so in proportion for the rest. By this method, the money of this nation will be more by one third than it is at present; and we shall content ourselves with not quite one fifth part of the current cash of our loving subjects; which will but barely suffice to clear the interest of those sums in which we stand indebted to our most dear brother and ancient ally. We are glad of this opportunity of shewing such an instance of our goodness to our subjects, by this our royal edict, which shall be read in every parish church in Great Britain, immediately after the celebration of high mass. For such is our pleasure."

## No. 19. FRIDAY, FEBRUARY 24.

Pulchrum est bene facere reipublicæ; etiam bene dicere haud absurdum est.
SALL.

It has been usual these many years for writers, who have approved the scheme of government which has taken place, to explain to the people the reasonableness of those principles which have prevailed, and to justify the conduct of those who act in conformity to such principles. It therefore happens well for the party which is undermost, when a work of this nature falls into the hands of those who content themselves to attack their principles, without exposing their persons, or singling out any particular objects for satire and ridicule. This manner of proceeding is no inconsiderable piece of merit in writers, who are often more influenced by a desire of fame, than a regard to the public good; and who, by this means, lose many fair opportunities of shewing their own wit, or of gratifying the ill-nature of their readers.

When a man thinks a party engaged in such measures as tend to the ruin of his country, it is certainly a very laudable and virtuous action in him to make war after this manner upon the whole body. But as several casuists are of opinion, that in a battle you should discharge upon the gross of the enemy, without levelling your piece at any particular person; so in this kind of combat also, I cannot think it fair to aim at any one man, and make his character the mark of your hostilities. There is now to be seen in the castle of Milan, a cannon bullet, inscribed, 'This to the Mareschal de Crequi,' which was the very ball that shot him. An author who points his satire at a great man is to be looked upon in the same view with the engineer who signalized himself by this ungenerous practice.

But as the spirit of the whigs and tories shews itself, upon every occasion, to be very widely different from one another; so is it particularly visible in the writings of this kind, which have been published by each party. The latter may, indeed, assign one reason to justify themselves in this practice; that having nothing of any manner of weight to offer against the principles of their antagonists, if they speak at all, it must be against their persons. When they cannot refute an adversary, the shortest way is to libel him; and to endeavour at the making his person odious, when they cannot represent his notions as absurd.

The Examiner was a paper, in the last reign, which was the favourite work of the party. It was ushered into the world by a letter from a secretary of state, setting forth the great genius of the author, the usefulness of his design, and the mighty consequences that were to be expected from it. It is said to have been written by those among them whom they looked upon as their most celebrated wits and politicians, and was dispersed into all quarters of the nation with great industry and expense. Who would not have expected, that at least the rules of decency and candour would be observed in such a performance? but, instead of this, you saw all the great men, who had done eminent services to their country but a few years before, draughted out one by one, and baited in their turns. No sanctity of character, or privilege of sex, exempted persons from this barbarous usage. Several of our prelates were the standing marks of public raillery, and many ladies of the first quality branded by name for matters of fact, which, as they were false, were not heeded, and, if they had been true, were innocent. The dead themselves were not spared. And here I cannot forbear taking notice of a kind of wit which has lately grown into fashion among the versifiers, epigrammatists, and other authors, who think it sufficient to distinguish themselves by their zeal for what they call the high church, while they sport with the most tremendous parts of revealed religion. Every one has seen epigrams upon the deceased fathers of our church, where the whole thought has turned upon hell-fire. Patriots, who ought to be remembered with honour by their posterity, have been introduced as speakers in a state of torments. There is something dreadful even in repeating these execrable pieces of wit, which no man who really believes another life, can peruse without fear and trembling. It is astonishing to see readers who call themselves Christians, applauding such diabolical mirth, and seeming to rejoice in the doom which is pronounced against their enemies, by such abandoned scribblers. A wit of this kind may, with great truth, be compared to the fool in the Proverbs, 'who plays with arrows, fire-brands, and death, and says, Am I not in sport!'

I must, in justice to the more sober and considerate of that party, confess, that many of them were highly scandalized at that personal slander and reflection which was flung out so freely by the libellers of the last reign, as well as by those profane liberties which have been since continued. And as for those who are either the authors or admirers of such compositions, I would have them consider with themselves, whether the name of a good churchman can atone for the want of that charity which is the most essential part of Christianity. They would likewise do well to reflect, how, by these methods, the poison has run freely into the minds of the weak and ignorant: heightened their rage against many of their fellow-subjects; and almost divested them of the common sentiments of humanity.

In the former part of this paper, I have hinted that the design of it is to oppose the principles of those who are enemies to the present government, and the main body of that party who espouse those principles. But even in such general attacks there are certain measures to be kept, which may have a tendency rather to gain, than to irritate those who differ with you in their sentiments. The Examiner would not allow such as were of a contrary opinion to him, to be either Christians or fellow-subjects. With him they were all atheists, deists, or apostates, and a separate commonwealth among themselves, that ought either to be extirpated, or, when he was in a better humour, only to be banished out of their native country. They were often put in mind of some approaching execution, and therefore all of them advised to prepare themselves for it, as men who had then nothing to take care of, but how to die decently. In short, the Examiner seemed to make no distinction between conquest and destruction.

The conduct of this work has hitherto been regulated by different views, and shall continue to be so; unless the party it has to deal with, draw upon themselves another kind of treatment. For if they shall persist in pointing their batteries against particular persons, there are no laws of war, that forbid the making of reprisals. In the mean time, this undertaking shall be managed with that generous spirit which was so remarkable among the Romans, who did not subdue a country in order to put the inhabitants to fire and sword, but to incorporate them into their own community, and make them happy in the same government with themselves.

---

## No. 20. MONDAY, FEBRUARY 27.

Privatus illis census erat brevis,
Commune magnum———

HOR.

It is very unlucky for those who make it their business to raise popular murmurs and discontents against his Majesty's government, that they find so very few and so very improper occasions for them. To shew how hard they are set in this particular, there are several, who for want of other materials, are forced to represent the bill which has passed this session, for laying an additional tax of two shillings in the pound upon land, as a kind of grievance upon the subject. If this be a matter of complaint, it ought in justice to fall upon those who have made it necessary. Had there been no rebellion, there would have been no increase of the land-tax: so that in proportion as a man declares his aversion to the one, he ought to testify his abhorrence of the other. But it is very remarkable that those, who would persuade the people that they are aggrieved by this additional burden, are the very persons who endeavour, in their ordinary conversation, to extenuate the heinousness of the rebellion, and who express the greatest tenderness for the persons of the rebels. They shew a particular indulgence for that unnatural insurrection which has drawn this load upon us, and are angry at the means which were necessary for suppressing it. There needs no clearer proof of the spirit and intention with which they act; I shall, therefore, advise my fellow-freeholders to consider the character of any person who would possess them with the notion of a hardship that is put upon the country by this tax. If he be one of known affection to the present establishment, they may imagine there is some reason for complaint. But if, on the contrary, he be one who has shewn himself indifferent as to the success of the present rebellion, or is suspected as a private abettor of it, they may take it for granted, his complaint against the land-tax is either the rage of a disappointed man, or the artifice of one who would alienate their affections from the present government.

The expence which will arise to the nation from this rebellion, is already computed at near a million. And it is a melancholy consideration for the freeholders of Great Britain, that the treason of their fellow-subjects should bring upon them as great a charge as the war with France. At the same time every reasonable man among them will pay a tax with at least as great cheerfulness for stifling a civil war in its birth, as for carrying on a war in a foreign country. Had not our first supplies been effectual for the crushing of our domestic enemies, we should immediately have beheld the whole kingdom a scene of slaughter and desolation: whereas, if we had failed in our first attempts upon a distant nation, we might have repaired the losses of one campaign by the advantages of another, and after several victories gained over us, might still have kept the enemy from our gates.

As it was thus absolutely necessary to raise a sum that might enable the government to put a speedy stop to the rebellion, so could there be no method thought of for raising such a sum more proper, than this of laying an additional tax of two shillings in the pound upon land.

In the first place: this tax has been so often tried, that we know the exact produce of it, which in any new project is always very doubtful and uncertain. As we are thus acquainted with the produce of this tax, we find it is adequate to the services for which it is designed, and that the additional tax is proportioned to the supernumerary expence, which falls upon the kingdom this year by the unnatural rebellion, as it has been above stated.

In the next place: no other tax could have been thought of, upon which so much money would have been immediately advanced as was necessary in so critical a juncture for pushing our successes against the rebels, and preventing the attempts of their friends and confederates both at home and abroad. No body cares to make loans upon a new and untried project; whereas men never fail to bring in their money upon a land-tax, when the premium or interest allowed them, is suited to the hazard they run by such loans to the government. And here one cannot but bewail the misfortune of our country, when we consider, that the house of commons had last year reduced this interest to four per cent., by which means there was a considerable saving to the nation; but that this year they have been forced to give six per cent., as well knowing the fatal consequences that might have ensued, had there not been an interest allowed, which would certainly encourage the lender to venture, in such a time of danger, what was indispensably necessary for the exigences of the public.

Besides; this is a method for raising a sum of money, that, with the ordinary taxes, will in all probability defray the whole expence of the year: so that there is no burden laid upon our posterity, who have been sufficiently loaded by other means of raising money; nor any deficiency to be hereafter made up by ourselves; which has been our case in so many other subsidies.

To this we may add; that we have no example of any other tax, which in its nature would so particularly affect the enemies to his Majesty's government. Multitudes of Papists and Nonjurors will be obliged to furnish a double proportion out of their revenues towards the clearing of that expence, which by their open and secret practices they have been instrumental in bringing upon their fellow-subjects.

I shall only mention one consideration more; that no other tax is so likely to cease as this is, when there is no farther occasion for it. This tax is established by a house of commons, which, by virtue of an act of parliament passed a few years ago, must consist for the most part of landed men; so that a great share of the weight of it must necessarily fall upon the members of their own body. As this is an instance of their public spirit, so we may be sure they would not have exerted it, had there not been an absolute necessity: nor can we doubt, that for the same reasons, when this necessity ceases, they will take the first opportunity of easing themselves in this particular, as well as those whom they represent. It is a celebrated notion of a patriot, who signally distinguished himself for the liberties of his country, that a house of commons should never grant such subsidies as are easy to be raised, and give no pain to the people, lest the nation should acquiesce under a burden they did not feel, and see it perpetuated without repining. Whether this notion might not be too refined, I shall not determine; but by what has been already said, I think we may promise ourselves, that this additional tax of two shillings in the pound, will not be continued another year, because we may hope the rebellion will be entirely ended in this.

And here, I believe, it must be obvious to every one's reflection, that the rebellion might not have concluded so soon, had not this method been made use of for that end. A foreign potentate trembles at the thought of entering into a war with so wealthy an enemy as the British nation, when he finds the whole landed interest of the kingdom engaged to oppose him with their united force; and at all times ready to employ against him such a part of their revenues, as shall be sufficient to baffle his designs upon their country: especially when none can imagine, that he expects an encouragement from those, whose fortunes are either lodged in the funds, or employed in trade.

The wisdom, therefore, of the present house of commons has by this tax, not only enabled the king to subdue those of his own subjects, who have been actually in arms against him, but to divert any of his neighbours from the hopes of lending them a competent assistance.

## No. 21. FRIDAY, MARCH, 2.

Qualis in Eurotæ ripis, aut per juga Cynthi,
Exercet Diana choros: quam mille secutæ
Hinc atque hinc glomerantur Oreades: illa pharetram
Fert humero, gradiensque Deas supereminet omnes.
VIRG.

It is not easy for any one who saw the magnificence of yesterday in the court of Great Britain,[a] to turn his thoughts for some time after on any other subject. It was a solemnity every way suited to the birth-day of a princess, who is the delight of our nation, and the glory of her sex. Homer tells us, that when the daughter of Jupiter presented herself among a crowd of goddesses, she was distinguished from the rest by her graceful stature, and known by her superior beauty, notwithstanding they were all beautiful. Such was the appearance of the Princess of Wales among our British ladies; or (to use a more solemn phrase) of 'the King's daughter among her honourable women.' Her Royal Highness, in the midst of such a circle, raises in the beholder the idea of a fine picture, where (notwithstanding the diversity of pleasing objects that fill up the canvas) the principal figure immediately takes the eye, and fixes the attention.

When this excellent princess was yet in her father's court, she was so celebrated for the beauty of her person, and the accomplishments of her mind, that there was no prince in the empire who had room for such an alliance, that was not ambitious of gaining her into his family, either as a daughter, or as a consort. He, who is now the chief of the crowned heads in Europe, and was then King of Spain, and heir to all the dominions of the house of Austria, sought her in marriage. Could her mind have been captivated with the glories of this world, she had them

[a] The author rises with his subject. This panegyric is extremely well written.

all laid before her; but she generously declined them, because she saw the acceptance of them was inconsistent with what she esteems more than all the glories of this world, the enjoyment of her religion. Providence, however, kept in store a reward for such an exalted virtue; and, by the secret methods of its wisdom, opened a way for her to become the greatest of her sex, among those who profess that faith to which she adhered with so much christian magnanimity.

This her illustrious conduct might, in the eye of the world, have lost its merit, had so accomplished a prince as his Royal Highness declared his passion for the same alliance at that time: it would then have been no wonder that all other proposals had been rejected. But it was the fame of this heroic constancy that determined his Royal Highness to desire in marriage a princess whose personal charms, which had before been so universally admired, were now become the least part of her character. We, of the British nation, have reason to rejoice, that such a proposal was made and accepted; and that her Royal Highness, with regard to these two successive treaties of marriage, shewed as much prudence in her compliance with the one, as piety in her refusal of the other.

The princess was no sooner arrived at Hanover, than she improved the lustre of that court, which was before reckoned among the politest in Europe; and increased the satisfaction of that people, who were before looked upon as the happiest in the empire. She immediately became the darling of the Princess Sophia, who was acknowledged in all the courts of Europe the most accomplished woman of the age in which she lived, and who was not a little pleased with the conversation of one in whom she saw so lively an image of her own youth.

But I shall insist no longer on that reputation which her Royal Highness has acquired in other countries. We daily discover those admirable qualities for which she is so justly famed, and rejoice to see them exerted in our own country, where we ourselves are made happy by their influence. We are the more pleased to behold the throne of these kingdoms surrounded by a numerous and beautiful progeny, when we consider the virtues of those from whom they descend. Not only the features, but the mind of the parent, is often copied out in the offspring. But the princess we are speaking of takes the surest method of making her royal issue like herself, by instilling early into their minds all the principles of religion, virtue, and honour, and seasoning their tender years with all that knowledge which they are capable of receiving. What may we not hope from such an uncommon care in the education of the children of Great Britain, who are directed by such precepts, and will be formed by such an example!

The conjugal virtues are so remarkable in her Royal Highness, as to deserve those just and generous returns of love and tenderness, for which the prince, her husband, is so universally celebrated.

But there is no part of her Royal Highness's character which we observe with greater pleasure, than that behaviour by which she has so much endeared herself to his Majesty; though, indeed, we have no reason to be surprised at this mutual intercourse of duty and affection, when we consider so wise and virtuous a princess possessing, in the same sacred person, the kindest of fathers and the best of kings. And here it is natural for us to congratulate our own good fortune, who see our sovereign blessed with a numerous issue, among whom are heirs male in two direct descents, which has not happened in the reign of any English king since the time of his Majesty's great ancestor Edward the third, and is a felicity not enjoyed by the subjects of any other of the kings of Europe who are his contemporaries. We are like men entertained with the view of a spacious landscape, where the eye passes over one pleasing prospect into another, till the sight is lost by degrees in a succession of delightful objects, and leaves us in the persuasion that there remain still more behind.

But if we regard her Royal Highness in that light which diffuses the greatest glory round a human character, we shall find the christian no less conspicuous than the princess. She is as eminent for a sincere piety in the practice of religion, as for an inviolable adherence to its principles. She is constant in her attendance on the daily offices of our church, and by her serious and devout comportment on these solemn occasions, gives an example that is very often too much wanted in courts.

Her religion is equally free from the weakness of superstition, and the sourness of enthusiasm. It is not of that uncomfortable melancholy nature which disappoints its own end, by appearing unamiable to those whom it would gain to its interests. It discovers itself in the genuine effects of Christianity, in affability compassion, benevolence, evenness of mind, and all the offices of an active and universal charity.

As a cheerful temper is the necessary result of these virtues, so it shines out in all the parts of her conversation, and dissipates those apprehensions which naturally hang on the timorous or the modest, when they are admitted to the honour of her presence. There is none that does not listen with pleasure to a person in so high a station, who condescends to make herself thus agreeable, by mirth without levity, and wit without ill-nature.

Her Royal Highness is, indeed, possessed of all those talents which make conversation either delightful or improving. As she has a fine taste of the elegant arts, and is skilled in several modern languages, her discourse is not confined to the ordinary subjects or forms of conversation, but can adapt itself with an uncommon grace to every occasion, and entertain the politest persons of different nations. I need not mention, what is observed by every one, that agreeable turn which appears in her sentiments upon the most ordinary affairs of life, and which is so suitable to the delicacy of her sex, the politeness of her education, and the splendour of her quality.

It would be vain to think of drawing into the compass of this paper, the many eminent virtues which adorn the character of this great princess; but as it is one chief end of this undertaking to make the people sensible of the blessings which they enjoy under his Majesty's reign, I could not but lay hold on this opportunity to speak of that which ought, in justice, to be reckoned among the greatest of them.

---

## No. 22.[a] MONDAY, MARCH 5.

Studiis rudis, sermone barbarus, impetu strenuus, manu promptus, cogitatione celer.
VELL. PATERC.

FOR the honour of his Majesty, and the safety of his government, we cannot but observe, that those who have appeared the greatest enemies to both, are of that rank of men, who are commonly distinguished by the title of Fox-hunters. As several of

[a] This Freeholder, together with the 44th and 47th, on a tory fox-hunter have all the ease and gaiety of the best Spectators on Sir Roger de Coverley And, in general, we may observe, that the gentle graces of Mr. Addison never forsake him, in a paper of humour; the bent of his genius lying so strongly that way.

If he any where writes beneath himself in the Freeholder, it is in those graver parts, which seem scarce susceptible of embellishment, (as those on the habeas-corpus, and the land-tax), or which require more time and recollection in a writer who would do justice to his subject (as those on trade, and government) than he had to bestow upon them. Not but another reason might be, that he purposely restrained his wit, on many occasions, the better to adapt himself to the apprehension of his plainer readers, whom he was chiefly concerned to manage, and whose idiot prejudices he wanted to remove.

these have had no part of their education in cities, camps, or courts, it is doubtful whether they are of greater ornament or use to the nation in which they live. It would be an everlasting reproach to politics, should such men be able to overturn an establishment which has been formed by the wisest laws, and is supported by the ablest heads. The wrong notions and prejudices which cleave to many of these country gentlemen, who have always lived out of the way of being better informed, are not easy to be conceived by a person who has never conversed with them.

That I may give my readers an image of these rural statesmen, I shall, without farther preface, set down an account of a discourse I chanced to have with one of them some time ago. I was travelling towards one of the remote parts of England, when about three o'clock in the afternoon, seeing a country gentleman trotting before me with a spaniel by his horse's side, I made up to him. Our conversation opened, as usual, upon the weather; in which we were very unanimous; having both agreed that it was too dry for the season of the year. My fellow-traveller, upon this, observed to me, that there had been no good weather since the revolution. I was a little startled at so extraordinary a remark, but would not interrupt him till he proceeded to tell me of the fine weather they used to have in King Charles the second's reign. I only answered that I did not see how the badness of the weather could be the king's fault; and, without waiting for his reply, asked him whose house it was we saw upon a rising ground at a little distance from us. He told me it belonged to an old fanatical cur, Mr. Such-a-one, 'You must have heard of him,' says he, 'he's one of the Rump.' I knew the gentleman's character upon hearing his name, but assured him, that to my knowledge he was a good churchman: 'Ay!' says he, with a kind of surprise, 'We were told in the country, that he spoke twice, in the Queen's time, against taking off the duties upon French claret.' This naturally led us in the proceedings of late parliaments, upon which occasion he affirmed roundly, that there had not been one good law passed since King William's accession to the throne, except the act for preserving the game. I had a mind to see him out, and therefore did not care for contradicting him. 'Is it not hard,' says he, 'that honest gentlemen should be taken into custody of messengers to prevent them from acting according to their consciences? But,' says he, 'what can we expect when a parcel of factious sons of whores——' He was going on in great passion, but chanced to miss his dog, who was amusing himself about a bush, that grew at some distance behind us. We stood still till he had whistled him up; when he fell into a long panegyric upon his spaniel, who seemed, indeed, excellent in his kind: but I found the most remarkable adventure of his life was, that he had once like to have worried a dissenting-teacher. The master could hardly sit on his horse for laughing all the while he was giving me the particulars of this story, which I found had mightily endeared his dog to him, and as he himself told me, had made him a great favourite among all the honest gentlemen of the country. We were at length diverted from this piece of mirth by a post-boy, who winding his horn at us, my companion gave him two or three curses, and left the way clear for him. 'I fancy,' said I, 'that post brings news from Scotland. I shall long to see the next Gazette.' 'Sir,' says he, 'I make it a rule never to believe any of your printed news. We never see, sir, how things go, except now and then in Dyer's Letter, and I read that more for the style than the news. The man has a clever pen, it must be owned. But is it not strange that we should be making war upon Church of England men, with Dutch and Swiss soldiers, men of antimonarchical principles? these foreigners will never be loved in England, sir; they have not that wit and good-breeding that we have.' I must confess I did not expect to hear my new acquaintance value himself upon these qualifications, but finding him such a critic upon foreigners, I asked him if he had ever travelled; he told me, he did not know what travelling was good for, but to teach a man to ride the great horse, to jabber French, and to talk against passive obedience to which he added, that he scarce ever knew a traveller in his life who had not forsook his principles, and lost his hunting-seat. 'For my part,' says he, 'I and my father before me have always been for passive-obedience, and shall be always for opposing a prince who makes use of ministers that are of another opinion. But where do you intend to inn to-night? (for we were now come in sight of the next town) I can help you to a very good landlord if you will go along with me. He is a lusty, jolly fellow, that lives well, at least three yards in the girt, and the best Church of England man upon the road.' I had a curiosity to see this high-church inn-keeper, as well as to enjoy more of the conversation of my fellow-traveller, and therefore readily consented to set our horses together for that night. As we rode side by side through the town, I was let into the characters of all the principal inhabitants whom we met in our way. One was a dog, another a whelp, another a cur, and another the son of a bitch, under which several denominations were comprehended all that voted on the whig side, in the last election of burgesses. As for those of his own party, he distinguished them by a nod of his head, and asking them how they did by their christian names. Upon our arrival at the inn, my companion fetched out the jolly landlord, who knew him by his whistle. Many endearments and private whispers passed between them; though it was easy to see, by the landlord's scratching his head, that things did not go to their wishes. The landlord had swelled his body to a prodigious size, and worked up his complection to a standing crimson by his zeal for the prosperity of the church, which he expressed every hour of the day, as his customers dropt in, by repeated bumpers. He had not time to go to church himself, but, as my friend told me in my ear, had headed a mob at the pulling down of two or three meeting-houses. While supper was preparing, he enlarged upon the happiness of the neighbouring shire; 'For,' says he, 'there is scarce a Presbyterian in the whole county, except the bishop.' In short, I found by his discourse that he had learned a great deal of politics, but not one word of religion, from the parson of his parish; and, indeed, that he had scarce any other notion of religion, but that it consisted in hating Presbyterians. I had a remarkable instance of his notions in this particular. Upon seeing a poor decrepid old woman pass under the window where we sat, he desired me to take notice of her; and afterwards informed me, that she was generally reputed a witch by the country people, but that, for his part, he was apt to believe she was a Presbyterian.

Supper was no sooner served in, than he took occasion, from a shoulder of mutton that lay before us, to cry up the plenty of England, which would be the happiest country in the world, provided we would live within ourselves. Upon which, he expatiated on the inconveniences of trade, that carried from us the commodities of our country, and made a parcel of upstarts as rich as men of the most ancient families of England. He then declared frankly, that he had always been against all treaties and alliances with foreigners; 'Our wooden walls,' says he, 'are our security, and we may bid defiance to the whole world, especially if they should attack us when the militia is out.' I ventured to reply, that I had as great an opinion of the English fleet as he had; but I could not see how they could be paid, and manned, and fitted out, unless we encouraged trade and navigation. He replied, with some vehemence, that he would undertake to prove trade would be the ruin of the English nation. I would fain have put him upon it; but he contented himself with affirming it more eagerly, to which he added two or three curses upon the London merchants, not forgetting the directors of the bank. After supper, he asked me if I was an admirer of punch: and immediately called for a sneaker. I took this occasion to insinuate the advantages of trade, by observing to him, that water was the only native of England that could be made use of on this occasion; but that the lemons, the brandy, the sugar, and the nutmeg, were all foreigners. This put him into some confusion; but the landlord, who overheard me, brought him off, by affirming, that for constant use, there was no liquor like a cup of English water, provided it had malt enough in it. My 'squire laughed heartily at the conceit, and made the landlord sit down with us. We sat pretty late over our punch; and, amidst a great deal of improving discourse, drank the healths of several persons in the country, whom I had never heard of, that, they both assured me, were the ablest statesmen in the nation; and of some Londoners, whom they extolled to the skies for their wit, and who, I knew, passed in town for silly fellows. It being now midnight, and my friend perceiving by his almanac that the moon was up, he called for his horses, and took a sudden resolution to go to his house, which was at three miles distance from the town, after having bethought himself that he never slept well out of his own bed. He shook me very heartily by the hand at parting, and discovered a great air of satisfaction in his looks, that he had met with an opportunity of shewing his parts, and left me a much wiser man than he found me.

## NO. 23. FRIDAY, MARCH 9.

Illis ira modum supra est, et sæpe venenum
Morsibus inspirant.—— VIRG.

IN the wars of Europe which were waged among our forefathers, it was usual for the enemy, when there was a king in the field, to demand by a trumpet in what part of the camp he resided, that they might avoid firing upon the royal pavilion. Our party-contests in England were heretofore managed with the same kind of decency and good-breeding. The person of the prince was always looked upon as sacred; and whatever severe usage his friends or ministers met with, none presumed to direct their hostilities at their sovereign. The enemies of our present settlement are of such a coarse kind of make, and so equally void of loyalty and good manners, that they are grown scurrilous upon the royal family, and treat the most exalted characters with the most opprobrious language.

This petulance in conversation is particularly observed to prevail among some of that sex where it appears the most unbecoming and the most unnatural. Many of these act with the greater licentiousness, because they know they can act with the greater impunity. This consideration, indeed, engages the most generous and well-bred even of our she malecontents, to make no ill use of the indulgence of our law-givers; and to discover in their debates at least the delicacy of the woman, if not the duty of the subject. But it is generally remarked, that every one of them who is a shrew in domestic life, is now become a scold in politics. And as for those of the party, who are of a superior rank and unblemished virtue, it must be a melancholy reflection for them to consider that all the common women of the town are of their side; for which reason they ought to preserve a more than ordinary modesty in their satirical excursions, that their characters may not be liable to suspicion.

If there is not some method found out for allaying these heats and animosities among the fair sex, one does not know to what outrages they may proceed. I remember a hero in Scarron, who, finding himself opposed by a mixed multitude of both sexes with a great deal of virulent language, after having brought them to a submission, gave order (to keep them from doing farther mischief) that the men should be disarmed of their clubs, and that the women should have their nails pared. We are not yet reduced to the necessity of applying such violent remedies; but as we daily receive accounts of ladies battling it on both sides, and that those who appear against the constitution, make war upon their antagonists by many unfair practices and unwarrantable methods, I think it is very convenient there should be a cartel settled between them. If they have not yet agreed upon any thing of this nature among themselves, I would propose to them the following plan, in which I have sketched our several rules suited to the politest sex in one of the most civilized nations:

That in every political rencounter between woman and woman, no weapon shall be made use of but the tongue.

That in the course of the engagement, if either of the combatants, finding herself hard pressed by her adversary, shall proceed to personal reflections, or discovery of secrets, they shall be parted by the standers by.

That when both sides are drawn up in a full assembly, it shall not be lawful for above five of them to talk at the same time.

That if any shall detract from a lady's character, (unless she be absent) the said detractress shall be forthwith ordered to the lowest place of the room.

That none presume to speak disrespectfully of his Majesty, or any of the royal family, on pain of three hours silence.

That none be permitted to speak spightfully of the court, unless they can produce vouchers that they have been there.

That the making use of news which goes about in whisper, unless the author be produced, or the fact well attested, shall be deemed fighting with white powder, and contrary to the laws of war.

That any one who produces libels or lampoons, shall be regarded in the same manner, as one who shoots with poisoned bullets.

That when a lady is thoroughly convinced of the falsehood of any story she has related, she shall give her parole not to tell it for a certain truth that winter.

That when any matter of doubt arises, which cannot otherwise be decided, appeal shall be made to a toast, if there be any such in the company.

That no coquette, notwithstanding she can do it with a good air, shall be allowed to sigh for the danger of the church, or to shiver at the apprehensions of fanaticism.

That when a woman has talked an hour and a half, it shall be lawful to call her down to order.

As this civil discord among the sisterhood of Great Britain is likely to engage them in a long and lingering war, consisting altogether of drawn battles, it is the more necessary that there should be a cartel settled among them. Besides, as our English ladies are at present the greatest stateswomen in Europe, they will be in danger of making themselves the most unamiable part of their sex, if they continue to give a loose to intemperate language, and to a low kind of ribaldry, which is not used among the women of fashion in any other country.

Discretion and good-nature have been always looked upon as

the distinguishing ornaments of female conversation. The woman, 'whose price is above rubies,' has no particular in the character given of her by the wise man, more endearing, than that 'she openeth her mouth with wisdom, and in her tongue is the law of kindness.' Besides, every fierce she-zealot should consider, that however any of the other sex may seem to applaud her as a partizan, there is none of them who would not be afraid of associating himself with her in any of the more private relations of life.

I shall only add, that there is no talent so pernicious as eloquence, to those who have it not under command: For which reason, women who are so liberally gifted by nature in this particular, ought to study, with the greatest application, the rules of female oratory, delivered in that excellent treatise, entitled, 'the Government of the Tongue.' Had that author foreseen the political ferment which is now raised among the sex, he would probably have made his book larger by some chapters than it is at present: but what is wanting in that work may, I hope, in some measure, be supplied by the above-written cartel.

---

## No. 24. MONDAY, MARCH 12.

Bellum importunum, cives, cum gente deorum,
Invictisque viris geritis——— — VIRG.

A PHYSICIAN makes use of various methods for the recovery of sick persons; and though some of them are painful, and all of them disagreeable, his patients are never angry at him, because they know he has nothing in view besides the restoring of them to a good state of health. I am forced to treat the disaffected part of his Majesty's subjects in the same manner, and may, therefore, reasonably expect the same returns of good-will I propose nothing to myself but their happiness as the end of all my endeavours; and am forced to adapt different remedies to those different constitutions, which are to be found in such a distempered multitude. Some of them can see the unreasonable, and some of them the ridiculous side of wrong principles, and, according to the different frame of their minds, reject an opinion as it carries in it either the appearance of wickedness, or of danger, or of folly.

I have endeavoured to expose in these several lights the notions and practices of those who are enemies to our present establishment. But there is a set of arguments, which I have not yet touched upon, and which often succeed, when all others fail. There are many who will not quit a project, though they find it pernicious, or absurd; but will readily desist from it, when they are convinced it is impracticable. An attempt to subvert the present government is, God be thanked, of this nature. I shall, therefore, apply the considerations of this paper rather to the discretion than the virtue of our malecontents, who should act in the present juncture of affairs like experienced gamesters, that throw up their cards when they know the game is in the enemies hand, without giving themselves any unnecessary vexation in playing it out.

In the reign of our two last British sovereigns, those who did not favour their interest might be ungenerous enough to act upon the prospect of a change, considering the precarious condition of their health, and their want of issue to succeed them.

But at present we enjoy a king of a long-lived family, who is in the vigour of his age, and blest with a numerous progeny. To this we may add his remarkable steadiness in adhering to those schemes which he has formed upon the maturest deliberation, and that submissive deference of his Royal Highness both from duty and inclination, to all the measures of his Royal Father. Nor must we omit that personal valour so peculiar to his Majesty and his illustrious house, which would be sufficient to vanquish, as we find it actually deters, both his foreign and domestic enemies.

This great prince is supported by the whole Protestant interest of Europe, and strengthened with a long range of alliances that reach from one end of the continent to the other. He has a great and powerful king for his son-in-law; and can himself command, when he pleases, the whole strength of an electorate in the empire. Such a combination of sovereigns puts one in mind of the apparition of gods which discouraged Æneas from opposing the will of heaven. When his eyes were cleared of that mortal cloud which hung upon them, he saw the several celestial deities acting in a confederacy against him, and immediately gave up a cause which was excluded from all possibility of success.

But it is the greatest happiness, as well as the greatest pleasure of our sovereign, that his chief strength lies in his own kingdoms. Both the branches of our legislature espouse his cause and interest with a becoming duty and zeal. The most considerable and wealthy of his subjects are convinced, that the prosperity of our sovereign and his people are inseparable: and we are very well satisfied, that his Majesty, if the necessity of affairs should require it, might find among the most dutiful of his subjects, men celebrated for their military characters, above any of the age in which they live. There is no question but his Majesty will be as generally valued and beloved in his British as he is in his German dominions, when he shall have time to make his royal virtues equally known among us. In the mean while we have the satisfaction to find, that his enemies have been only able to make ill impressions upon the low and ignorant rabble of the nation; and to put the dregs of the people into a ferment.

We have already seen how poor and contemptible a force has

been raised by those who have dared to appear openly against his Majesty, and how they were headed and encouraged by men whose sense of their guilt made them desperate in forming so rash an enterprise, and dispirited in the execution of it. But we have not yet seen that strength which would be exerted in the defence of his Majesty, the Protestant religion, and the British liberties, were the danger great enough to require it. Should the king be reduced to the necessity of setting up the royal standard, how many thousands would range themselves under it! what a concourse would there be of nobles and patriots! we should see men of another spirit than what has appeared among the enemies to our country, and such as would out-shine the rebellious part of their fellow-subjects as much in their gallantry as in their cause.

I shall not so much suspect the understandings of our adversaries, as to think it necessary to enforce these considerations, by putting them in mind of that fidelity and allegiance which is so visible in his Majesty's fleet and army, or of many other particulars which, in all human probability, will perpetuate our present form of government, and which may be suggested to them by their own private thoughts.

The party, indeed, that is opposite to our present happy settlement, seem to be driven out of the hopes of all human methods for carrying on their cause, and are, therefore, reduced to the poor comfort of prodigies and old women's fables. They begin to see armies in the clouds,[a] when all upon the earth hath forsaken them. Nay, I have been lately shewn a written prophecy that is handed among them with great secrecy, by which it appears their chief reliance at present is upon a Cheshire miller who was born with two thumbs upon one hand.

[a] The superstition of the people is always ready to *catch*, in times of public commotion; and a remarkable *aurora borealis* happened to set fire to it, at that time.

I have addressed this whole paper to the despair of our malecontents, not with a design to aggravate the pain of it, but to use it as a means[a] of making them happy. Let them seriously consider the vexation and disquietude of mind that they are treasuring up for themselves, by struggling with a power which will be always too hard for them; and by converting his Majesty's reign into their own misfortune, which every impartial man must look upon as the greatest blessing to his country. Let them extinguish those passions, which can only imbitter their lives to them, and deprive them of their share in the happiness of the community. They may conclude that his Majesty, in spite of any opposition they can form against him, will maintain his just authority over them; and whatever uneasiness they may give themselves, they can create none in him, excepting only because they prevent him from exerting equally his natural goodness and benevolence to every subject in his dominions

---

## No. 25. FRIDAY, MARCH 17.

Quid est sapientia? semper idem velle atque idem nolle.—SENEC.

IF we may believe the observation which is made of us by foreigners, there is no nation in Europe so much given to change as the English. There are some who ascribe this to the fickleness of our climate; and others to the freedom of our govern-

[a] *As a means*] The use of the word *means*, in English, is remarkable, and may be thought capricious. It seems to be of French extraction. The French have, *le moyen*, frequently but seldom *les moyens*: we, on the contrary, prefer the plural termination, *means*; yet still, for the most part (though not always) we use it as a noun of the singular number, or as the French *le moyen*. It is one of those anomalies, which use hath introduced and established, in spite of *analogy*. We should not be allowed to say—*a mean* of making men happy.

ment. From one or both of these causes their writers derive that variety of humours which appears among the people in general, and that inconsistency of character which is to be found in almost every particular person. But as a man should always be upon his guard against the vices to which he is most exposed, so we should take a more than ordinary care not to lie at the mercy of the weather in our moral conduct, nor to make a capricious use of that liberty which we enjoy by the happiness of our civil constitution.

This instability of temper ought in a particular manner to be checked, when it shows itself in political affairs, and disposes men to wander from one scheme of government to another: since such a fickleness of behaviour in public measures, cannot but be attended with very fatal effects to our country.

In the first place; it hinders any great undertaking, which requires length of time for its accomplishment, from being brought to its due perfection. There is not any instance in history which better confirms this observation, than that which is still fresh in every one's memory. We engaged in the late war with a design to reduce an exorbitant growth of power in the most dangerous enemy to Great Britain. We gained a long and wonderful series of victories, and had scarce any thing left to do, but to reap the fruits of them: when on a sudden our patience failed us; we grew tired of our undertaking; and received terms from those, who were upon the point of giving us whatever we could have demanded of them.

This mutability of mind in the English, makes the ancient friends of our nation very backward to engage with us in such alliances as are necessary for our mutual defence and security. It is a common notion among foreigners, that the English are good confederates in an enterprise which may be dispatched within a short compass of time; but that they are not to be depended upon in a work which cannot be finished without constancy and perseverance. Our late measures have so blemished our national credit in this particular, that those potentates who are entered into treaties with his present Majesty, have been solely encouraged to it by their confidence in his personal firmness and integrity.

I need not, after this suggest to my reader the ignominy and reproach that falls upon a nation, which distinguishes itself among its neighbours by such a wavering and unsettled conduct.

This our inconsistency in the pursuit of schemes which have been thoroughly digested, has as bad an influence on our domestic as on our foreign affairs. We are told, that the famous prince of Conde used to ask the English ambassador, upon the arrival of a mail, 'Who was Secretary of State in England by that post?' as a piece of raillery upon the fickleness of our politics. But what has rendered this a misfortune to our country, is that public ministers have no sooner made themselves masters of their business, than they have been dismissed from their employments; and that this disgrace has befallen very many of them, not because they have deserved it, but because the people love to see new faces in high posts of honour.

It is a double misfortune to a nation, which is thus given to change, when they have a sovereign at the head of them, that is prone to fall in with all the turns and veerings of the people. Sallust, the gravest of all the Roman historians, who had formed his notions of regal authority from the manner in which he saw it exerted among the barbarous nations, makes the following remark: *Plerumque Regiæ voluntates, uti vehementes, sic mobiles, sæpe ipsæ sibi adversæ.* 'The wills of kings, as they are generally vehement, are likewise very fickle, and at different times opposite to themselves.' Were there any colour for this general observation, how much does it redound to the honour of such princes who are exceptions to it!

The natural consequence of an unsteady government, is the perpetuating of strife and faction among a divided people. Whereas a king who persists in those schemes which he has laid, and has no other view in them but the good of his subjects, extinguishes all hopes of advancement in those who would grow great by an opposition to his measures, and insensibly unites the contending parties in their common interest.

Queen Elizabeth, who makes the greatest figure among our English sovereigns, was most eminently remarkable for that steadiness and uniformity which ran through all her actions, during that long and glorious reign. She kept up to her chosen motto in every part of her life; and never lost sight of those great ends, which she proposed to herself on her accession to the throne, the happiness of her people, and the strengthening of the Protestant interest. She often interposed her royal authority to break the cabals which were forming against her first ministers, who grew old and died in those stations which they filled with so great abilities. By this means she baffled the many attempts of her foreign and domestic enemies, and entirely broke the whole force and spirit of that party among her subjects, which was popishly affected, and which was not a little formidable in the beginning of her reign.

The frequent changes and alterations in public proceedings, the multiplicity of schemes introduced one upon another, with the variety of short-lived favourites, that prevailed in their several turns under the government of her successors, have by degrees broken us into those unhappy distinctions and parties, which have given so much uneasiness to our kings, and so often endangered the safety of their people.

I question not but every impartial reader hath been beforehand with me, in considering, on this occasion, the happiness of our country under the government of his present Majesty; who is so deservedly famous for an inflexible adherence to those counsels which have a visible tendency to the public good, and to those persons who heartily concur with him in promoting these his generous designs.

A prince of this character will be dreaded by his enemies, and served with courage and zeal by his friends; and will either instruct us by his example, to fix the unsteadiness of our politics, or by his conduct hinder it from doing us any prejudice.

Upon the whole, as there is no temper of mind more unmanly in a private person, nor more pernicious to the public in a member of a community, than that changeableness with which we are too justly branded by all our neighbours, it is to be hoped that the sound part of the nation will give no farther occasion for this reproach but continue steady to that happy establishment which has now taken place among us. And as obstinacy in prejudices which are detrimental to our country, ought not to be mistaken for that virtuous resolution and firmness of mind which is necessary to our preservation, it is to be wished that the enemies to our constitution would so far indulge themselves in this national humour, as to come into one change more, by falling in with that plan of government which at present they think fit to oppose. At least we may expect they will be so wise as to shew a legal obedience to the best of kings, who profess the duty of passive obedience to the worst.

## No. 26. MONDAY, MARCH 19.

Bella viri pacemque gerant, queis bella gerenda.—VIRG.

WHEN the Athenians had long contended against the power of Philip, he demanded of them to give up their orators, as well knowing their opposition would be soon at an end if it were not irritated from time to time by these tongue-warriors. I have endeavoured, for the same reason, to gain our female adversaries, and by that means to disarm the party of its principal strength. Let them give us up their women, and we know by experience how inconsiderable a resistance we are to expect from their men.

This sharp political humour has but lately prevailed in so great a measure as it now does among the beautiful part of our species. They used to employ themselves wholly in the scenes of a domestic life, and provided a woman could keep her house in order, she never troubled herself about regulating the commonwealth. The eye of the mistress was wont to make her pewter shine, and to inspect every part of her household furniture as much as her looking-glass. But at present our discontented matrons are so conversant in matters of state, that they wholly neglect their private affairs: for we may always observe that a gossip in politics is a slattern in her family.

It is indeed a melancholy thing to see the disorders of a household that is under the conduct of an angry stateswoman, who lays out all her thoughts upon the public, and is only attentive to find out miscarriages in the ministry. Several women of this turn are so earnest in contending for hereditary right, that they wholly neglect the education of their sons and heirs; and are so taken up with their zeal for the church, that they cannot find time to teach their children their catechism. A lady who thus intrudes into the province of the men, was so astonishing a character among the old Romans, that when Amæsia [a] presented herself to speak before the senate, they looked upon it as a prodigy, and sent messengers to inquire of the oracle, what it might portend to the commonwealth?

It would be manifestly to the disadvantage of the British cause, should our pretty loyalists profess an indifference in state-affairs, while their disaffected sisters are thus industrious to the prejudice of their country; and accordingly we have the satisfaction to find our she-associates are not idle upon this occasion. It is owing to the good principles of these his Majesty's fair and faithful subjects, that our country-women appear no less amiable in the eyes of the male-world, than they have done in former ages. For where a great number of flowers grow, the ground at a distance seems entirely covered with them, and we must walk into it, before we can distinguish the several weeds that spring up in such a beautiful mass of colours. Our great concern is, to find deformity can arise among so many charms, and that the most lovely parts of the creation can make themselves the most disagreeable. But it is an observation of the philosophers, that the best things may be corrupted into the worst; and the ancients did not scruple to affirm, that the furies and the graces were of the same sex.

As I should do the nation and themselves good service, if I could draw the ladies, who still hold out against his Majesty, into the interest of our present establishment, I shall propose to their serious consideration, the several inconveniences which those

[a] *Amæsia.* The story is told in Plutarch, [Numa, p. 77. Ed. Par. 1624,] with this difference, that no name is mentioned, and, that the pleading was in the *forum*, and not before the senate.

Dacier, indeed, in his notes on this place, mentions an *Amasia Sentia*, who pleaded before the Prætor in a capital cause, but refers to no authority, and says nothing of consulting the oracle. Mr. A. seems to have jumbled these two stories together, and to have put *Amæsia* for *Amasia.*

among them undergo, who have not yet surrendered to the government.

They should first reflect on the great sufferings and persecutions to which they expose themselves by the obstinacy of their behaviour. They lose their elections in every club where they are set up for toasts. They are obliged by their principles to stick a patch on the most unbecoming side of their fore-heads. They forego the advantage of birth-day suits. They are insulted by the loyalty of claps and hisses every time they appear at a play. They receive no benefit from the army, and are never the better for all the young fellows that wear hats and feathers. They are forced to live in the country and feed their chickens; at the same time that they might shew themselves at court, and appear in brocade, if they behaved themselves well. In short, what must go to the heart of every fine woman, they throw themselves quite out of the fashion.

The above-mentioned motive must have an influence upon the gay part of the sex; and as for those who are acted by more sublime and moral principles, they should consider, that they cannot signalize themselves as malecontents, without breaking through all the amiable instincts and softer virtues, which are peculiarly ornamental to womankind. Their timorous, gentle, modest behaviour; their affability, meekness, good-breeding, and many other beautiful dispositions of mind must be sacrificed to a blind and furious zeal for they do not know what. A man is startled when he sees a pretty bosom heaving with such party-rage, as is disagreeable even in that sex which is of a more coarse and rugged make. And yet such is our misfortune, that we sometimes see a pair of stays ready to burst with sedition: and hear the most masculine passions exprest in the sweetest voices. I have lately been told of a country-gentlewoman, pretty much famed for this virility of behaviour in party-disputes, who, upon venting her notions very freely in a strange place, was carried before an honest justice of the peace. This prudent magistrate observing her to be a large black woman, and finding by her discourse that she was no better than a rebel in a riding-hood, began to suspect her for my Lord Nithisdale; till a stranger came to her rescue, who assured him, with tears in his eyes, that he was her husband.

In the next place, our British ladies may consider, that by interesting themselves so zealously in the affairs of the public, they are engaged, without any necessity, in the crimes which are often committed even by the best of parties, and which they are naturally exempted from by the privilege of their sex. The worst character a female could formerly arrive at, was of being an ill woman; but by their present conduct, she may likewise deserve the character of an ill subject. They come in for their share of political guilt, and have found a way to make themselves much greater criminals, than their mothers before them.

I have great hopes that these motives, when they are assisted by their own reflections, will incline the fair ones of the adverse party to come over to the national interest, in which their own is so highly concerned; especially if they consider, that by these superfluous employments which they take upon them as partisans, they do not only dip themselves in an unnecessary guilt, but are obnoxious to a grief and anguish of mind, which doth not properly fall within their lot. And here I would advise every one of these exasperated ladies, who indulges that opprobrious eloquence which is so much in fashion, to reflect on Æsop's fable of the viper. "This little animal, (says the old moralist) chancing to meet with a file, began to lick it with her tongue till the blood came; which gave her a very silly satisfaction, as imagining the blood came from the file, notwithstanding all the smart was in her own tongue."

## No. 27. FRIDAY, MARCH 23.

——dii visa secundant. –LUCB.

It is an old observation, that a time of peace is always a time of prodigies; for as our news-writers must adorn their papers with that which the critics call, 'The Marvellous,' they are forced in a dead calm of affairs, to ransack every element for proper amusements, and either to astonish their readers from time to time with a strange and wonderful sight, or be content to lose their custom. The sea is generally filled with monsters when there are no fleets upon it. Mount Ætna immediately began to rage upon the extinction of the rebellion: and woe to the people of Catanea, if the peace continues; for they are sure to be shaken every week with earthquakes, till they are relieved by the siege of some other great town in Europe. The air has likewise contributed its quota of prodigies. We had a blazing star by the last mail from Genoa; and in the present dearth of battles, have been very opportunely entertained, by persons of undoubted credit, with a civil war in the clouds, where our sharp-sighted malecontents discovered many objects invisible to an eye that is dimmed by whig-principles.

I question not but this paper will fall in with the present humour, since it contains a very remarkable vision of a highland seer,[a] who is famous among the mountains, and known by the name of second-sighted Sawney. Had he been able to write, we might probably have seen this vision sooner in print; for it happened to him very early in the late hard winter; and is transmitted to me by a student at Glasgow, who took the whole relation from him, and stuck close to the facts, though he has delivered them in his own style.

[a] Mr. A. is much too complaisant to his *Highland-seer*, in giving him the honour of so fine a vision as the following. He might have introduced it, as a *dream* of his own, with more propriety

"SAWNEY was descended of an ancient family, very much renowned for their skill in prognostics. Most of his ancestors were second-sighted and his mother but narrowly escaped being burnt for a witch. As he was going out one morning very early to steal a sheep, he was seized on the sudden with a fit of second-sight. The face of the whole country about him was changed in the twinkling of an eye, and presented him with a wide prospect of new scenes and objects, which he had never seen till that day.

"He discovered at a great distance from him a large fabric, which cast such a glistering light about it, that it looked like a huge rock of diamond. Upon the top of it was planted a standard, streaming in a strong northern wind, and embroidered with a mixture of thistles and flower-de-luces. As he was amusing himself with this strange sight, he heard a bagpipe at some distance behind him, and, turning about, saw a general, who seemed very much animated by the sound of it, marching towards him at the head of a numerous army. He learnt, upon inquiry, that they were making a procession to the structure which stood before him, and which he found was the Temple of Rebellion. He immediately struck in with them; but described this march to the temple with so much horror, that he shivered every joint all the while he spoke of it. They were forced to clamber over so many rocks, and to tread upon the brink of so many precipices, that they were very often in danger of their lives. Sawney declared, that, for his own part, he walked in fear of his neck every step he took. Upon their coming within a few furlongs of the temple, they passed through a very thick grove, consecrated to a deity who was known by the name of Treason. They here dispersed themselves into abundance of labyrinths and covered walks which led to the temple. The path was so very slippery, the shade so exceeding gloomy, and the whole wood so full of echoes that they were forced to march with the greatest wariness, circumspection, and silence. They at length arrived at a great gate, which was the principal avenue to the magnificent fabric. Sawney stood some time at the entrance to observe the splendor of the building, and was not a little entertained with a prodigious number of statues, which were planted up and down in a spacious court that lay before it; but, upon examining it more nicely, he found the whole fabric, which made such a glittering appearance, and seemed impregnable, was composed of ice, and that the several statues which seemed at a distance to be made of the whitest marble, were nothing else but so many figures in snow. The front of the temple was very curiously adorned with stars and garters, ducal coronets, generals' staffs, and many other emblems of honour wrought in the most beautiful frost-work. After having stood at gaze some time before this great gate, he discovered on it an inscription, signifying it to be the Gate of Perjury. There was erected near it a great Colossus in snow that had two faces, and was drest like a Jesuit, with one of its hands upon a book, and the other grasping a dagger. Upon entering into the court, he took a particular survey of several of the figures. There was Sedition with a trumpet in her hand, and Rapine in the garb of a Highlander: Ambition, Envy, Disgrace, Poverty, and Disappointment, were all of them represented under their proper emblems. Among other statues, he observed that of Rumour whispering an idiot in the ear, who was the representative of credulity; and Faction embracing with her hundred arms an old-fashioned figure in a steeple-crowned hat, that was designed to express a cunning old gypsy, called Passive-obedience. Zeal, too, had a place among the rest, with a bandage over her eyes, though one would not have expected to have seen her represented in snow. But the most remarkable object in this court-yard, was a huge tree that grew up before the porch of the temple, and was of the same kind with that, which Virgil tells us flourished at the entrance of the infernal regions. For it bore nothing but dreams, which hung in clusters under every leaf of it. The travellers refreshed themselves in the shade of this tree before they entered the Temple of Rebellion, and after their frights and fatigues, received great comfort in the fruit which fell from it. At length the gates of the temple flew open, and the crowd rushed into it. In the centre of it was a grim idol, with a sword in the right hand, and a firebrand in the left. The forepart of the pedestal was curiously embossed with a triumph, while the back-part, that lay more out of sight, was filled with gibbets and axes. This dreadful idol is worshipped, like several of old, with human sacrifices, and his votaries were consulting among themselves, how to gratify him with hecatombs; when, on a sudden, they were surprised with the alarm of a great light which appeared in the southern part of the heavens, and made its progress directly towards them. This light appeared as a great mass of flame, or rather glory, like that of the sun in its strength. There were three figures in the midst of it, who were known by their several hieroglyphics, to be Religion, Loyalty, and Valour. The last had a graceful air, a blooming countenance, and a star upon its breast, which shot forth several pointed beams of a peculiar lustre. The glory which encompassed them, covered the place, and darted its rays with so much strength, that the whole fabric and all its ornaments began to melt. The several emblems of honour, which were wrought on the front in the brittle materials above mentioned, trickled away under the first impressions of the heat. In short, the thaw was so violent, that the temple and statues ran off in a sudden torrent, and the whole winter-piece was dissolved. The covered walks were laid open by the light which shone through every part of them, and the dream-tree withered like the famous gourd that was smitten by the noonday sun. As for the votaries, they left the place with the greatest precipitation, and dispersed themselves by flight into a thousand different paths among the mountains."

---

## No. 28. MONDAY, MARCH 26.

———Incendia lumen
Præbebant, aliquisque malo fuit usus in illo.—Ovid Met.

Sir Francis Bacon, in the dedication before his history of Henry the seventh, observes, that peaceable times are the best to live in, though not so proper to furnish materials for a writer: as hilly countries afford the most entertaining prospects, though a man would chuse to travel through a plain one. To this we may add, that the times, which are full of disorders and tumults, are likewise the fullest of instruction. History, indeed, furnishes us with very distinct accounts of factions, conspiracies, civil wars, and rebellions, with the fatal consequences that attend them: but they do not make such deep and lasting impressions on our minds, as events of the same nature, to which we have ourselves been witnesses, and in which we, or our friends and acquaintance, have been sufferers. As adversity makes a man wise in his private affairs, civil calamities give him prudence and circumspection in his public conduct.

The miseries of the civil war, under the reign of King Charles the first, and the consequences which ensued upon them, did, for many years, deter the inhabitants of our island from the thoughts of engaging anew in such desperate undertakings: and convinced them, by fatal experience, that nothing could be so pernicious to the English, and so opposite to the genius of the people, as the subversion of monarchy. In the like manner we may hope that the great expences brought upon the nation by the present rebellion; the sufferings of innocent people, who have lived in that place which was the scene of it; with that dreadful prospect of ruin and confusion which must have followed its success; will secure us from the like attempts for the future, and fix his Majesty upon the throne of Great Britain; especially when those who are prompted to such wicked practices reflect upon the punishments to which the criminals have exposed themselves, and the miseries in which they have involved their relations, friends, and families.

It will be likewise worth their while to consider, how such tumults and riots, as have been encouraged by many, who we may hope did not propose to themselves such fatal consequences, lead to a civil war: and how naturally that seditious kind of conversation, which many seem to think consistent with their religion and morality, ends in an open rebellion. I question not but the more virtuous and considerate part of our malecontents, are now stung with a very just remorse for this their manner of proceeding, which has so visibly tended to the destruction of their friends, and the sufferings of their country. This may, at the same time, prove an instructive lesson to the boldest and bravest among the disaffected, not to build any hopes upon the talkative zealots of their party; who have shewn by their whole behaviour, that their hearts are equally filled with treason and cowardice. An army of trumpeters would give as great a strength to a cause, as this confederacy of tongue-warriors; who, like those military musicians, content themselves with animating their friends to battle, and run out of the engagement upon the first onset.

But one of the most useful maxims we can learn from the present rebellion, is, that nothing can be more contemptible and insignificant, than the scum of a people, when they are instigated against a king, who is supported by the two branches of the legislature. A mob may pull down a meeting-house, but will never be able to overturn a government, which has a courageous and wise prince at the head of it, and one who is zealously assisted by the great council of the nation, that best know the value of him. The authority of the Lords and Commons of Great Britain, in conjunction with that of our sovereign, is not to be controlled by a tumultuary rabble. It is big with fleets and armies, can fortify itself with what laws it shall judge proper for its own defence, can command the wealth of the kingdom for the security of the people, and engage the whole Protestant interest of Europe in so good and just a cause. A disorderly multitude contending with the body of the legislature, is like a man in a fit under the conduct of one in the fullness of his health and strength. Such a one is sure to be over-ruled in a little time, though he deals about his blows, and exerts himself in the most furious convulsions while the distemper is upon him.

We may farther learn from the course of the present rebellion, who, among the foreign states in our neighbourhood, are the true and natural friends of Great Britain, if we observe which of them gave us their assistance in reducing our country to a state of peace and tranquillity; and which of them used their endeavours to heighten our confusions, and plunge us into all the evils of a civil war. I shall only take notice under this head, that in former ages it was the constant policy of France to raise and cherish intestine feuds and discords in the isle of Great Britain, that we might either fall a prey into their hands, or that they might prosecute their designs upon the continent with less interruption. Innumerable instances of this nature occur in history. The most remarkable one was that in the reign of King Charles the first. Though that prince was married to a daughter of France, and was personally beloved and esteemed in the French court, it is well known that they abetted both parties in the civil war, and always furnished supplies to the weaker side, lest there should be an end put to those fatal divisions.

We might also observe, that this rebellion has been a means of discovering to his Majesty,[a] how much he may depend upon the professions and principles of the several parties among his own subjects; who are those persons that have espoused his interests with zeal or indifference; and who among them are influenced to their allegiance by places, duty, or affection. But as these, and several other considerations, are obvious to the thoughts of every reader, I shall conclude, with observing how naturally many of those, who distinguish themselves by the name of the High-Church, unite themselves to the cause of Popery; since it is manifest that all the Protestants concerned in the rebellion, were such as gloried in this distinction.

It would be very unjust, to charge all who have ranged themselves under this new denomination, as if they had done it with a design to favour the interests of Popery. But it is certain that many of them, who at their first setting out were most averse to[b] the doctrines of the church of Rome, have, by the cunning of our adversaries, been inspired with such an unreasonable aversion to their Protestant brethren, and taught to think so favourably of the Roman Catholic principles, (not to mention the endeavours that have been used to reconcile the doctrines of the two churches, which are in themselves as opposite as light and darkness) that they have been drawn over insensibly into its interests. It is no wonder, therefore, that so many of

[a] *A means of discovering to his Majesty.* The verb, *discover*, implies the exertion of personal faculties, and therefore cannot be used thus absolutely; I mean, without a reference to some agent. He might have said, *that by means of this rebellion, his Majesty has discovered how much*, &c.

[b] *Averse to—aversion to.* Many would now say, *averse from*; some, perhaps, *aversion from.* The case seems clearer in the use of the *adjective*, than the *substantive.* Yet the Latins have, *averso* IN *me animo—aversus lucro—aversus defensioni*, &c. But see the note on *dissent with*, in *Whig-Examiner*, No. I. 446.

these deluded zealots have been engaged in a cause which they at first abhorred, and have wished or acted for the success of an enterprise, that might have ended in the extirpation of the Protestant religion in this kingdom, and in all Europe. In short, they are like the Syrians, who were first smitten with blindness, and unknowingly led out of their way into the capital of their enemy's country; insomuch that the text tells us, 'When they opened their eyes, they found themselves in the midst of Samaria.'

---

## NO. 29. FRIDAY, MARCH 30.

Dis te minorem quod geris, imperas.
Hinc omne principium, huc refer exitum.
Dii multa neglecti dederunt
Hesperiæ mala luctuosæ.—Hor.

This being a day in which the thoughts of our countrymen are, or ought to be, employed on serious subjects, I shall take the opportunity of that disposition of mind in my readers, to recommend to them the practice of those religious and moral virtues, without which all policy is vain, and the best cause deprived of its greatest ornament and support.

Common sense, as well as the experience of all ages, teaches us, that no government can flourish which doth not encourage and propagate religion and morality among all its particular members. It was an observation of the ancient Romans, that their empire had not more increased by the strength of their arms, than by the sanctity of their manners: and Cicero, who seems to have been better versed than any of them, both in the theory and the practice of politics, makes it a doubt, whether it were possible for a community to exist, that had not a prevailing mixture of piety in its constitution. Justice, temperance, humi lity, and almost every other moral virtue, do not only derive the blessings of Providence upon those who exercise them, but are the natural means for acquiring the public prosperity.[a] Besides; religious motives and instincts are so busy in the heart of every reasonable creature, that a man who would hope to govern a society without any regard to these principles, is as much to be contemned for his folly, as to be detested for his impiety.

To this we may add, that the world is never sunk into such a state of degeneracy, but they pay a natural veneration to men of virtue; and rejoice to see themselves conducted by those, who act under the awe of a Supreme Being, and who think themselves accountable for all their proceedings to the great judge and superintendent of human affairs.

Those of our fellow-subjects, who are sensible of the happiness they enjoy in his Majesty's accession to the throne, are obliged, by all the duties of gratitude, to adore that Providence which has so signally interposed in our behalf, by clearing a way to the Protestant succession through such difficulties as seemed insuperable; by detecting the conspiracies which have been formed against it; and, by many wonderful events, weakening the hands and baffling the attempts of all his Majesty's enemies, both foreign and domestic.

The party who distinguish themselves by their zeal for the present establishment, should be careful, in a particular manner, to discover in their whole conduct such a reverence for religion,

[a] *Means for acquiring the public prosperity. Acquire,* is another of those verbs that imply personal agency. See the note on *discover,* in the last paper. It should be, *are the natural means by which men acquire those blessings*—or, *by which states acquire prosperity.* Our grammars are very defective in their account of *verbs active,* which differ widely from each other, though they take the same common name. In some, we regard little more than the transitive effect; in others, some energy of the efficient is chiefly respected. *Procure,* and *acquire,* may, to some, appear synonymous: yet, trade may *procure* that wealth, which the tradesman only *acquires.*

as may shew how groundless that reproach is which is cast upon them by their enemies, of being averse to our national worship. While others engross to themselves the name of the Church, and, in a manner, excommunicate the best part of their fellow-subjects; let us shew ourselves the genuine sons of it, by practising the doctrines which it teaches. The advantage will be visibly on our side, if we stick to its essentials; while they triumph in that empty denomination which they bestow upon themselves. Too many of them are already dipt in the guilt of perjury and sedition; and as we remain unblemished in these particulars, let us endeavour to excel them in all the other parts of religion, and we shall quickly find, that a regular morality is, in its own nature, more popular, as well as more meritorious, than an intemperate zeal.

We have likewise, in the present times of confusion and disorder, an opportunity of shewing our abhorrence of several principles which have been ascribed to us by the malice of our enemies. A disaffection to kings and kingly government, with a proneness to rebellion, have been often very unjustly charged on that party which goes by the name of whigs. Our steady and continued adherence to his Majesty and the present happy settlement, will the most effectually confute this calumny. Our adversaries, who know very well how odious commonwealth principles are to the English nation, have inverted the very sense of words and things, rather than not continue to brand us with this imaginary guilt: for with some of these men, at present, loyalty to our king is republicanism, and rebellion passive obedience.

It has been an old objection to the principles of the whigs, that several of their leaders, who have been zealous for redressing the grievances of government, have not behaved themselves better than the tories in domestic scenes of life; but at the same time have been public patriots and private oppressors. This objec tion, were it true, has no weight in it, since the misbehaviour of particular persons does not at all affect their cause, and since a man may act laudably in some respects, who does not so in others. However, it were to be wished, that men would not give occasion even to such invectives; but at the same time they consult the happiness of the whole, that they would promote it to their utmost in all their private dealings among those who lie more immediately within their influence. In the mean while I must observe, that this reproach, which may be often met with in print and conversation, tends in reality to the honour of the whigs, as it supposes that a greater regard to justice and humanity is to be expected from them, than from those of the opposite party: and it is certain we cannot better recommend our principles, than by such actions as are their natural and genuine fruits.

Were we thus careful to guard ourselves in a particular manner against these groundless imputations of our enemies, and to rise above them as much in our morality as in our politics, our cause would be always as flourishing as it is just. It is certain, that our notions have a more natural tendency to such a practice, as we espouse the Protestant interest in opposition to that of Popery, which is so far from advancing morality by its doctrines, that it has weakened, or entirely subverted, many of the duties even of natural religion.

I shall conclude, with recommending one virtue more to the friends of the present establishment, wherein the whigs have been remarkably deficient; which is, a general unanimity and concurrence in the pursuit of such measures as are necessary for the well-being of their country. As it is a laudable freedom of thought which unshackles their minds from the poor and narrow prejudices of education, and opens their eyes to a more extensive view of the public good; the same freedom of thought disposes several of them to the embracing of particular schemes and maxims, and to a certain singularity of opinion which proves highly prejudicial to their cause; especially when they are encouraged in them by a vain breath of popularity, or by the artificial praises which are bestowed on them by the opposite party. This temper of mind, though the effect of a noble principle, very often betrays their friends, and brings into power the most pernicious and implacable of their enemies. In cases of this nature, it is the duty of an honest and prudent man, to sacrifice a doubtful opinion to the concurring judgment of those whom he believes to be well-intentioned to their country, and who have better opportunities of looking into all its most complicated interests. An honest party of men, acting with unanimity, are of infinitely greater consequence than the same party aiming at the same end by different views: as a large diamond is of a thousand times greater value whilst it remains entire, than when it is cut into a multitude of smaller stones, notwithstanding they may each of them be very curiously set, and are all of the same water.

---

## No. 30. MONDAY, APRIL 2.

——I, verbis virtutem illude superbis.

VIRG.

As I was some years ago engaged in conversation with a fashionable French abbé upon a subject which the people of that kingdom love to start in discourse, the comparative greatness of the two nations; he asked me, 'How many souls I thought there might be in London?' I replied, being willing to do my country all the honour I fairly could, 'That there were several who computed them at near a million:' but not finding that surprise I expected in his countenance, I returned the question upon him, how many he thought there might be in Paris ? to which he answered, with a certain grimace of coldness and indifference, 'about ten or twelve millions.'

It would, indeed, be incredible to a man who has never been in France, should one relate the extravagant notion they entertain of themselves, and the mean opinion they have of their neighbours. There are certainly (notwithstanding the visible decay of learning and taste which has appeared among them of late years) many particular persons in that country, who are eminent in the highest degree for their good sense as well as for their knowledge in all the arts and sciences. But I believe every one, who is acquainted with them, will allow, that the people in general fall short of those, who border upon them, in strength and solidity of understanding. One would therefore no more wonder to see the most shallow nation of Europe the most vain, than to find the most empty fellows in every distinct nation more conceited and censorious than the rest of their countrymen. Prejudice and self-sufficiency naturally proceed from inexperience of the world, and ignorance of mankind. As it requires but very small abilities to discover the imperfections of another, we find that none are more apt to turn their neighbours into ridicule, than those who are the most ridiculous in their own private conduct.

Those among the French, who have seen nothing but their own country, can scarce bring themselves to believe, that a nation, which lies never so little north of them, is not full of Goths and Vandals. Nay, those among them who travel into foreign parts are so prejudiced in favour of their own imaginary politeness, that they are apt to look upon every thing as barbarous in proportion as it deviates from what they find at home. No less a man than an ambassador of France, being in conversation with our king of glorious memory, and willing to encourage his Majesty, told him, that he talked like a Frenchman. The king smiled at the encomium which was given hin. and only replied, 'sir, I am sure you do.' An eminent writer of the last age was so offended at this kind of insolence, which shewed itself very plentifully in one of their travellers who gave an account of England, that he vindicated the honour of his country in a book full of just satire and ingenuity. I need not acquaint my reader, that I mean Bishop Sprat's answer to Sorbiere.

Since I am upon this head, I cannot forbear mentioning some profound remarks that I have been lately shewn in a French book, the author of which lived, it seems, some time in England. 'The English,' says this curious traveller, 'very much delight in pudding. This is the favourite dish, not only of the clergy, but of the people in general. Provided there be a pudding upon the table, no matter what are the other dishes; they are sure to make a feast. They think themselves so happy when they have a pudding before them, that if any one would tell a friend he is arrived in a lucky juncture, the ordinary salutation is, 'sir, I am glad to see you; you are come in pudding-time.'

One cannot have the heart to be angry at this judicious observer, notwithstanding he has treated us like a race of Hottentots, because he only taxes us with our inordinate love of pudding, which, it must be confessed, is not so elegant a dish as frog and sallad. Every one who has been at Paris, knows that *Un gros milord Anglois* is a frequent jest upon the French stage; as if corpulence was a proper subject for satire, or a man of honour could help his being fat, who eats suitable[a] to his quality.

It would be endless to recount the invectives which are to be met with among the French historians, and even in Mezeray himself, against the manners of our countrymen. Their authors, in other kinds of writing, are likewise very liberal in characters of

[a] He should have said *suitably;* and he would have said it, but for the jingle that hurt his ear, in *quality.*

the same nature. I cannot forbear mentioning the learned Monsieur Patin in particular; who tells us in so many words, 'That the English are a people, whom he naturally abhors;' and in another place, 'that he looks upon the English among the several nations of men, as he does upon wolves among the several species of beasts.' A British writer would be very justly charged with want of politeness, who, in return to this civility, should look upon the French as that part of mankind which answers to a species in the brute creation, whom we call in English by the name of monkies.

If the French load us with these indignities, we may observe, for our comfort, that they give the rest of their borderers no better quarter. If we are a dull, heavy, phlegmatic people, we are, it seems, no worse than our neighbours. As an instance, I shall set down at large a remarkable passage in a famous book entitled Chevræana, written many years ago by the celebrated Monsieur Chevreau; after having advertised my reader that the duchess of Hanover, and the princess Elizabeth of Bohemia, who are mentioned in it, were the late excellent princess Sophia and her sister.

'Tilenus pour un Allemand, parle et ecrit bien François,' dit Scaliger: 'Gretzer a bien de l'esprit pour un Allemand,' dit le Cardinal du Perron: Et le P. Bonhours met en question, si un Allemand peut être bel esprit? on ne doit juger ni bien ni mal d'une nation par un particulier ni d'un particulier par sa nation. Il y a des Allemands, comme des François, qui n'ont point d'esprit; des Allemands, qui ont scû plus d'Hebreu, plus de Grec, que, Scaliger & le Cardinal du Perron: J'honore fort le P. Bouhours, qui a du merite; mais J'ose dire, que la France n'a point de plus bel Esprit que Madame la Duchese de Hanovre d'aujourdhui, ni de personne plus solidement savante en philoso phie que l'etoit Madame la Princesse Elizabeth de Boheme, sa

Sœur : Et je ne croi pas que 'on refuse le même titre à beaucoup d'Academiciens d'Allemagne dont les Ouvrages meriteroient bien d'être traduits. Il y a d' autres Princesses en Allemagne, qui ont infiniment de l'esprit. Les François disent c'est un Allemand, pour exprimer un homme pesant, brutal : & les Allemands comme les Italiens, c'est un François, pour dire un fou & un étourdi. C'est aller trop loin : comme le Prince de Salé dit de Ruyter, Il est honnête homme, c'est bien dommage qu'il soit Chrétien. *Chevræana, tom. I.*

" 'Tilenus,' says Scaliger, 'speaks and writes well for a German.' 'Gretzer has a great deal of wit for a German,' says Cardinal Perron. And Father Bouhours makes it a question, whether a German can be a wit? One ought not to judge well or ill of a nation from a particular person, nor of a particular person from his nation. There are Germans as there are French, who have no wit; and Germans who are better skilled in Greek and Hebrew than either Scaliger or the Cardinal du Perron. I have a great honour for Father Bouhours, who is a man of merit; but will be bold to say, that there is not in all France, a person of more wit than the present Duchess of Hanover; nor more thoroughly knowing in philosophy than was the late Princess Elizabeth of Bohemia, her sister; and I believe none can refuse the same title to many academicians in Germany, whose works very well deserve to be translated into our tongue. There are other Princesses in Germany who have also an infinite deal of wit. The French say of a man, that he is a German, when they would signify that he is dull and heavy; and the Germans, as well as the Italians, when they would call a man a hair-brain'd coxcomb, say he is a Frenchman. This is going too far, and is like the Governor of Sallee's saying of De Ruyter, the Dutch admiral, 'He is an honest man, 'tis a great pity he is a Christian.' "

Having already run my paper out to its usual length, I have not room for many reflections on that which is the subject of it. The last cited author has been before-hand with me in its proper moral. I shall only add to it, that there has been an unaccountable disposition among the English of late years, to fetch the fashion from the French, not only in their dress and behaviour, but even in their judgments and opinions of mankind. It will, however, be reasonable for us, if we concur with them in their contempt of other neighbouring nations, that we should likewise regard ourselves[a] under the same view in which they are wont to place us. The representations they make of us, are as of a nation the least favoured by them; and, as these are agreeable to the natural aversion they have for us, are more disadvantageous than the pictures they have drawn of any other people in Europe.

---

## No. 31. FRIDAY, APRIL 6.

Omnes homines, P. C. qui de rebus dubiis consultant, ab odio, amicitia, ira, atque misericordia vacuos esse decet. CÆSAR APUD SALLUST.

I HAVE purposely avoided, during the whole course of this paper, to speak any thing concerning the treatment which is due to such persons as have been concerned in the late rebellion, because I would not seem to irritate justice against those who are under the prosecution of the law, nor incense any of my readers against unhappy, though guilty men. But when we find the proceedings of our government, in this particular, traduced and misrepresented, it is the duty of every good subject to set them in their proper light.

[a] *Reasonable for us, that we should regard ourselves.* Improperly expressed. It should either be—*reasonable that we should regard ourselves.* Or else—*reasonable for us to regard ourselves.*

I am the more prompted to this undertaking by a pamphlet, entitled, 'An argument to prove the affections of the people of England to be the best security of the government; humbly offered to the consideration of the patrons of severity, and applied to the present juncture of affairs.' Had the whole scope of the author been answerable to his title, he would have only undertaken to prove, what every man in his wits is already convinced of. But the drift of the pamphlet is, to stir up our compassion towards the rebels, and our indignation against the government. The author, who knew that such a design as this could not be carried on without a great deal of artifice and sophistry, has puzzled and perplexed his cause, by throwing his thoughts together in such a studied confusion, that upon this account, if upon any, his pamphlet is, as the party have represented it, unanswerable.

The famous Monsieur Bayle compares the answering of an immethodical author to the hunting of a duck: when you have him full in your sight, and fancy yourself within reach of him, he gives you the slip, and becomes invisible. His argument is lost in such a variety of matter, that you must catch it where you can, as it rises and disappears in the several parts of his discourse.

The writer of this pamphlet could, doubtless, have ranged his thoughts in much better order, if he had pleased; but he knew very well that error is not to be advanced by perspicuity. In order, therefore, to answer this pamphlet, I must reduce the substance of it under proper heads; and disembroil the thoughts of the author, since he did not think fit to do it himself.

In the first place I shall observe, that the terms which the author makes use of, are loose, general, and undefined, as will be shewn in the sequel of this paper; and, what less becomes a fair reasoner, he puts wrong and invidious names on every thing, to colour a false way of arguing. He allows that the rebels indisputably merit to be severely chastised; that they deserve it according to law; and that, if they are punished, they have none to thank but themselves. (p. 7.) How can a man, after such a concession, make use sometimes of the word 'cruelty,' but generally of 'revenge,' when he pleads against the exercise of what, according to his own notion, is at the most but rigid justice? Or why are such executions, which, according to his own opinion, are legal, so often to be called violences and slaughters? Not to mention the appellations given to those who do not agree with him in his opinions for clemency, as the blood-thirsty, the political butchers, state chirurgeons, and the like.

But I shall now speak of that point, which is the great and reigning fallacy of the pamphlet, and runs, more or less, through every paragraph. His whole argument turns upon this single consideration; Whether the king should exert mercy or justice towards those who have openly appeared in the present rebellion? By mercy, he means a general pardon; by justice, a general punishment: so that he supposes no other method practicable in this juncture, than either the forgiving all, or the executing all. Thus he puts the question; 'Whether it be the interest of the prince to destroy the rebels by fire, sword, or gibbet?' (p. 4.) And, speaking of the 'zealots for the government,' he tells us, 'they think no remedy so good, as to make clear work; and that they declare for the utter extirpation of all who are its enemies in the most minute circumstances; as if amputation were the sole remedy these political butchers could find out for the distempers of a state; or that they thought the only way to make the top flourish, were to lop off the under branches.' (p. 5.) He then speaks of the 'coffee-house politicians, and the casuists in red coats; who,' he tells us, 'are for the utmost rigour that their laws of war, or laws of convenience, can inspire them with.' (p. 5.) Again, 'it is represented,' says he, that the rebels deserve the highest punish ment the laws can inflict.' (p. 7.) And afterwards tells us, 'the question is, Whether the government shall shew mercy, or take a reverend divine's advice, to slay man and woman, infant and suckling?' (p. 8.) Thus again he tells us, 'the friends to severe counsels alledge, that the government ought not to be moved by compassion; and that the law should have its course.' (p. 9.) And in another place puts these words in their mouths, 'He may still retain their affection, and yet let the laws have their course in punishing the guilty.' (p. 18.) He goes upon the same supposition in the following passages: 'It is impracticable, in so general a corruption, to destroy all who are infected; and, unless you destroy all, you do nothing to the purpose.' (p. 10.) 'Shall our rightful king shew himself less the true father of his people, and afford his pardon to none of those people, who, like king Lear to his daughters, had so great a confidence in his virtue, as to give him all.' (p. 25.) I shall only add, that the concluding paragraph, which is worked up with so much artificial horror, goes upon a supposition answerable to the whole tenor of the pamphlet; and implies, that the impeached lords were to be executed without exception or discrimination.

Thus we see what is the author's idea of that justice against which all his arguments are levelled. If, in the next place, we consider the nature of that clemency which he recommends, we find it to be no less universal and unrestrained.

He declares for a general act of indemnity, (p. 20.) and tells us, 'It is the sense of every dispassionate man of the kingdom, that the rebels may, and ought to be pardoned.' (p. 19.) 'One popular act,' says he, 'would even yet retrieve all.' (p. 21.) He declares himself not 'over fond of the doctrines of making examples of traitors;' (ibid.) and that 'the way to prevent things from being brought to an extremity, is to deal mildly with those unfortunate gentlemen engaged in the rebellion.'

The reader may now see in how fallacious a manner this writer has stated the controversy; he supposes there are but two methods of treating the rebels; that is, by cutting off every one of them to a man, or pardoning every one of them without distinction. Now, if there be a third method between these two extremes, which is on all accounts more eligible than either of them, it is certain that the whole course of his argumentation comes to nothing. Every man of the plainest understanding will easily conclude, that in the case before us, as in most others, we ought to avoid both extremes; that, to destroy every rebel, would be an excessive severity; and, to forgive every one of them, an unreasonable weakness. The proper method of proceeding is that which the author has purposely omitted; namely, to temper justice with mercy; and, according to the different circumstances that aggravate or alleviate the guilt of the offenders, to restrain the force of the laws, or to let them take their proper course. Punishments are necessary to shew there is justice in a government, and pardons to shew there is mercy; and, both together, convince the people, that our constitution, under a good administration, does not only make a difference between the guilty and the innocent, but even among the guilty, between such as are more or less criminal.

This middle method, which has been always practised by wise and good governors, has hitherto been made use of by our sovereign. If, indeed, a stranger, and one who is altogether unacquainted with his Majesty's conduct, should read this pamphlet, he would conclude that every person engaged in the rebellion, was to die by the sword, the halter, or the axe; nay, that their friends and abettors were involved in the same fate. Would it be possible for him to imagine, that of the several thousands openly taken in arms, and liable to death by the laws of their country, not above forty have yet suffered? How would he be surprised to hear, that, notwithstanding his Majesty's troops have been victorious in every engagement, more of his friends have lost their lives in this rebellion, than of his traitorous subjects; though we add to those who have died by the hand of justice those of them who fell in battle? and yet we find a more popular compassion endeavoured to be raised[a] for the deaths of the guilty, who have brought such calamities on their country, than for the innocent who perished in the defence of it.

This middle method of proceeding, which has been pursued by his Majesty, and is wilfully overlooked by the author, best answers the ends of government; which is to maintain the safety of the public by rewards and punishments. It is also incumbent on a governor, according to the received dictates of religion; which instructs us, 'That he beareth not the sword in vain; but ought to be a terror to evil-doers, and a praise to them that do well.' It is likewise in a particular manner the duty of a British king, who obliges himself by his coronation oath to execute 'justice in mercy,' that is, to mix them in his administration, and not to exercise either of them to the total exclusion of the other.

But if we consider the arguments which this author gives for clemency, from the good effects it would produce, we shall find, that they hold true only when applied to such a mercy as serves rather to mitigate than exclude justice. The excellence of that unlimited clemency which the author contends for, is recommended by the following arguments.

[a] *Compassion endeavoured to be raised.—Endeavour* seems to be one of those neutrals which do not admit the passive form after the auxiliary *to be*: we say, *I have endeavoured*, but not, *I am, or it is endeavoured.* Besides the two participles passive, *endeavoured* to be *raised*, coming so near together, have an ill effect. He might have said—*and yet we find him endeavouring to raise a more popular compassion*, &c.

First, That it endears a prince to his people. This he descants on in several parts of his book. 'Clemency will endear his person to the nation; and then they will neither have the power nor will to disturb him.' (p. 8.) 'Was there ever a cruel prince that was not hated by his subjects?' (p. 24.) 'A merciful good-natured disposition is of all others the most amiable quality, and in princes always attended with a popular love.' (p. 18.)

It is certain, that such a popular love will always rise towards a good prince, who exercises such a mercy as I have before described, which is consistent with the safety of the constitution, and the good of his kingdom. But if it be thrown away at random, it loses its virtue, lessens the esteem and authority of a prince, and cannot long recommend him, even to the weakest of his subjects, who will find all the effects of cruelty in such an ill-grounded compassion. It was a famous saying of William Rufus, and is quoted to his honour by historians: "Whosoever spares perjured men, robbers, plunderers, and traitors, deprives all good men of their peace and quietness, and lays a foundation of innumerable mischiefs to the virtuous and innocent."

Another argument for unlimited clemency, is, that it shews a courageous temper; 'Clemency is likewise an argument of fearlessness; whereas cruelty not only betrays a weak, abject, depraved spirit, but also is for the most part a certain sign of cowardice. (p. 19.) He had a truly great soul, and such will always disdain the coward's virtue, which is fear; and the consequence of it, which is revenge.' (p. 27.) This panegyric on clemency, when it is governed by reason, is likewise very right; but it may so happen, that the putting of laws in execution against traitors to their country, may be the argument of fearlessness, when our governors are told that they dare not do it; and such methods may be made use of to extort pardons, as would make it look like cowardice to grant them. In this last case the author should have remembered his own words, that 'then only mercy is meritorious when it is voluntary, and not extorted by the necessity of affairs.' (p. 13.) Besides, the author should have considered, that another argument which he makes use of for his clemency, are the resentments that may arise from the execution of a rebel: an argument adapted to a cowardly, not a fearless temper. This he infers from the disposition of 'the friends, well-wishers, or associates of the sufferers.' (p. 4.) 'Resentment will inflame some; in others compassion will, by degrees, rise into resentment. This will naturally beget a disposition to overturn what they dislike, and then there will want only a fair opportunity.' (p. 12.) This argument, like most of the others, pleads equally for malefactors of all kinds, whom the government can never bring to justice, without disobliging their friends, well-wishers, or associates. But, I believe, if the author would converse with any friend, well-wisher, or associate of these sufferers, he would find them rather deterred from their practices by their sufferings, than disposed to rise in a new rebellion to revenge them. A government must be in a very weak and melancholy condition, that is not armed with a sufficient power for its own defence against the resentment of its enemies, and is afraid of being overturned if it does justice on those who attempt it. But I am afraid the main reason, why these friends, well-wishers, and associates, are against punishing any of the rebels, is that which must be an argument with every wise governor for doing justice upon some of them; namely, that it is a likely means to come at the bottom of this conspiracy, and to detect those who have been the private abettors of it, and who are still at work in the same design; if we give credit to the suggestions of our malecontents themselves, who labour to make us believe that there is still life in this wicked project.

I am wonderfully surprised to see another argument made

use of for a general pardon, which might have been urged more properly for a general execution. The words are these: 'The generality will never be brought to believe, but that those who suffer only for treason have very hard measure, nor can you with all your severity, undeceive them of their error.' If the generality of the English have such a favourable opinion of treason, nothing can so well cure them of an error so fatal to their country, as the punishment of those who are guilty of it. It is evident, that a general impunity would confirm them in such an opinion: for the vulgar will never be brought to believe, that there is a crime where they see no penalty. As it is certain no error can be more destructive to the very being of government than this, a proper remedy ought to be applied to it; and I would ask this author, Whether upon this occasion, 'The doctrine of making examples of traitors, be not very seasonable; though he declares himself 'not over fond of it.' The way to awaken men's minds to the sense of this guilt, is to let them see, by the sufferings of some who have incurred it, how heinous a crime it is in the eye of the law.

The foregoing answer may be applied, likewise, to another argument of the same nature. 'If the faction be as numerous as is pretended; if the spirit has spread itself over the whole kingdom; if it has mixed with the mass of the people; then certainly all bloody measures will but whet men the more for revenge.' If justice inflicted on a few of the flagrant criminals, with mercy extended to the multitude, may be called 'bloody measures,' they are without doubt absolutely necessary, in case the spirit of faction be thus spread among the mass of the people; who will readily conclude, that if open rebellion goes unpunished, every degree of faction which leads to it must be altogether innocent.

I am come now to another argument for pardoning all the rebels, w' ich is, that it would inspire them all with gratitude, and reduce them to their allegiance. 'It is truly heroic to overcome the hearts of one's enemies; and when it is compassed, the undertaking is truly politic. (p. 8.) He has now a fair opportunity of conquering more enemies by one act of clemency, than the most successful general will be able to do in many campaigns. (p. 9.) Are there not infinite numbers who would become most dutiful upon any fair invitation, upon the least appearance of grace? (p. 13.) Which of the rebels could be ungrateful enough to resist or abuse goodness exemplified in practice, as well as extolled in theory?' (p. 20.) Has not his Majesty then shewn the least appearance of grace in that generous forgiveness which he has already extended to such great numbers of his rebellious subjects, who must have died by the laws of their country, had not his mercy interposed in their behalf? But if the author means (as he doth, through this whole pamphlet by the like expressions) an universal forgiveness, no unprejudiced man can be of his opinion, that it would have had this good effect. We may see how little the conversion of rebels is to be depended on, when we observe, that several of the leaders in this rebellion were men who had been pardoned for practices of the same nature: and that most of those who have suffered, have avowed their perseverance in their rebellious principles, when they spoke their minds at the place of execution, notwithstanding their professions to the contrary, while they solicited forgiveness. Besides, were pardon extended indifferently to all, which of them would think himself under any particular obligation? Whereas, by that prudent discrimination which his Majesty has made between the offenders of different degrees, he naturally obliges those whom he has considered with so much tenderness, and distinguished as the most proper objects of mercy. In short, those who are pardoned would not have known the value of grace, if none had felt the effects of justice.

I must not omit another reason which the author makes use of against punishments: 'Because,' he says, 'those very means, or the apprehensions of them, have brought things to the pass in which they are, and consequently will reduce them from bad to worse.' (p. 10.) And afterwards, 'This growth of disaffection is in a great measure owing to the groundless jealousies men entertained of the present administration, as if they were to expect nothing but cruelty under it.' If our author would have spoken out, and have applied these effects to the real cause, he could ascribe this change of affections among the people to nothing else but the change of the ministry: for we find that a great many persons lost their loyalty with their places; and that their friends have ever since made use of the most base methods to infuse those groundless discontents into the minds of the common people, which have brought so many of them to the brink of destruction, and proved so detrimental to their fellow-subjects. However, this proceeding has shewn how dangerous it would have been for his Majesty to have continued in their places of trust a set of men, some of whom have since actually joined with the pretender to his crown: while others may be justly suspected never to have been faithful to him in their hearts, or, at least, whose principles are precarious, and visibly conducted by their interest. In a word, if the removal of these persons from their posts has produced such popular commotions, the continuance of them might have produced something much more fatal to their king and country, and have brought about that revolution, which has now been in vain attempted. The condition of a British king would be very poor, indeed, should a party of his subjects threaten him with a rebellion upon his bringing malefactors to justice, or upon his refusing to employ those whom he dares not trust.

I shall only mention another argument against the punish

ment of any of the rebels, whose executions he represents as very shocking to the people, because they are their countrymen (p. 12.) And again, 'The quality of the sufferers, their alliances, their characters, their being Englishmen, with a thousand other circumstances, will contribute to breed more ill blood than all the state-chirurgeons can possibly let out.' (p. 12.) The impeached lords, likewise, in the last paragraph of the pamphlet, are recommended to our pity, because they are our countrymen. By this way of reasoning, no man that is a gentleman, or born within the three seas, should be subject to capital punishment. Besides, who can be guilty of rebellion that are not our countrymen? As for the endearing name of Englishmen, which he bestows upon every one of the criminals, he should consider, that a man deservedly cuts himself off from the affections as well as the privileges of that community, which he endeavours to subvert.

These are the several arguments which appear in different forms and expressions through this whole pamphlet, and under which every one that is urged in it may be reduced. There is, indeed, another set of them, derived from the example and authority of great persons, which the author produces in favour of his own scheme. These are William the Conqueror, Henry the fourth of France, our late King William, King Solomon, and the Pretender. If a man were disposed to draw arguments for severity out of history, how many instances might one find of it among the greatest princes of every nation? but as different princes may act very laudably by different methods in different conjunctures, I cannot think this a conclusive way of reasoning. However, let us examine this set of arguments, and we shall find them no less defective than those above-mentioned.

'One of the greatest of our English monarchs, (says our author,) was William the Conqueror; and he was the greater, because he put to death only one person of quality that we read of, and him after repeated treacheries; yet he was a foreigner, had power sufficient, and did not want provocations to have been more bloody.' (p. 27.) This person of quality was the Earl Waltheof, who being overtaken with wine, engaged in a conspiracy against this monarch, but repenting of it the next morning, repaired to the king, who was then in Normandy, and discovered the whole matter. Notwithstanding which, he was beheaded upon the defeat of the conspiracy, for having but thus far tampered in it. And as for the rest of the conspirators, who rose in an actual rebellion, the king used them with the utmost rigour, he cut off the hands of some, put out the eyes of others, some were hanged upon gibbets, and those who fared the best, were sent into banishment. There are, indeed, the most dreadful examples of severity in this reign: though it must be confessed, that, after the manner of those times, the nobility generally escaped with their lives, though[a] multitudes of them were punished with banishment, perpetual imprisonment, forfeitures, and other great severities: while the poor people, who had been deluded by these their ring-leaders, were executed with the utmost rigour. A partiality which I believe no commoner of England will ever think to be either just or reasonable.

The next instance is Henry the fourth of France, 'who (says our author) so handsomely expressed his tenderness for his people, when, at signing the treaty of Vervins, he said, that by one dash of his pen he had overcome more enemies, than he could ever be able to do with his sword.' Would not an ordinary reader think that this treaty of Vervins was a treaty between Henry the fourth, and a party of his subjects? for otherwise how can it have a place in the present argument? But instead of

[a] This sentence is rendered awkward and involved by a double *though* —"*though* it must be confessed—*though* multitudes of them."—The way to reform it is, to put a full stop at *reign*, and to begin the next sentence thus —*It must be confessed*, &c.

that, it was a treaty between France and Spain; so that the speech expressed an equal tenderness to the Spaniards and French; as multitudes of either nation must have fallen in that war, had it continued longer. As for this king's treatment of conspirators, (though he is quoted thrice in the pamphlet as an example of clemency) you have an eminent instance of it in his behaviour to the Mareschal de Biron, who had been his old faithful servant, and had contributed more than any one to his advancement to the throne. This Mareschal, upon some discontent, was entered [a] into a conspiracy against his master, and refusing to open the whole secret to the king, he was sent to the Bastile, and there beheaded, notwithstanding he sought for mercy with great importunities, and in the most moving manner. There are other instances in this king's reign, who notwithstanding was remarkable for his clemency, of rebels and conspirators who were hanged, beheaded, or broken alive on the wheel.

The late King William was not disturbed by any rebellion from those who had once submitted to him. But we know he treated the persons concerned in the assassination-plot as so horrid a conspiracy deserved. As for the saying which this author imputes to that monarch, it being a piece of secret history, one doth not know when it was spoken, or what it alluded to, unless the author had been more particular in the account of it.

The author proceeds, in the next place, to no less an authority, than that of Solomon: "Among all the general observations of the wisest princes we know of, I think there is none holds more universally than, Mercy and truth preserve a king, and his throne is established in mercy.' (p. 18.) If we compare the different sayings of this wise king, which relate to the conduct of princes, we cannot question but that he means by this mercy, that

[a] See the note on—*endeavoured*, p. 140, and the judicious remark of the author of—*A Short Introduction to English Grammar*, p. 70, 1767.

kind of it, which is consistent with reason and government, and by which we hope to see his Majesty's throne established. But our author should consider that the same wise man has said, in another place, that 'an evil man seeketh rebellion, therefore a cruel messenger shall be sent against him.' Accordingly his practice was agreeable to his proverb: no prince having ever given a greater testimony of his abhorrence to undertakings of this treasonable nature. For he dispatched such a cruel messenger as is here mentioned to those who had been engaged in a rebellion many years before he himself was on the throne, and even to his elder brother, upon the bare suspicion that he was projecting so wicked an enterprise.

How the example of the pretender came into this argument, I am at a loss to find out. 'The pretender declared a general pardon to all: and shall our rightful king shew himself less the true father of his people, and afford his pardon to none,' &c. (p. 25.) The pretender's general pardon was to a people who were not in his power; and had he ever reduced them under it, it was only promised to such as immediately joined with him for the recovery of what he called his right. It was such a general pardon as would have been consistent with the execution of more than nine parts in ten of the kingdom.

There is but one more historical argument, which is drawn from King Philip's treatment of the Catalans. 'I think it would not be unseasonable for some men to recollect what their own notions, were of the treatment of the Catalans; how many declamations were made on the barbarity used towards them by King Philip,' &c. (p. 29.) If the author remembers, these declamations as he calls them, were not made so much on the barbarity used towards them by King Philip, as on the barbarity used towards them by the English government. King Philip might have some colour for treating them as rebels, but we ought to have regarded them as allies; and were obliged, by all the ties of honour, conscience, and public faith, to have sheltered them from those sufferings, which were brought upon them by a firm and inviolable adherence to our interest. However, none can draw into a parallel the cruelties which have been inflicted on that unhappy people, with those few instances of severity which our government has been obliged to exert towards the British rebels. I say, no man would make such a parallel, unless his mind be so blinded with passion and prejudice, as to assert, in the language of this pamphlet, 'That no instances can be produced of the least lenity under the present administration, from the hour it commenced to this day,' (p. 20.) with other astonishing reflections of the same nature, which are contradicted by such innumerable matters of fact, that it would be an affront to a reader's understanding to endeavour to[a] confute them. But to return to the Catalans; 'During the whole course of the war, (says the author,) which ever of them submitted to discretion, were received to mercy.' (p. 22.) This is so far from being truly related, that in the beginning of the war, they were executed without mercy. But when, in conjunction with their allies, they became superior to King Philip's party in strength, and extended their conquests up to the very gates of Madrid, it cannot be supposed the Spanish court would be so infatuated as to persist in their first severities, against an enemy that could make such terrible reprisals. However, when this reason of state ceased, how dreadful was the havoc made among this brave, but unhappy people! The whole kingdom, without any distinction to[b] the many thousands of its innocent inhabitants, was stript of its immunities, and reduced to a state of slavery. Barcelona was filled with ex-

[a] *To endeavour to.* To avoid the two infinitives he might have said—*should I endeavour to confute them.*

[b] *Distinction to*—rather—*distinction of.*

ecutions; and all the patriots of their ancient liberties either beheaded, stowed in dungeons, or condemned to work in the mines of America.

God be thanked, we have a king who punishes with reluctancy, and is averse to such cruelties as were used among the Catalans, as much as to those practised on the persons concerned in Monmouth's rebellion. Our author, indeed, condemns these western assizes in King James's reign (p. 26). And it would be well if all those who still adhere to the cause of that unfortunate king, and are clamorous at the proceedings of his present Majesty, would remember, that notwithstanding that rebellion fell very much short of this, both in the number and strength of the rebels, and had no tendency either to destroy the national religion, to introduce an arbitrary government, or to subject us to a foreign power; not only the chief of the rebels was beheaded, but even a lady, who had only harboured one of the offenders in her house, was in her extreme old age put to the same kind of death: that about two hundred and thirty were hanged, drawn, and quartered, and their limbs dispersed through several parts of the country, and set up as spectacles of terror to their fellow-subjects. It would be too tedious a work to run through the numberless fines, imprisonments, corporal punishments, and transportations, which were then likewise practised as wholesome severities.

We have now seen how fallaciously the author has stated the cause he has undertaken, by supposing that nothing but unlimited mercy, or unlimited punishment, are the methods that can be made use of in our present treatment of the rebels: that he has omitted the middle way of proceeding between these two extremes: that this middle way is the method in which his Majesty like all other wise and good kings, has chosen to proceed: that it is agreeable to the nature of government, religion, and our British constitution: and that every argument which the author has produced from reason and example, would have been a true one, had it been urged for that restrained clemency which his Majesty has exercised: but is a false one, when applied to such a general, undistinguishing mercy as the author would recommend.

Having thus answered that which is the main drift and design of this pamphlet, I shall touch upon those other parts of it, which are interwoven with the arguments, to put men out of humour with the present government.

And here we may observe, that it is our author's method to suppose matters of fact which are not in being, and afterwards to descant upon them. As he is very sensible that the cause will not bear the test of reason, he has indeed every where chosen rather topics for declamation than argument. Thus he entertains us with a laboured invective against a standing army. But what has this to do in the present case? I suppose he would not advise his Majesty to disband his forces while there is an army of rebels in his dominions. I cannot imagine he would think the affections of the people of England a security of the government in such a juncture, were it not at the same time defended with a sufficient body of troops. No prince has ever given a greater instance of his inclinations to rule without a standing army, if we consider, that upon the very first news of the defeat of the rebels, he declared to both houses of parliament, that he had put an immediate stop to the levies which he had begun to raise at their request, and that he would not make use of the power which they had intrusted him with, unless any new preparations of the enemy should make it necessary for our defence. This speech was received with the greatest gratitude by both houses; and it is said, that in the house of commons a very candid and honourable gentleman (who generally votes with the minority) declared, that he had not heard so gracious a speech from the throne for many years last past.

In another place, he supposes that the government has not endeavoured to gain the applause of the vulgar, by doing something for the church; and very gravely makes excuses for this their pretended neglect. What greater instances could his Majesty have given of his love to the church of England, than those he has exhibited by his most solemn declarations; by his daily example; and by his promotions of the most eminent among the clergy to such vacancies as have happened in his reign? To which we must add, for the honour of his government in this particular, that it has done more for the advantage of the clergy, than those, who are the most zealous for their interest, could have expected in so short a time; which will farther appear, if we reflect upon the valuable and royal donative to one of our universities, and the provision made for those who are to officiate in the fifty new churches. His Majesty is, indeed, a prince of too much magnanimity and truth, to make use of the name of the church for drawing his people into any thing that may be prejudicial to them; for what our author says, to this purpose, redounds as much to the honour of the present administration, as to the disgrace of others. 'Nay, I wish with all my soul they had stooped a little *ad captum vulgi*, to take in those shallow fluttering hearts, which are to be caught by any thing baited with the name of church.' (p. 11.)

Again; the author asks, 'Whether terror is to become the only national principle?' with other questions of the same nature; and in several parts of his book, harangues very plentifully against such a notion. Where he talks in generals upon this topic, there is no question but every whig and tory in the kingdom perfectly agrees with him in what he says. But if he would insinuate, as he seems to do in several places, that there should be no impres sions of awe upon the mind of a subject, and that a government should not create terror in those who are disposed to do ill, as well as encourage those that do their duty; in short, if he is for an entire exclusion of that principle of fear which is supposed to have some influence in every law, he opposes himself to the form of every government in the world, and to the common sense of mankind.

The artifice of this author in starting objections to the friends of the government, and the foolish answers which he supposes they return to them, is so very visible, that every one sees they are designed rather to divert his reader, than to instruct him.

I have now examined this whole pamphlet, which, indeed, is written with a great deal of art, and as much argument as the cause would bear: and after having stated the true notion of clemency, mercy, compassion, good-nature, humanity, or whatever else it may be called, so far as it is consistent with wisdom, and the good of mankind, or, in other words, so far as it is a moral virtue, I shall readily concur with the author in the highest panegyrics that he has bestowed upon it. As, likewise, I heartily join with him in every thing he has said against justice, if it includes, as his pamphlet supposes, the extirpation of every criminal, and is not exercised with a much greater mixture of clemency than rigour. Mercy, in the true sense of the word, is that virtue by which a prince approaches nearest to him, whom he represents; and whilst he is neither remiss nor extreme to animadvert upon those who offend him, that logic will hold true of him which is applied to the great Judge of all the earth; 'With thee there is mercy, therefore shalt thou be feared.'[a]

[a] The reasoning, in this long paper, is close and solid; and the expression, generally, what it ought to be, pure and perspicuous, but unadorned.

## No. 32. MONDAY, APRIL 9.

Heu miseræ cives! non hostem, inimicaque castra
Argivum; vestras spes uritis—— VIRG.

I QUESTION not but the British ladies are very well pleased with the compliment I have paid them in the course of my papers, by regarding them, not only as the most amiable, but as the most important part of our community. They ought, indeed, to resent the treatment they have met with from other authors, who have never troubled their heads about them, but addressed all their arguments to the male half of their fellow-subjects, and taken it for granted, that if they could bring these into their measures, the females, would of course follow their political mates. The arguments they have made use of, are like Hudibras's spur, which he applied to one side of his horse, as not doubting but the other would keep pace with it. These writers seem to have regarded the fair sex but as the garniture of a nation; and when they consider them as parts of the commonwealth, it is only as they are of use to the consumption of our manufacture. 'Could we persuade our British women (says one of our eminent merchants in a letter to his friend in the country upon the subject of commerce) to clothe themselves in the comely apparel which might be made out of the wool of their own country; and instead of coffee, tea, and chocolate, to delight in those wholesome and palatahle liquors which may be extracted from our British simples; they would be of great advantage to trade, and therein to the public weal.'

It is now, however, become necessary to treat our women as members of the body politic; since it is visible, that great numbers of them have of late eloped from their allegiance, and that they do not believe themselves obliged to draw with us, as yoke-fellows in the constitution. They will judge for themselves look into the state of the nation with their own eyes; and be no longer led blindfold by a male legislature. A friend of mine was lately complaining to me, that his wife had turned off one of the best cook-maids in England, because the wench had said something to her fellow-servants, which seemed to favour the suspension of the Habeas Corpus act.

When errors and prejudices are thus spread among the sex, it is the hardest thing in the world to root them out. Arguments, which are the only proper means for it, are of little use: they have a very short answer to all reasonings that turn against them, 'make us believe that, if you can;' which is in Latin, if I may upon this occasion be allowed the pedantry of a quotation, *non persuadebis, etiamsi persuaseris.* I could not but smile at a young university disputant, who was complaining the other day of the unreasonableness of a lady with whom he was engaged in a point of controversy. Being left alone with her, he took the opportunity of pursuing an argument which had been before started in discourse, and put it to her in a syllogism: upon which, as he informed us with some heat, she granted him both the major and the minor, but denied him the conclusion.

The best method, therefore, that can be made use of with these polemical ladies, who are much more easy to be refuted than silenced, is to shew them the ridiculous side of their cause, and to make them laugh at their own politics. It is a kind of ill manners to offer objections to a fine woman; and a man would be out of countenance that should gain the superiority in such a contest. A coquette logician may be rallied, but not contradicted. Those who would make use of solid arguments and strong reasonings to a reader or hearer of so delicate a turn, would be like that foolish people whom Ælian speaks of, that worshipped a fly, and sacrificed an ox to it.

The truth of it is, a man must be of a very disputatious temper, that enters into state-controversies with any of the fair sex. If the malignant be not beautiful, she cannot do much mischief; and if she is, her arguments will be so enforced by the charms of her person, that her antagonist may be in danger of betraying his own cause. Milton puts this confession into the mouth of our father Adam; who, though he asserts his superiority of reason in his debates with the mother of mankind, adds,

> ————Yet when I approach
> Her loveliness, so absolute she seems,
> And in herself complete; so well to know
> Her own, that what she wills to do or say,
> Seems wisest, virtuousest, discreetest, best:
> All higher knowledge in her presence falls
> Degraded, wisdom in discourse with her
> Loses, discountenanced, and like folly shews;
> Authority and reason on her wait————

If there is such a native loveliness in the sex, as to make them victorious even when they are in the wrong, how resistless is their power when they are on the side of truth! And, indeed, it is a peculiar good fortune to the government, that our fair malecontents are so much over-matched in beauty, as well as number, by those who are loyal to their king, and friends to their country.

Every paper, which I have hitherto addressed to our beautiful incendiaries, hath been filled with considerations of a different kind; by which means I have taken care that those, who are enemies to the sex, or to myself, may not accuse me of tautology, or pretend that I attack them with their own weapon. For this reason I shall here lay together a new set of remarks, and observe the several artifices by which the enemies to our establishment do raise such unaccountable passions and prejudices in the minds of our discontented females.

In the first place; it is usual among the most cunning of our adversaries, to represent all the rebels as very handsome men. If the name of a traitor be mentioned, they are very particular in describing his person; and when they are not able to extenuate his treason, commend his shape. This has so good an effect in one of our female audiences, that they represent to themselves a thousand poor, tall, innocent, fresh-coloured young gentlemen, who are dispersed among the several prisons of Great Britain; and extend their generous compassion towards a multitude of agreeable fellows that never were in being.

Another artifice is, to instil jealousies into their minds, of designs upon the anvil to retrench the privileges of the sex. Some represent the whigs as enemies to Flanders' lace: others had spread a report, that in the late act of parliament for four shillings in the pound upon land, there would be inserted a clause for raising a tax upon pin-money. That the ladies may be the better upon their guard against suggestions of this nature, I shall beg leave to put them in mind of the story of Papirius, the son of a Roman senator. This young gentleman, after having been present in public debates, was usually teased by his mother to inform her of what had passed. In order to deliver himself from this importunity, he told her one day, upon his return from the senate-house, that there had been a motion made for a decree to allow every man two wives. The good lady said nothing; but managed matters so well among the Roman matrons, that the next day they met together in a body before the senate-house, and presented a petition to the fathers against so unreasonable a law. This groundless credulity raised so much raillery upon the petitioners, that we do not find the ladies offered to direct the lawgivers of their country ever after.

There has been another method lately made use of, which has been practised with extraordinary success; I mean the spreading abroad reports of prodigies, which has wonderfully gratified the curiosity, as well as the hopes, of our fair malignants. Their managers turn water into blood for them; frighten them with sea-monsters; make them see armies in the air; and give them their word, the more to ingratiate themselves with them, that they signify nothing less than future slaughter and desolation. The disloyal part of the sex immediately hug themselves at the news of the bloody fountain; look upon these fish as their friends; have great expectations from the clouds; and are very angry with you, if you think they do not all portend ruin to their country.

Secret history and scandal have always had their allurements; and I have in other discourses shewn the great advantage that is made of them in the present ferment among the fair ones.

But the master engine, to overturn the minds of the female world, is the "danger of the church.' I am not so uncharitable as to think there is any thing in an observation made by several of the whigs, that there is scarce a woman in England who is troubled with the vapours, but is more or less affected with this cry: or, to remark with others, that it is not uttered in any part of the nation with so much bitterness of tongue and heart, as in the districts of Drury-lane. On the contrary, I believe there are many devout and honourable women who are deluded in this point by the artifice of designing men. To these, therefore, I would apply myself, in a more serious manner, and desire them to consider how that laudable piety, which is natural to the sex, is apt to degenerate into a groundless and furious zeal, when it is not kept within the bounds of charity and reason. Female zeal, though proceeding from so good a principle, has been infinitely detrimental to society, and to religion itself. If we may believe the French historians, it often put a stop to the proceedings of their kings, which might have ended in a reformation. For, upon their breaking with the Pope, the queens frequently inter posed, and by their importunities reconciled them to the usurpations of the Church of Rome. Nay, it was this vicious zeal which gave a remarkable check to the first progress of Christianity, as we find it recorded by a sacred historian in the following passage, which I shall leave to the consideration of my female readers. 'But the Jews stirred up the devout and honourable women, and the chief men of the city, and raised a persecution against Paul and Barnabas, and expelled them out of their coasts.'

---

## No. 33. FRIDAY, APRIL 13.

Nulli adversus magistratus ac reges gratiores sunt; nec immerito; nullis enim plus præstant quam quibus frui tranquillo otio licet. Itaque hi quibus ad propositum bene vivendi confert securitas publica, necesse est auctorem hujus boni ut parentem colant.

SENEC. EP. 73.

WE find by our public papers, the university of Dublin have lately presented to the Prince of Wales, in a most humble and dutiful manner, their diploma for constituting his Royal Highness chancellor of that learned body; and that the prince received this their offer with the goodness and condescension which is natural to his illustrious house. As the college of Dublin have been long famous for their great learning, they have now given us an instance of their good sense; and it is with pleasure that we find such a disposition in this famous nursery of letters to propagate sound principles, and to act, in its proper sphere, for the honour and dignity of the royal family. We hope that such an example will have its influence on other societies of the same nature; and cannot but rejoice to see the heir of Great Britain vouchsafing to patronise, in so peculiar a manner, that noble seminary, which is, perhaps, at this time training up such persons as may hereafter be ornaments to his reign.

When men of learning are acted thus by a knowledge of the world as well as of books, and shew that their studies naturally inspire them with a love to their king and country; they give a reputation to literature, and convince the world of its usefulness. But when arts and sciences are so perverted, as to dispose men to act in contradiction to the rest of the community, and to set up for a kind of separate republic among themselves, they draw upon them the indignation of the wise, and the contempt of the ignorant.

It has, indeed, been observed, that persons who are very much esteemed for their knowledge and ingenuity in their private characters, have acted like strangers to mankind, and to the dictates of right reason, when joined together in a body. Like several chemical waters, that are each of them clear and transparent when separate, but ferment into a thick troubled liquor when they are mixed in the same vial.

There is a piece of mythology which bears very hard upon learned men, and which I shall here relate, rather for the delicacy of the satire, than for the justness of the moral. When the city of Athens was finished, we are told that Neptune and Minerva presented themselves as candidates for the guardianship of the place. The Athenians, after a full debate upon the matter, came to an election, and made choice of Minerva. Upon which Neptune, who very much resented the indignity, upbraided them with their stupidity and ignorance, that a maritime town should reject the patronage of him who was the god of the seas, and could defend them against all the attacks of their enemies. He concluded with a curse upon the inhabitants, which was to stick to them and their posterity, namely, 'that they should be all fools.' When Minerva, their tutelary goddess, who presides over arts and sciences, came among them to receive the honour they had conferred upon her, they made heavy complaints of the curse which Neptune had laid upon the city, and begged her, if possible, to take it off. But she told them it was not in her power, for that one deity could not reverse the act of another. 'However,' said she, 'I may alleviate the curse which I cannot remove: it is not possible for me to hinder you from being fools, but I will take care that you shall be learned.'

There is nothing which bodies of learned men should be more careful of, than, by all due methods, to cultivate the favour of the great and powerful. The indulgence of a prince is absolutely necessary to the propagation, the defence, the honour, and support of learning. It naturally creates in men's minds an ambition to distinguish themselves by letters, and multiplies the number of those who are dedicated to the pursuits of knowledge. It protects them against the violence of brutal men; and gives them opportunities to pursue their studies in a state of peace and tranquillity. It puts the learned in countenance, and gives them a place among the fashionable part of mankind. It distributes rewards, and encourages speculative persons, who have neither opportunity nor a turn of mind to increase their own fortunes, with all the incentives of place, profit, and preferment. On the contrary, nothing is in itself so pernicious to communities of learned men, nor more apprehended by those that wish them well, than the displeasure of their prince, which those may justly expect to feel, who would make use of his favour to his own prejudice, and put in practice all the methods that lie within their power to vilify his person, and distress his government. In both these cases, a learned body is in a more particular manner exposed to the influence of their king, as described by the wisest of men, 'The wrath of a king is as the roaring of a lion; but his favour is as the dew upon the grass.'

We find in our English histories, that the Empress Matilda (who was the great ancestor of his present Majesty, and whose grand-daughter of the same name has a place upon several of the Hanover medals), was particularly favoured by the university of Oxford, and defended in that place, when most parts of the kingdom had revolted against her. Nor is it to be questioned, but an university so famous for learning and sound knowledge, will shew the same zeal for her illustrious descendant, as they will every day discern his Majesty's royal virtues, through those prejudices which have been raised in their minds by artful and designing men. It is with much pleasure we see this great fountain of learning already beginning to run clear, and recovering its natural purity and brightness. None can imagine that a community which is taxed by the worst of its enemies, only for over-straining the notions of loyalty even to bad princes, will fall short of a due allegiance to the best.

When this happy temper of mind is fully established among them, we may justly hope to see the largest share of his Majesty's favours fall upon that university, which is the greatest, and upon all accounts the most considerable, not only in his dominions, but in all Europe.

I shall conclude this paper with a quotation out of Cambden's History of Queen Elizabeth, who, after having described that queen's reception at Oxford, gives an account of the speech which she made to them at her departure; concluding with a piece of advice to that university. Her counsel was, 'That they would first serve God, not after the curiosity of some, but according to the laws of God and the land; that they would not go before the laws, but follow them; nor dispute whether better might be prescribed, but keep those prescribed already; obey their superiors; and, lastly, embrace one another in brotherly piety and concord.'

## No. 34. MONDAY, APRIL 16.

——— sævus apertam
In rabiem cœpit verti jocus——— Hor.

It is very justly, as well as frequently observed, that if our nation be ever ruined, it must be by itself. The parties and divisions which reign among us may several ways bring destruction upon our country, at the same time that our united force would be sufficient to secure us against all the attempts of a foreign enemy. Whatever expedients, therefore, can be found to allay those heats and animosities, which break us into different factions and interests, cannot but be useful to the public, and highly tend to its safety, strength, and reputation.

This dangerous dissension among us discovers itself in all the most indifferent circumstances of life. We keep it up, and cherish it with as much pains, as if it were a kind of national blessing. It insinuates itself into all our discourses, mixes in our parties of pleasure, has a share in our diversions, and is an ingredient in most of our public entertainments.

I was, not long ago, at the play called Sir Courtly Nice, where, to the eternal reproach of good sense, I found the whole audience had very gravely ranged themselves into two parties, under Hot-head and Testimony. Hot-head was the applauded hero of the tories, and Testimony no less the favourite of the whigs. Each party followed their champion. It was wonderful to see so polite an assembly distinguishing themselves by such extraordinary representatives, and avowing their principles as conformable either to the zeal of Hot-head, or the moderation of Testimony. Thus the two parts which were designed to expose the faults of both sides, and were accordingly received by our ancestors in King Charles the second's reign, meet with a kind of sanction from the applauses which are respectively bestowed on them by their wise posterity. We seem to imagine that they were written as patterns for imitation, not as objects of ridicule.

This humour runs so far, that most of our late comedies owe their success to it. The audience listens after nothing else. I have seen little Dicky place himself, with great approbation, at the head of the tories, for five acts together, and Pinky espouse the interest of the whigs with no less success. I do not find that either party has yet thrown themselves under the patronage of Scaramouch, or that Harlequin has violated that neutrality, which, upon his late arrival in Great Britain, he professed to both parties, and which it is thought he will punctually observe, being allowed on all sides to be a man of honour. It is true, that upon his first appearance, a violent whig tradesman, in the pit, begun to compliment him with a clap, as overjoyed to see him mount a ladder, and fancying him to be dressed in a highland plaid.

I question not but my readers will be surprised to find me animadverting on a practice that has been always favourable to the cause which now prevails. The British theatre was whig even in the worst of times; and in the last reign did not scruple to testify its zeal for the good of our country, by many magnanimous claps in its lower regions, answered with loud huzzas from the upper gallery. This good disposition is so much heightened of late, that the whole neighbourhood of the Drury-lane theatre very often shakes with the loyalty of the audience. It is said that a young author, who very much relies on this prevailing humour, is now writing a farce to be called A Match out of Newgate, in allusion to the title of a comedy called A Match in Newgate: and that his chief person is a round-shouldered man, with a pretty large nose, and a wide mouth, making his addresses to a lovely black woman, that passes for a peeress of Great Britain. In short, the whole play is built upon the late escape of General Forster, who is supposed, upon the road, to fall in love with my Lord Nithisdale, whom the ingenious author imagines to be still in his riding-hood.

But notwithstanding the good principles of a British audience in this one particular, it were to be wished that every thing should be banished the stage which has a tendency to exasperate men's minds, and inflame that party rage which makes us such a miserable and divided people. And that, in the first place, because such a proceeding as this disappoints the very design of all public diversions and entertainments. The institution of sports and shews was intended, by all governments, to turn off the thoughts of the people from busying themselves in matters of state, which did not belong to them ; to reconcile them to one another by the common participations of mirth and pleasure; and to wear out of their minds that rancour which they might have contracted by the interfering views of interest and ambition. It would therefore be for the benefit of every society, that is disturbed by contending factions, to encourage such innocent amusements as may thus disembitter the minds of men, and make them mutually rejoice in the same agreeable satisfactions. When people are accustomed to sit together with pleasure, it is a step towards reconciliation; but, as we manage matters, our politest assemblies are like boisterous clubs, that meet over a glass of wine, and, before they have done, throw bottles at one another's heads. Instead of multiplying those desirable opportunities, where we may agree in points that are indifferent, we let the spirit of contention into those very methods that are not only foreign to it, but should in their nature dispose us to be friends. This our anger in our mirth is like poison in a perfume, which taints the spirits instead of chearing and refreshing them.

Another manifest inconvenience which arises from this abuse of public entertainments is, that it naturally destroys the taste of an audience. I do not deny, but that several performances have been justly applauded for their wit, which have been written with an eye to this predominant humour of the town; but it is visible even in these, that it is not the excellence, but the application of the sentiment, that has raised applause. An author is very much disappointed to find the best parts of his productions received with indifference, and to see the audience discovering beauties which he never intended. The actors, in the midst of an innocent old play, are often startled with unexpected claps or hisses; and do not know whether they have been talking like good subjects, or have spoken treason. In short, we seem to have such a relish for faction, as to have lost that of wit; and are so used to the bitterness of party rage, that we cannot be gratified with the highest entertainment that has not this kind of seasoning in it.

But as no work must expect to live long which draws all its beauty from the colour of the times; so neither can that pleasure be of greater continuance, which arises from the prejudice or malice of its hearers.

To conclude; since the present hatred and violence of parties is so unspeakably pernicious to the community, and none can do a better service to their country than those who use their utmost endeavours to extinguish it, we may reasonably hope, that the more elegant part of the nation will give a good example to the rest; and put an end to so absurd and foolish a practice, which makes our most refined diversions detrimental to the public, and, in a particular manner, destructive of all politeness.

## No. 35. FRIDAY, APRIL 20.

Atheniensium res gestæ, sicut ego existumo, satis amplæ magnificæque fuere, verum aliquanto minores tamen quam fama feruntur: sed, quia provenere ibi magna scriptorum ingenia, per terrarum orbem Atheniensium facta pro maxumis celebrantur. Ita eorum, qui ea fecere, virtus tanta habetur, quantum verbis ea potuere extollere præclara ingenia.
SALLUST.

GRATIAN, among his maxims for raising a man to the most consummate character of greatness, advises, first, to perform extraordinary actions; and, in the next place, to secure a good historian. Without the last, he considers the first as thrown away; as, indeed, they are, in a great measure, by such illustrious persons, as make fame and reputation the end of their undertakings. The most shining merit goes down to posterity with disadvantage when it is not placed by writers in its proper light.

The misfortune is, that there are more instances of men who deserve this kind of immortality, than of authors who are able to bestow it. Our country, which has produced writers of the first figure in every other kind of work, has been very barren in good historians. We have had several who have been able to compile matters of fact, but very few who have been able to digest them with that purity and elegance of style, that nicety and strength of reflection, that subtilty, and discernment in the unravelling of a character, and that choice of circumstances for enlivening the whole narration, which we so justly admire in the ancient historians of Greece and Rome, and in some authors of our neighbouring nations.

Those who have succeeded best in works of this kind, are such, who, besides their natural good sense and learning, have themselves been versed in public business, and thereby acquired a thorough knowledge of men and things. It was the advice of the great Duke of Schomberg, to an eminent historian of his acquaintance, who was an ecclesiastic, that he should avoid being too particular in the drawing up of an army, and other circumstances of the day of battle; for that he had always observed most notorious blunders and absurdities committed on that occasion, by such writers as were not conversant in the art of war. We may reasonably expect the like mistakes in every other kind of public matters, recorded by those who have only a distant theory of such affairs. Besides, it is not very probable that men, who have passed all their time in a low and vulgar life, should have a suitable idea of the several beauties and blemishes in the actions or characters of great men. For this reason I find an old law, quoted by the famous Monsieur Bayle, that no person below the dignity of a Roman knight should presume to write an history.

In England there is scarce any one, who has had a tincture of reading or study, that is not apt to fancy himself equal to so great a task; though it is plain, that many of our countrymen, who have tampered in history, frequently show, that they do not understand the very nature of those transactions which they recount. Nay, nothing is more usual than to see every man, who is versed in any particular way of business, finding fault with several of these authors, so far as they treat of matters within his sphere.

There is a race of men lately sprung up among this sort of writers, whom one cannot reflect upon without indignation as well as contempt. These are Grub-street biographers, who watch for the death of a great man, like so many undertakers, on purpose to make a penny of him. He is no sooner laid in his grave, but he falls into the hands of an historian; who, to swell a volume, ascribes to him works which he never wrote, and actions which he never performed; celebrates virtues which he was never famous for, and excuses faults which he was never guilty of. They fetch their only authentic records out of Doctors Commons; and when they have got a copy of his last will and testament, they fancy themselves furnished with sufficient materials for his history. This might, indeed, enable them in some measure to write the history of his death; but what can we expect from an author that undertakes to write the life of a great man, who is furnished with no other matters of fact, besides legacies; and instead of being able to tell us what he did, can only tell us what he bequeathed? This manner of exposing the private concerns of families, and sacrificing the secrets of the dead to the curiosity of the living, is one of those licentious practices which might well deserve the animadversion of our government, when it has time to contrive expedients for remedying the many crying abuses of the press. In the mean while, what a poor idea must strangers conceive of those persons, who have been famous among us in their generation, should they form their notions of them from the writings of these our historiographers! What would our posterity think of their illustrious forefathers, should they only see them in such weak and disadvantageous lights! But, to our comfort, works of this nature are so short-lived, that they cannot possibly diminish the memory of those patriots which they are not able to preserve.

The truth of it is, as the lives of great men cannot be written with any tolerable degree of elegance or exactness, within a short space after their decease; so neither is it fit that the history of a person, who has acted among us in a public character, should appear, till envy and friendship are laid asleep, and the prejudice both of his antagonists and adherents be, in some degree, softened and subdued. There is no question but there are several eminent persons in each party, however they may represent one another at present, who will have the same admirers among posterity, and be equally celebrated by those, whose minds will not be distempered by interest, passion, or partiality. It were happy for us, could we prevail upon ourselves to imagine, that one, who differs from us in opinion, may possibly be an honest man; and that we might do the same justice to one another, which will be done us hereafter by those who shall make their appearance in the world, when this generation is no more. But in our present miserable and divided condition, how just soever a man's pretensions may be to a great or blameless reputation, he must expect his share of obloquy and reproach; and, even with regard to his posthumous character, content himself with such a kind of consideration, as induced the famous Sir Francis Bacon, after having bequeathed his soul to God, and his body to the earth, to leave his fame to foreign nations; and after some years, to his own country.

---

## No. 36. MONDAY, APRIL 23.

——————Illa se jactet in aula,—VIRG.

AMONG all the paradoxes in politics which have been advanced by some among us, there is none so absurd and shocking to the most ordinary understanding, as that it is possible for Great Britain to be quietly governed by a Popish sovereign. King Henry the fourth found it impracticable for a Protestant to reign even in France, notwithstanding the reformed religion does not engage a prince to the persecution of any other; and notwithstanding the authority of the sovereign in that country is more able to support itself, and command the obedience of the people, than in any other European monarchy. We are convinced by the experience of our own times, that our constitution is not able to bear a Popish prince at the head of it. King James the second was endowed with many royal virtues, and might have made a nation of Roman Catholics happy under his administration. The grievances we suffered in his reign proceeded purely from his religion: but they were such as made the whole body of the nobility, clergy, and commonalty, rise up as one man against him, and oblige him to quit the throne of his ancestors. The truth of it is, we have only the vices of a Protestant prince to fear, and may be made happy by his virtues: but in a Popish prince we have no chance for our prosperity; his very piety obliges him to our destruction; and in proportion as he is more religious, he becomes more insupportable. One would wonder, therefore, to find many who call themselves Protestants, favouring the pretensions of a person who has been bred up in the utmost bitterness and bigotry of the church of Rome; and who, in all probability, within less than a twelvemonth, would be opposed by those very men that are industrious to set him upon the throne, were it possible for so wicked and unnatural an attempt to succeed.

I was some months ago in a company, that diverted themselves with the Declaration which he had then published, and particularly with the date of it, 'In the fourteenth year of our reign.' The company was surprised to find there was a king in Europe who had reigned so long and made such a secret of it. This gave occasion to one of them, who is now in France, to inquire into the history of this remarkable reign, which he has digested into annals, and lately transmitted hither for the perusal of his friends. I have suppressed such personal reflections as are mixed in this short chronicle, as not being to the purpose; and find that the whole history of his regal conduct and exploits may be comprised in the remaining part of this half-sheet.

*The history of the Pretender's fourteen years reign digested into annals.*

Anno Regni 1°. He made choice of his ministry, the first of whom was his confessor. This was a person recommended by the society of Jesuits, who represented him as one very proper to guide the conscience of a king, that hoped to rule over an island which is not within the pale of the church. He then proceeded to name the president of his council, his secretaries of state, and gave away a very honourable sinecure to his principal favourite, by constituting him his lord-high-treasurer. He likewise signed a dormant commission for another to be his high-admiral, with orders to produce it whenever he had sea-room for his employment.

Anno Regni 2°. He perfected himself in the minuet step.

Anno Regni 3°. He grew half a foot.

Anno Regni 4°. He wrote a letter to the Pope, desiring him to be as kind to him as his predecessor had been, who was his godfather. In the same year he ordered the lord high-treasurer to pay off the debts of the crown, which had been contracted since his accession to the throne; particularly, a milk-score of three years standing.

Anno Regni 5°. He very much improved himself in all princely learning, having read over the legends of the saints, with the history of those several martyrs in England, who had attempted to blow up a whole parliament of heretics.

Anno Regni 6°. He applied himself to the arts of government with more than ordinary diligence; took a plan of the Bastile with his own hand; visited the galleys; and studied the edicts of his great patron Louis XIV.

Anno Regni 7°. Being now grown up to years of maturity, he resolved to seek adventures; but was very much divided in his mind, whether he should make an expedition to Scotland, or a pilgrimage to Loretto: being taught to look upon the latter in a religious sense, as the place of his nativity. At length he resolved upon his Scotch expedition; and, as the first exertion of that royal authority, which he was going to assume, he knighted himself. After a short piece of errantry upon the seas, he got safe to Dunkirk, where he paid his devotions to St. Anthony, for having delivered him from the dangers of the seas, and Sir George Byng.

Anno Regni 8°. He made a campaign in Flanders, where, by the help of a telescope, he saw the battle of Oudenarde, and the prince of Hanover's horse shot under him: being posted on a high tower with two French princes of the blood.

Anno Regni 9°. He made a second campaign in Flanders; and upon his return to the French court, gained a great reputation, by his performance in a rigadoon.

Anno Regni 10°. The Pope having heard the fame of these his military achievements, made him the offer of a cardinal's cap; which he was advised not to accept by some of his friends in England.

Anno Regni 11°. He retired to Lorrain, where every morning he made great havoc among the wild-fowl, by the advice, and with the assistance of his privy-council. He is said, this summer, to have shot with his own hands fifty brace of pheasants, and one wild pig; to have set thirty coveys of partridges; and to have hunted down forty brace of hares; to which he might have added as many foxes, had not most of them made their escape, by running out of his friend's dominions, before his dogs could finish the chase. He was particularly animated to these diversions by his ministry, who thought they would not a little recommend him to the good opinion and kind offices of several British fox-hunters.

Anno Regni 12°. He made a visit to the Duke d'Aumont, and passed for a French marquis in a masquerade.

Anno Regni 13°. He visited several convents, and gathered subscriptions from all the well-disposed monks and nuns, to whom he communicated his design of an attempt upon Great Britain.

Anno Regni 14°. He now made great preparations for the invasion of England, and got together vast stores of ammunition, consisting of reliques, gun-powder, and cannon-ball. He received from the Pope a very large contribution, one moiety in money, and the other in indulgences. An Irish priest brought him an authentic tooth of St. Thomas à Becket, and it is thought, was to have for his reward the archbishopric of Canterbury. Every monastery contributed something; one gave him a thousand pounds; and another as many masses.

This year, containing farther the battles which he fought in Scotland, and the towns which he took, is so fresh in every one's memory, that we shall say no more of it.

---

## No. 37. FRIDAY, APRIL 27.

———quod si
Frigida curarum fomenta relinquere posses;
Quo te cælestis sapientia duceret, ires.
Hoc opus, hoc studium parvi properemus et ampli,
Si patriæ volumus, si nobis vivere cari.—Hor.

It is a melancholy reflection, that our country, which in times of Popery was called the nation of saints, should now have less appearance of religion in it, than any other neighbouring state or kingdom; whether they be such as continue still immersed in the errors of the church of Rome, or such as are recovered out of them. This is a truth that is obvious to every one, who has been conversant in foreign parts. It was formerly thought dangerous for a young man to travel, lest he should return an atheist to his native country: but at present it is certain, that an Englishman, who has any tolerable degree of reflection, cannot be better awakened to a sense of religion in general, than by observing how the minds of all mankind are set upon this important point; how every nation is serious and attentive to the great business of their being; and that in other countries a man is not out of the fashion, who is bold and open in the profession and practice of all Christian duties.

This decay of piety is by no means to be imputed to the Reformation, which in its first establishment produced its proper fruits, and distinguished the whole age with shining instances of virtue and morality. If we would trace out the original of that flagrant and avowed impiety, which has prevailed among us for some years, we should find that it owes its rise to that opposite extreme of cant and hypocrisy, which had taken possession of the people's minds in the times of the great rebellion, and of the usurpation that succeeded it. The practices of these men, under the covert of a feigned zeal, made even the appearances of sincere devotion ridiculous and unpopular. The raillery of the wits and courtiers, in King Charles the second's reign, upon every thing which they then called precise, was carried to so great an extravagance, that it almost put Christianity out of countenance. The ridicule grew so strong and licentious, that from this time we may date that remarkable turn in the behaviour of our fashionable Englishmen, that makes them shame-faced in the exercise of those duties which they were sent into the world to perform.

The late cry of the church has been an artifice of the same kind with that made use of by the hypocrites of the last age, and has had as fatal an influence upon religion. If a man would but seriously consider how much greater comfort he would receive in the last moments of his life from a reflection that he has made one virtuous man, than that he has made a thousand tories, we should not see the zeal of so many good men turned off from its proper end, and employed in making such a kind of converts.

What satisfaction will it be to an immoral man, at such a time, to think he is a good whig! or to one that is conscious of sedition, perjury, or rebellion, that he dies with the reputation of a high churchman!

But to consider how this cry of the church has corrupted the morals of both parties. Those, who are the loudest in it, regard themselves rather as a political, than a religious communion; and are held together rather by state-notions, than by articles of faith. This fills the minds of weak men, who fall into the snare, with groundless fears and apprehensions, unspeakable rage towards their fellow-subjects, wrong ideas of persons whom they are not acquainted with, and uncharitable interpretations of those actions of which they are not competent judges. It instils into their minds the utmost virulence and bitterness, instead of that charity, which is the perfection and ornament of religion, and the most indispensable and necessary means for attaining the end of it. In a word, among these mistaken zealots, it sanctifies cruelty and injustice, riots and treason.

The effects which this cry of the church has had on the other party, are no less manifest and deplorable. They see themselves unjustly aspersed by it, and vindicate themselves in terms no less opprobrious, than those by which they are attacked. Their indignation and resentment rises in proportion to the malice of their adversaries. The unthinking part of them are apt to contract an unreasonable aversion even to that ecclesiastical constitution to which they are represented as enemies; and not only to particular persons, but to that order of men in general, which will be always held sacred and honourable, so long as there is reason and religion in the world.

I might mention many other corruptions common to both parties, which naturally flow from this source; and might easily shew, upon a full display of them, that this clamour which pro tends to be raised[a] for the safety of religion, has almost worn out the very appearance of it; and rendered us not only the most divided, but the most immoral people upon the face of the earth.

When our nation is overflowed with such a deluge of impiety, it must be a great pleasure to find any expedient take place, that has a tendency to recover it out of so dismal a condition. This is one great reason why an honest man may rejoice to see an act so near taking effect, for making elections of members to serve in parliament less frequent. I find myself prevented by other writings (which have considered the act now depending in this particular light) from expatiating upon this subject. I shall only mention two short pieces which I have been just now reading, under the following titles, 'Arguments about the alteration of the triennial elections of Parliament:' and, 'The alteration in the triennial act considered.'

The reasons for this law, as it is necessary for settling his Majesty in his throne; for extinguishing the spirit of rebellion; for procuring foreign alliances; and other advantages of the like nature; carry a great weight with them. But I am particularly pleased with it, as it may compose our unnatural feuds and animosities, revive an honest spirit of industry in the nation, and cut off frequent occasions of brutal rage and intemperance. In short, as it will make us not only a more safe, a more flourishing, and a more happy, but also a more virtuous people.

[a] *Pretends to be raised.* When we speak of any thing as *pretending*, it is *to do something*, not *to be acted upon.* The impropriety might have been avoided by saying—*pretends to respect the safety of religion*—or some such thing.

## No. 38. MONDAY APRIL 30.

———Longum, formosa, vale.———VIRG.

It is the ambition of the male part of the world to make themselves esteemed, and of the female to make themselves beloved. As this is the last paper which I shall address to my fair readers; I cannot perhaps oblige them more, than by leaving them, as a kind of legacy, a certain secret which seldom fails of procuring this affection, which they are naturally formed both to desire and to obtain. This nostrum is comprised in the following sentence of Seneca, which I shall translate for the service of my country-women. *Ego tibi monstrabo amatorium sine medicamento, sine herbâ, sine ullius veneffcæ carmine: si vis amari, ama.* 'I will discover to you a philter that has neither drug, nor simple, nor enchantment in it: love, if you would raise love.' If there be any truth in this discovery, and this be such a speci fic as the author pretends, there is nothing which makes the sex more unamiable than party-rage. The finest woman, in a transport of fury, loses the use of her face. Instead of charming her beholders, she frights both friend and foe. The latter can never be smitten by so bitter an enemy, nor the former captivated by a nymph, who, upon occasion, can be so very angry. The most endearing of our beautiful fellow-subjects, are those whose minds are the least imbittered with the passions and prejudices of either side; and who discover the native sweetness of the sex in every part of their conversation and behaviour. A lovely woman, who thus flourishes[a] in her innocence and good humour, amidst that mutual spite and rancour which prevails among her exasperated sisterhood, appears more amiable by the singularity of her charac-

[a] *Flourishes* in her innocence—*exasperated* sisterhood. These finely chosen words introduce, very happily, the quotation from Solomon.

ter; and may be compared, with Solomon's bride, to 'a lily among thorns.'

A stateswoman is as ridiculous a creature as a cotquean. Each of the sexes should keep within its particular bounds, and content themselves to excel within their respective districts. When Venus complained to Jupiter of the wound which she had received in battle, the father of the gods smiled upon her, and put her in mind, that instead of mixing in a war, which was not her business she should have been officiating in her proper ministry, and carrying on the delights of marriage. The delicacy of several modern critics has been offended with Homer's Billingsgate warriors; but a scolding hero is, at the worst, a more tolerable character than a bully in petticoats. To which we may add, that the keenest satirist among the ancients, looked upon nothing as a more proper subject of raillery and invective, than a female gladiator.

I am the more disposed to take into consideration these ladies of fire and politics, because it would be very monstrous to see feuds and animosities kept up among the soft sex, when they are in so hopeful a way of being composed among the men, by the septennial bill, which is now ready for the royal assent. As this is likely to produce a cessation of arms, till the expiration of the present parliament, among one half of our island, it is very reasonable that the more beautiful moiety of his Majesty's subjects should establish a truce among themselves for the same term of years. Or rather it were to be wished, that they would summon together a kind of senate, or parliament, of the fairest and wisest of our sister subjects, in order to enact a perpetual neutrality among the sex. They might at least appoint something like a committee, chosen from among the ladies residing in London and Westminster, in order to prepare a bill to be laid before the assembly upon the first opportunity of their meeting. The regulation might be as follows:

'That a committee of toasts be forthwith appointed; to consider the present state of the sex in the British nation.

"That this committee do meet at the house of every respective member of it on her visiting-day; and that every one who comes to it shall have a vote, and a dish of tea.

"That the committee be empowered to send for billet-doux, libels, lampoons, lists of toasts, or any other the like papers and records.

"That it be an instruction to the said committee, to consider of proper ways and methods to reclaim the obstinately opprobrious and virulent; and how to make the ducking-stool more useful."

Being always willing to contribute my assistances to my country-women, I would propose a preamble, setting forth, "That the late civil war among the sex has tended very much to the lessening of that ancient and undoubted authority, which they have claimed over the male part of the island; to the ruin of good house-wifery; and to the betraying of many important secrets: that it has produced much bitterness of speech, many sharp and violent contests, and a great effusion of citron-water: that it has raised animosities in their hearts, and heats in their faces, that it has broke out in their ribbons, and caused unspeakable confusions in their dress: and, above all, that it has introduced a certain frown into the features, and a sourness into the air of our British ladies, to the great damage of their charms, and visible decay of the national beauty."

As for the enacting part of the bill, it may consist of many particulars which will naturally arise from the debates of the tea-table; and must, therefore, be left to the discretion and ex perience of the committee. Perhaps it might not be amiss to enact, among other things,

"That the discoursing on politics shall be looked upon as dull as[a] talking on the weather.

"That if any man troubles a female assembly with parliament-news, he shall be marked out as a blockhead, or an incendiary.

"That no woman shall henceforth presume to stick a patch upon her forehead, unless it be in the very middle, that is, in the neutral part of it.

"That all fans and snuff-boxes, of what principles soever, shall be called in: and that orders be given to Motteux and Mathers, to deliver out, in exchange for them, such as have no tincture of party in them.

"That when any lady bespeaks a play, she shall take effectual care that the audience be pretty equally checquered with whigs and tories.

"That no woman, of any party, presume to influence the legislature.

"That there be a general amnesty and oblivion of all former hostilities and distinctions, all public and private failings on either side: and that every one who comes into this neutrality within the space of          weeks, shall be allowed an ell extraordinary, above the present standard, in the circumference of her petticoat.

"Provided always, nevertheless, That nothing herein contained shall extend, or be construed to extend, to any person or persons, inhabiting and practising within the hundreds of Drury, or to any other of that society in what part soever of the nation

[a] *Looked upon as dull.* Elliptically expressed to avoid the repetition of *as.* The sentence, if drawn out at length, would be *looked upon as being as dull as.*

in like manner practising and residing; who are still at liberty to rail, calumniate, scold, frown, and pout, as in afore-times, any thing in this act to the contrary notwithstanding."

---

## No. 39. FRIDAY, MAY 4.

Prodesse quam conspici.

It often happens, that extirpating the love of glory, which is observed to take the deepest root in noble minds, tears up several virtues with it; and that suppressing the desire of fame, is apt to reduce men to a state of indolence and supineness. But when, without any incentive of vanity, a person of great abilities is zealous for the good of mankind; and as solicitous for the concealment, as the performance of illustrious actions; we may be sure that he has something more than ordinary in his composition, and has a heart filled with goodness and magnanimity.

There is not perhaps, in all history, a greater instance of this temper of mind, than what appeared in that excellent person, whose motto I have placed at the head of this paper. He had worn himself out in his application to such studies as made him useful or ornamental to the world, in concerting schemes for the welfare of his country, and in prosecuting such measures as were necessary for making those schemes effectual: but all this was done with a view to the public good that should rise out of these generous endeavours, and not to the fame which should accrue to himself. Let the reputation of the action fall where it would; so[a] his country reaped the benefit of it, he was satisfied. As his turn of mind threw off, in a great measure, the oppositions of

[a] *So*, is here used, as it often is, in our language, in the sense of *provided that.*

envy and competition, it enabled him to gain the most vain and impracticable into his designs, and to bring about several great events for the safety and advantage of the public, which must have died in their birth, had he been as desirous of appearing beneficial to mankind, as of being so.

As he was admitted into the secret and most retired thoughts and counsels of his royal master, King William, a great share in the plan of the Protestant succession is universally ascribed to him. And if he did not entirely project the union of the two kingdoms, and the bill of regency, which seem to have been the only methods in human policy, for securing to us so inestimable a blessing, there is none who will deny him to have been the chief conductor in both these glorious works. For posterity are obliged to allow him that praise after his death, which he industriously declined while he was living. His life, indeed, seems[a] to have been prolonged beyond its natural term, under those indispositions which hung upon the latter part of it, that he might have the satisfaction of seeing the happy settlement take place, which he had proposed to himself as the principal end of all his public labours. Nor was it a small addition to his happiness, that by this means he saw those who had been always his most intimate friends, and who had concerted with him such measures for the guarantee of the Protestant succession, as drew upon them the displeasure of men who were averse to it, advanced to the highest posts of trust and honour under his present Majesty. I believe there are none of these patriots, who will think it a derogation from their merit to have it said, that they received many lights and advantages from their intimacy with my Lord Somers: who had such a general knowledge of affairs, and so tender a concern for his friends,

[a] *His life indeed seems, &c.* A natural reflection, in a panegyric on Lord Somers, and in a paper written professedly in honour of the *happy settlement.*

that whatever station they were in, they usually applied to him for his advice in every perplexity of business, and in affairs of the greatest difficulty.

His life was, in every part of it, set off with that graceful modesty and reserve, which made his virtues more beautiful, the more they were cast in such agreeable shades.

His religion was sincere, not ostentatious; and such as inspired him with an universal benevolence towards all his fellow-subjects, not with bitterness against any part of them. He shewed his firm adherence to it as modelled by our national constitution, and was constant to its offices of devotion, both in public and in his family. He appeared a champion for it, with great reputation, in the cause of the seven bishops, at a time when the church was really in danger. To which we may add, that he held a strict friendship and correspondence with the great Archbishop Tillotson, being acted by[a] the same spirit of candour and moderation; and moved rather with pity than indignation towards the persons of those who differed from him in the unessential parts of Christianity.

His great humanity appeared in the minutest circumstances of his conversation. You found it in the benevolence of his aspect, the complacency of his behaviour, and the tone of his voice. His great application to the severer studies of the law, had not infected his temper with any thing positive or litigious. He did not know what it was to wrangle on indifferent points, to triumph in the superiority of his understanding, or to be supercilious on the side of truth. He joined the greatest delicacy of good-breeding to the greatest strength of reason. By approving the sentiments of a person, with whom he conversed, in such particulars as were just, he won him over from those points in which

[a] *Being acted by.* We should now say, *being actuated with.* Besides, I doubt whether it be right to give to the neutral verb, *act*, a passive signification.

he was mistaken ; and had so agreeable a way of conveying knowledge, that whoever conferred with him grew the wiser, without perceiving that he had been instructed. We may probably ascribe to this masterly and engaging manner of conversation, the great esteem which he had gained with the late queen, while she pursued those measures which had carried the British nation to the highest pitch of glory ; notwithstanding she had entertained many unreasonable prejudices against him, before she was acquainted with his personal worth and behaviour.

As in his political capacity we have before seen how much he contributed to the establishment of the Protestant interest, and the good of his native country, he was always true to these great ends. His character was uniform and consistent with itself, and his whole conduct of a piece. His principles were founded in reason, and supported by virtue; and therefore did not lie at the mercy of ambition, avarice, or resentment. His notions were no less steady and unshaken, than just and upright. In a word, he concluded his course among the same well-chosen friendships and alliances, with which he began it.

This great man was not more conspicuous as a patriot and a statesman, than as a person of universal knowledge and learning. As by dividing his time between the public scenes of business, and the private retirements of life, he took care to keep up both the great and good man; so by the same means he accomplished himself not only in the knowledge of men and things, but in the skill of the most refined arts and sciences. That unwearied diligence, which followed him through all the stages of his life, gave him such a thorough insight into the laws of the land, that he passed for one of the greatest masters of his profession at his first appearance in it. Though he made a regular progress through the several honours of the long robe, he was always looked upon as one who deserved a superior station to that he was possessed of; till he arrived at the highest dignity to which those studies could advance him.

He enjoyed in the highest perfection two talents, which do not often meet in the same person, the greatest strength of good sense, and the most exquisite taste of politeness. Without the first, learning is but an incumbrance; and without the last, is ungraceful. My Lord Somers was master of these two qualifications in so eminent a degree, that all the parts of knowledge appeared in him with such an additional strength and beauty, as they want in the possession of others. If he delivered his opinion of a piece of poetry, a statue, or a picture, there was something so just and delicate in his observations, as naturally produced pleasure and assent in those who heard him.

His solidity and elegance, improved by the reading of the finest authors, both of the learned and modern languages, discovered itself in all his productions. His oratory was masculine and persuasive, free from every thing trivial and affected. His style in writing was chaste and pure, but at the same time full of spirit and politeness; and fit to convey the most intricate business to the understanding of the reader, with the utmost clearness and perspicuity. And here it is to be lamented, that this extraordinary person, out of his natural aversion to vainglory, wrote several pieces as well as performed several actions, which he did not assume the honour of: though at the same time so many works of this nature have appeared, which every one has ascribed to him, that I believe no author of the greatest eminence would deny my Lord Somers to have been the best writer of the age in which he lived.

This noble lord, for the great extent of his knowledge and capacity, has been often compared with the Lord Verulam, who had also been chancellor of England. But the conduct of these extraordinary persons, under the same circumstances, was vastly different. They were both impeached by a House of Commons. One of them, as he had given just occasion for it, sunk under it; and was reduced to such an abject submission, as very much diminished the lustre of so exalted a character: but my Lord Somers was too well fortified in his integrity to fear the impotence of an attempt upon his reputation; and though his accusers would gladly have dropped their impeachment, he was instant with them for the prosecution of it, and would not let that matter rest till it was brought to an issue. For the same virtue and greatness of mind which gave him a disregard of fame, made him impatient of an undeserved reproach.

There is no question but this wonderful man will make one of the most distinguished figures in the history of the present age; but we cannot expect that his merit will shine out in its proper light, since he wrote many things which are not published in his name; was at the bottom of many excellent counsels, in which he did not appear; did offices of friendship to many persons, who knew not from whom they were derived; and performed great services to his country, the glory of which was transferred to others: in short, since he made it his endeavour rather to do worthy actions, than to gain an illustrious character.

---

## No. 40. MONDAY, MAY 7.

Urit enim fulgore suo qui prægravat artes
Infra se positas: extinctus amabitur idem.—Hor.

It requires no small degree of resolution to be an author, in a country so facetious and satirical as this of Great Britain. Such a one raises a kind of alarm among his fellow-subjects, and by pretending to distinguish himself from the herd, becomes a mark of public censure, and sometimes a standing object of raillery and ridicule. Writing is, indeed, a provocation to the envious, and an affront to the ignorant. How often do we see a person, whose intentions are visibly to do good by the works which he publishes, treated in as scurrilous a manner, as if he were an enemy to mankind? All the little scramblers after fame fall upon him, publish every blot in his life, depend upon hearsay to defame him, and have recourse to their own invention, rather than suffer him to erect himself into an author with impunity. Even those who write on the most indifferent subjects, and are conversant only in works of taste, are looked upon as men that make a kind of insult upon society,[a] and ought to be humbled as disturbers of the public tranquillity. Not only the dull and the malicious, which make a formidable party in our island, but the whole fraternity of writers rise up in arms against every new intruder into the world of fame; and, a thousand to one,[b] before they have done, prove him not only to be a fool, but a knave. Successful authors do what they can to exclude a competitor; while the unsuccessful, with as much eagerness, lay in their claim to him as a brother. This natural antipathy to a man who breaks his ranks, and endeavours to signalize his parts in the world, has, very probably, hindered many persons from making their appearance in print, who might have enriched our country with better productions, in all kinds, than any that are now extant. The truth of it is, the active part of mankind, as they do most for the good of their contemporaries, very deservedly gain the greatest share in their applauses; whilst men of speculative endowments, who employ their talents in writing, as they may equally benefit or amuse succeeding ages, have, generally, the greatest

[a] *Make a kind of insult upon society. To make an insult* is not very exact English. He might have said, *as men that offer an insult to society*, or, *as men that make a kind of assault upon society.*

[b] *A thousand to one*—a familiar phrase, for, *most probably.*

share in the admiration of posterity. Both good and bad writers may receive great satisfaction from the prospects of futurity; as, in after-ages, the former will be remembered, and the latter forgotten.

Among all sets of authors, there are none who draw upon themselves more displeasure, than those who deal in political matters, which indeed is very often too justly incurred, considering that spirit of rancour and virulence with which works of this nature generally abound. These are not only regarded as authors, but as partisans, and are sure to exasperate at least one half of their readers. Other writers offend only the stupid or jealous among their countrymen; but these, let their cause be never so[a] just, must expect to irritate a supernumerary party of the self-interested, prejudiced, and ambitious. They may, however, comfort themselves with considering, that if they gain any unjust reproach from one side, they generally acquire more praise than they deserve from the other; and that writings of this kind, if conducted with candour and impartiality, have a more particular tendency to the good of their country, and of the present age, than any other compositions whatsoever.

To consider an author farther, as the subject of obloquy and detraction. We may observe with what pleasure a work is received by the invidious part of mankind, in which a writer falls short of himself, and does not answer the character which he has acquired by his former productions. It is a fine simile in one of Mr. Congreve's prologues, which compares a writer to a buttering gamester, that stakes all his winnings upon every cast: so that if he loses the last throw, he is sure to be undone. It would be

[a] *Never so.* We now say *ever so.* The other form, *never so*, seems to have a secret reference to an *opposition* conceived in the writer's or speaker's mind, but not explicitly declared, as, if we should complete the sentence, thus—*let their cause be* [not bad, but] *ever so just;* i. e. how-so ever just.

well for all authors, if, like that gentleman,[b] they knew when to give over, and to desist from any farther pursuits after fame, whilst they are in the full possession of it. On the other hand, there is not a more melancholy object in the learned world, than a man who has written himself down. As the public is more disposed to censure than to praise, his readers will ridicule him for his last works, when they have forgot to applaud those which preceded them. In this case, where a man has lost his spirit by old age and infirmity, one could wish that his friends and relations would keep him from the use of pen, ink, and paper, if he is not to be reclaimed by any other methods.

The author, indeed, often grows old before the man, especially if he treats on subjects of invention, or such as arise from reflections upon human nature; for, in this case, neither his own strength of mind, nor those parts of life which are commonly unobserved, will furnish him with sufficient materials to be at the same time both pleasing and voluminous. We find, even in the outward dress of poetry, that men, who write much without taking breath, very often return to the same phrases and forms of expression, as well as to the same manner of thinking. Authors, who have thus drawn off the spirit of their thoughts, should lie still for some time, till their minds have gathered fresh strength, and by reading, reflection, and conversation, laid in a new stock of elegancies, sentiments, and images of nature. The soil, that is worn with too frequent culture, must lie fallow for a while, till it has recruited its exhausted salts, and again enriched itself by the ventilations of the air, the dews of heaven, and the kindly influences of the sun.

[b] Mr. Congreve was a fashionable writer in his time; and Mr Addison, who had a friendship with him, speaks of him, as every body else did He had, indeed, a great deal of wit; but a man must have a furious passion for it, or very little taste, that can read his comedies, on which his reputation was founded, with pleasure, or even patience.

For my own part, notwithstanding this general malevolence towards those who communicate their thoughts in print, I cannot but look with a friendly regard on such as do it, provided there is no tendency in their writings to vice and profaneness. If the thoughts of such authors have nothing in them, they, at least, do no harm, and shew an honest industry, and a good intention in the composer. If they teach me any thing I did not know before, I cannot but look upon myself as obliged to the writer, and consider him as my particular benefactor, if he conveys to me one of the greatest gifts that is in the power of man to bestow, an improvement of my understanding, an innocent amusement, or an incentive to some moral virtue. Were not men of abilities thus communicative, their wisdom would be in a great measure useless, and their experience uninstructive. There would be no business in solitude, nor proper relaxations in business. By these assistances, the retired man lives in the world, if not above it; passion is composed; thought hindered from being barren and the mind from preying upon itself. That esteem, indeed, which is paid to good writers by their posterity, sufficiently shews the merit of persons who are thus employed. Who does not now more admire Cicero as an author, than as a consul of Rome? and does not oftener talk of the celebrated writers of our own country who lived in former ages, than of any other particular persons among their contemporaries and fellow-subjects.

When I consider myself as a British freeholder, I am in a particular manner pleased with the labours of those who have improved our language with the translation of old Latin and Greek authors; and by that means let us into the knowledge of what passed in the famous governments of Greece and Rome. We have already most of their historians in our own tongue: and, what is still more for the honour of our language t has been taught to express with elegance the greatest of their poets in each nation. The illiterate among our countrymen may learn to judge, from Dryden's Virgil, of the most perfect epic performance: and those parts of Homer, which have already been published by Mr. Pope,[a] give us reason to think that the Iliad will appear in English with as little disadvantage to that immortal poem.

There is another author, whom I have long wished to see well translated into English, as this work is filled with a spirit of liberty, and more directly tends to raise sentiments of honour and virtue in his reader, than any of the poetical writings of antiquity. I mean the Pharsalia of Lucan. This is the only author of consideration among the Latin poets, who was not explained for the use of the Dauphin, for a very obvious reason; because the whole Pharsalia would have been no less than a satire upon the French form of government. The translation of this author is now in the hands of Mr. Rowe,[b] who has already given the world some admirable specimens of it; and not only kept up the fire of the original, but delivered the sentiments with greater perspicuity, and in a finer turn of phrase and verse.

As undertakings of so difficult a nature require the greatest encouragements, one cannot but rejoice to see those general subscriptions which have been made to them; especially since, if the two works last mentioned are not finished by those masterly hands which are now employed in them, we may despair of seeing them attempted by others.

[a] For a comment on this panegyric on Mr. Pope's translation of the Illiad, see the life of Bishop Warburton, prefixed to the new edition of his works in quarto.

[b] He speaks like a friend, of Mr. Rowe, and, like a whig, of Lucan; but, as a *critic*, we know what his opinion was of the Latin poet, and of his friends undertaking, when he celebrates the translator for delivering the sentiments of his original, *with greater perspicuity, and in a finer turn of phrase and verse.*

## No. 41. FRIDAY, MAY 11.

Dissentientis conditionibus
Fœdis, et exemplo trahenti
Perniciem veniens in ævum.—HOR.

As the care of our national commerce redounds more to the riches and prosperity of the public, than any other act of government, it is pity that we do not see the state of it marked out in every particular reign with greater distinction and accuracy, than what is usual among our English historians. We may however observe, in general, that the best and wisest of our monarchs have not been less industrious to extend their trade, than their dominions; as it manifestly turns in a much higher degree to the welfare of the people, if not to the glory of the sovereign.

The first of our kings who carried our commerce, and consequently our navigation to a very great height, was Edward the third. This victorious prince, by his many excellent laws for the encouragement of trade, enabled his subjects to support him in his many glorious wars upon the continent, and turned the scale so much in favour of our English merchandise, that, by a balance of trade taken in his time, the exported commodities amounted to two hundred and ninety-four thousand pounds, and the imported but to thirty-eight thousand.

Those of his successors, under whose regulations our trade flourished most, were Henry the seventh, and Queen Elizabeth. As the first of these was, for his great wisdom, very often styled the English Solomon, he followed the example of that wise king in nothing more, than by advancing the traffic of his people. By this means he reconciled to him the minds of his subjects, strengthened himself in their affections, improved very much the navigation of the kingdom, and repelled the frequent attempts of his enemies.

As for Queen Elizabeth, she had always the trade of her kingdom very much at heart; and we may observe the effects of it through the whole course of her reign, in the love and obedience of her people, as well as in the defeats and disappointments of her enemies.

It is with great pleasure that we see our present sovereign applying his thoughts so successfully to the advancement of our traffic, and considering himself as the king of a trading island. His Majesty has already gained very considerable advantages for his people, and is still employed in concerting schemes, and forming treaties, for retrieving and enlarging our privileges in the world of commerce.

I shall only, in this paper, take notice of the treaty concluded at Madrid on the fourteenth of December last, 1715; and by comparing it with that concluded at Utrecht on the ninth of December, 1713, shew several particulars in which the treaty made with his present Majesty is more advantageous to Great Britain, than that which was made in the last reign; after this general observation, that it is equally surprising how so bad a treaty came to be made at the end of a glorious and successful war; and how so good a one has been obtained in the beginning of a reign disturbed by such intestine commotions. But we may learn from hence, that the wisdom of a sovereign, and the integrity of his ministers, are more necessary for bringing about works of such consequence for the public good, than any juncture of time, or any other the most favourable circumstance.

We must here premise, that by the treaty concluded at Madrid in 1667, the duties of importation payable upon the manufactures and products of Great Britain, amounted, upon the established valuation in the Spanish book of rates (after the deduction of the gratias), in Andalusia, to $11\frac{1}{3}$ per cent.; in Valentia, to 5 per cent.; and, in Catalonia, to about 7 per cent. or less:

and, consequently, upon the whole aforesaid trade, those duties could not exceed 10 per cent. in a medium.

After this short account of the state of our trade with Spain, before the treaty of Utrecht, under the late queen, we must observe, that by the explanatory articles of this last-mentioned treaty, the duties of importation upon the products and manufactures of Great Britain were augmented, in Andalusia, to 27½ per cent. at a medium.

But by the late treaty made with his present Majesty at Madrid, the said duties are again reduced, according to the aforesaid treaty of 1667, and the deduction of the gratias is established as an inviolable law; whereas, before, the gratias of the farmers, particularly, were altogether precarious, and depended entirely upon courtesy.

That the common reader may understand the nature of these gratias, he must know, that when the King of Spain had laid higher duties upon our English goods than what the merchants were able or willing to comply with, he used to abate a certain part: which indulgence, or abatement, went under the name of a gratia. But when he had farmed out these his customs to several of his subjects, the farmers, in order to draw more merchandise to their respective ports, and thereby to increase their own particular profits, used to make new abatements, or gratias, to the British merchants, endeavouring sometimes to outvy one another in such indulgences, and by that means to get a greater proportion of custom into their own hands.

But to proceed; the duties on exportation may be computed to be raised, by the Utrecht treaty, near as much as the aforesaid duties of importation; whereas, by the treaty made with his present Majesty, they are reduced to their ancient standard.

Complaint having been made, that the Spaniards, after the suspension of arms, had taken several New England and other

British ships gathering salt at the island of Tertuga, a very full and just report concerning that affair was laid before her late Majesty, of which I shall give the reader the following extract:

"Your Majesty's subjects have, from the first settlement of the continent of America, had a free access to this island; and have, without interruptions, unless in time of war, used to take what salt they pleased there: and we have proofs of that usage for above fifty years, as appears by certificates of persons who have been employed in that trade.

"It doth not appear, upon the strictest inquiry, that the Spaniards ever inhabited or settled on the said island; nor is it probable they ever did, it being either all barren rock, or dry sand, and having no fresh water or provisions in it.

"We take leave to lay before your Majesty, the consequence of your Majesty's subjects being prohibited to fetch salt at Tertuga; which will in part appear from the number of ships using that trade, being, as we are informed, one year with another, about a hundred sail.

"The salt carried from thence to New England is used chiefly for curing of fish, which is either cod, scale-fish, or mackrel; the former of which is the principal branch of the returns made from the continent to Great Britain by way of Spain, Portugal, and the Straits, for the woollen and other goods sent from this kingdom thither. Besides which, the scale-fish and mackrel are of such consequence, that the sugar-islands cannot subsist without them, their negroes being chiefly supported by this fish: so that if they were not supplied therewith from New England, (which they cannot be, if your Majesty's subjects are prohibited from getting salt at Tertuga) they would not be able to carry on their sugar-works. This hath been confirmed to us by several considerable planters concerned in those parts.

"Upon the whole, your Majesty's subjects having enjoyed an

uninterrupted usage of gathering salt at Tertuga, ever since the first settlement of the continent as aforesaid, we humbly submit to your Majesty the consequence of preserving that usage and right upon which the trade of your Majesty's plantations so much depends."

Notwithstanding it appears from what is above-written, that our sugar-islands were like to suffer considerably for want of fish from New England, no care was taken to have this matter remedied by the explanatory articles, which were posterior to the above-mentioned report.

However, in the third article of the treaty made with his present Majesty, this business is fully settled to our advantage.

The British merchants having had several hardships put upon them at Bilboa, which occasioned the decay of our trade at that place, the said merchants did make and execute, in the year 1700, a treaty of privileges with the magistrates and inhabitants of St. Ander, very much to the advantage of this kingdom, in order to their removing and settling there: the effect of which was prevented by the death of king Charles the second of Spain, and the war which soon after ensued. This matter, it seems, was slighted or neglected by the managers of the Utrecht treaty: for, by the fourteenth article of that treaty, there is only 'a liberty given to the British subjects to settle and dwell at St. Ander, upon the terms of the ninth and thirteenth articles of the treaty of 1667,' which are general. But no regard was had to the forementioned treaty of privileges in 1700; whereas, by the second article of the treaty now made with his present Majesty the forementioned treaty of privileges with St. Ander is confirmed and ratified.

Another considerable advantage is, that the French, by the treaty made with his present Majesty, are to pay the same duties at the dry ports, through which they pass by land-carriage, as we pay, upon importation or exportation by sea: which was not provided for by the Utrecht treaty.

By the cedulas annexed to the treaty of 1667, the valuable privileges of having judge conservators (appointed to make a more speedy and less expensive determination of all controversies arising in trade) was fully established. But by the fifteenth article of Utrecht that privilege was in effect given up. For it is therein only stipulated, 'That in case any other nation have that privilege, we shall in like manner enjoy it.' But by the fifth article of the treaty now made with his present Majesty, it is stipulated, that 'We shall enjoy all the rights, privileges, franchises, exemptions, and immunities whatsoever, which we enjoyed by virtue of the royal cedulas or ordinances by the treaty of 1667.' So that hereby the privilege of judge-conservators is again confirmed to us.

As nothing but the reputation of his Majesty in foreign countries, and of his fixed purposes to pursue the real good of his kingdoms, could bring about treaties of this nature: so it is impossible to reflect with patience on the folly and ingratitude of those men who labour to disturb him in the midst of these his royal cares, and to misrepresent his generous endeavours for the good of his people.

---

## No. 42. MONDAY, MAY 14.

O fortunatos mercatores!——— HOR.

SEVERAL authors have written on the advantage of trade in general; which is, indeed, so copious a subject, that as it is impossible to exhaust it in a short discourse, so it is very difficult to observe any thing new upon it. I shall, therefore, only con sider trade in this paper, as it is absolutely necessary and essen tial to the safety, strength, and prosperity of our own nation.

In the first place, as we are an island accommodated on all sides with convenient ports, and encompassed with navigable seas, we should be inexcusable, if we did not make these blessings of Providence and advantages of nature turn to their proper account. The most celebrated merchants in the world, and those who make the greatest figure in antiquity, were situated in the little island of Tyre, which, by the prodigious increase of its wealth and strength at sea, did very much influence the most considerable kingdoms and empires on the neighbouring continent, and gave birth to the Carthaginians, who afterwards exceeded all other nations in naval power. The old Tyre was, indeed, seated on the continent, from whence the inhabitants, after having been besieged by the great king of Assyria, for the space of thirteen years, withdrew themselves and their effects into the island of Tyre; where, by the benefit of such a situation, a trading people were enabled to hold out for many ages against the attempts of their enemies, and became the merchants of the world.

Further; as an island, we are accessible on every side; and exposed to perpetual invasions; against which it is impossible to fortify ourselves sufficiently, without such a power at sea, as is not to be kept up, but by a people who flourish in commerce. To which we must add, that our inland towns being destitute of fortifications, it is our indispensable concern to preserve this our naval strength, which is as a general bulwark to the British nation.

Besides; as an island, it has not been thought agreeable to the true British policy to make acquisitions upon the continent. In lieu, therefore, of such an increase of dominion, it is our business to extend to the utmost our trade and navigation. By this means, we reap the advantages of conquest, without violence or injustice; we not only strengthen ourselves, but gain the wealth of our neighbours in an honest way; and, without any act of hostility, lay the several nations of the world under a kind of contribution.

Secondly, Trade is fitted to the nature of our country, as it abounds with a great profusion of commodities of its own growth, very convenient for other countries, and is naturally destitute of many things suited to the exigencies, ornaments, and pleasures of life, which may be fetched from foreign parts. But, that which is more particularly to be remarked, our British products are of such kinds and quantities, as can turn the balance of trade to our advantage, and enable us to sell more to foreigners than we have occasion to buy from them.

To this we must add, that by extending a well-regulated trade, we are as great gainers by the commodities of many other countries, as by those of our own nation; and by supplying foreign markets with the growth and manufactures of the most distant regions, we receive the same profit from them, as if they were the produce of our own island.

Thirdly, We are not a little obliged to trade, as it has been a great means of civilizing our nation, and banishing out of it all the remains of its ancient barbarity. There are many bitter sayings against islanders in general, representing them as fierce, treacherous, and inhospitable. Those who live on the continent have such opportunities of a frequent intercourse with men of different religions and languages, and who live under different laws and governments, that they become more kind, benevolent, and open-hearted, to their fellow-creatures, than those who are the inhabitants of an island, that hath not such conversations with the rest of the species. Cæsar's observation upon our forefathers is very much to our present purpose; who remarks, that those of them that lived upon the coast or in sea-port towns, were much more civilized, than those who had their dwellings in the inland country, by reason of frequent communications with their neighbours on the continent.

In the last place. Trade is absolutely necessary for us, as our country is very populous. It employs multitudes of hands both by sea and land, and furnishes the poorest of our fellow-subjects with the opportunities of gaining an honest livelihood. The skilful or industrious find their account in it: and many, who have no fixed property in the soil of our country, can make themselves masters of as considerable estates, as those who have the greatest portions of the land descending to them by inheritance.

If what has been often charged upon us by our neighbours has any truth in it, That we are prone to sedition and delight in change, there is no cure more proper for this evil than trade, which thus supplies business to the active, and wealth to the indigent. When men are easy in their circumstances, they are naturally enemies to innovations; and, indeed, we see in the course of our English histories, many of our popular commotions have taken their rise from the decay of some branch of commerce, which created discontents among persons concerned in the manufactures of the kingdom. When men are soured with poverty, and unemployed, they easily give into any prospect of change, which may better their condition, and cannot make it much worse.

Since, therefore, it is manifest, that the promoting of our trade and commerce is necessary and essential to our security and strength, our peace and prosperity, it is our particular happiness to see a monarch on the throne, who is sensible of the true interest of his kingdoms, and applies himself with so much success to the advancement of our national commerce

The reader may see, in my last paper, the advantages which his Majesty has gained for us in our Spanish trade. In this, I shall give a short account of those procured for us from the Austrian low countries, by virtue of the twenty-sixth article of the barrier treaty made at Antwerp the fifteenth of November last.

This branch of our trade was regulated by a tariff, or declaration of the duties of import and export, in the year 1670, which was superseded by another made in 1680, that continued 'till this last tariff settled in 1715 with his present Majesty. As for the two former, those who are at the pains of perusing them will find, the tariff of 1670 laid higher duties on several considerable branches of our trade, than that of 1680, but in many particulars was more favourable to us than the latter. Now, by the present tariff of 1715, these duties are fixed and regulated for the future by those which were most favourable in either of the former tariffs, and all our products and manufactures (one only excepted, which I shall name by and by) settled upon rather an easier foot than ever.

Our woollen cloths, being the most profitable branch of our trade into these countries, have by this means, gained a very considerable advantage. For the tariff of 1680, having laid higher duties upon the finer sorts, and lower duties on ordinary cloth, than what were settled in the tariff of 1670, his Majesty has, by the present treaty, reduced the duties on the finer sorts to the tariff of 1670, and confirmed the duties on ordinary cloth according to the tariff of 1680. Insomuch that this present tariff of 1715, considered with relation to this valuable part of our trade, reduces the duties at least one sixth part, supposing the exportation of all sorts to be equal. But as there is always a much greater exportation of the ordinary cloth, than of the finer sorts the reduction of these duties becomes still much more considerable.

We must further observe, that there had been several innovations made to the detriment of the English merchant since the tariff of 1680; all which innovations are now entirely set aside upon every species of goods, except butter, which is here particularly mentioned, because we cannot be too minute and circumstantial in accounts of this nature. This article, however, is moderated, and is rated in proportion to what has been, and is still to be paid by the Dutch.

As our commerce with the Netherlands is thus settled to the advantage of our British merchants, so is it much to their satisfaction: and if his Majesty, in the several succeeding parts of his reign, (which we hope may be many years prolonged) should advance our commerce in the same proportion as he has already done, we may expect to see it in a more flourishing condition, than under any of his royal ancestors. He seems to place his greatness in the riches and prosperity of his people; and what may we not hope from him in a time of quiet and tranquillity? since, during the late distractions, he has done so much for the advantage of our trade, when we could not reasonably expect he should have been able to do any thing.

---

## No. 43. FRIDAY, MAY 18.

Hoc fonte derivata clades
In patriam populumque fluxit.—HOR.

ONE would wonder how any person, endowed, with the ordinary principles of prudence and humanity, should desire to be king of a country, in which the established religion is directly opposite to that which he himself professes. Were it possible for such a one to accomplish his designs, his own reason must tell him, there could not be a more uneasy prince, nor a more unhappy people. But how it can enter into the wishes of any private persons to be the subjects of a man, whose faith obliges him to use the most effectual means for extirpating their religion, is altogether incomprehensible, but upon the supposition, that whatever principles they seem to adhere to, their interest, ambition, or revenge, is much more active and predominant in their minds, than the love of their country, or of its national worship.

I have never heard of any particular benefit which either the Pretender himself, or the favourers of his cause, could promise to the British nation from the success of his pretensions; though the evils which would arise from it, are numberless and evident. These men content themselves with one general assertion, which often appears in their writings, and their discourse; that the kingdom will never be quiet till he is upon the throne. If by this position is meant, that those will never be quiet who would endeavour to place him there, it may possibly have some truth in it; though we hope even these will be reduced to their obedience by the care of their safety, if not by the sense of their duty. But on the other side, how ineffectual would this strange expedient be, for establishing the public quiet and tranquillity, should it ever take place! for, by way of argument, we may suppose impossibilities. Would that party of men which comprehends the most wealthy, and the most valiant of the kingdom, and which, were the cause put to a trial, would undoubtedly appear the most numerous, (for I am far from thinking all those who are distinguished by the name of tories, to be favourers of the Pretender) can we, I say, suppose these men would live quiet under a reign which they have hitherto opposod, and from which they apprehend such a manifest destruction to their country? Can we suppose our present royal family, who are so powerful in foreign dominions, so strong in their relations and alliances, and so universally supported by the Protestant interest of Europe, would continue quiet, and not make vigorous and repeated attempts for the recovery of their right, should it ever be wrested out of their hands? Can we imagine that our British clergy would be quiet under a prince, who is zealous for his religion, and obliged by it to subvert those doctrines, which it is their duty to defend and propagate? Nay, would any of those men themselves, who are the champions of this desperate cause, unless such of them as are professed Roman Catholics, or disposed to be so, live quiet under a government which, at the best, would make use of all indirect methods in favour of a religion, that is inconsistent with our laws and liberties, and would impose on us such a yoke, as neither we nor our fathers were able to bear? All the quiet that could be expected from such a reign, must be the result of absolute power on the one hand, and a despicable slavery on the other: and I believe every reasonable man will be of the Roman historian's opinion, that a disturbed liberty is better than a quiet servitude,

There is not, indeed, a greater absurdity than to imagine the quiet of a nation can arise from an establishment, in which the king would be of one communion, and the people of another; especially when the religion of the sovereign carries in it the utmost malignity to that of the subject. If any of our English monarchs might have hoped to reign quietly under such circumstances, it would have been King Charles the second, who was received with all the joy and good-will that are natural to a people, newly rescued from a tyranny which had long oppressed them in several shapes. But this monarch was too wise to own himself a Roman Catholic, even in that juncture of time; or to imagine it practicable for an avowed Popish prince to govern a Protestant people. His brother tried the experiment, and every one knows the success of it.

As speculations are best supported by facts, I shall add to these domestic examples one or two parallel instances out of the

Swedish history, which may be sufficient to shew us, that a scheme of government is impracticable in which the head does not agree with the body, in that point, which is of the greatest concern to reasonable creatures. Sweden is the only Protestant kingdom in Europe besides this of Great Britain, which has had the misfortune to see Popish princes upon the throne; and we find that they behaved themselves as we did, and as it is natural for men to do, upon the same occasion. Their King Sigismond having, contrary to the inclinations of his people, endeavoured, by several clandestine methods, to promote the Roman Catholic religion among his subjects, and shewn several marks of favour to their priests and jesuits, was, after a very short reign, deposed by the states of that kingdom, being represented as one who could neither be held by oaths nor promises, and over-ruled by the influence of his religion, which dispenses with the violation of the most sacred engagements that are opposite to its interests. The states, to shew farther their apprehensions of Popery, and how incompatible they thought the principles of the church of Rome in a sovereign were with those of the reformed religion in his subjects, agreed that his son should succeed to the throne, provided he were brought up a Protestant. This the father seemingly complied with; but afterwards refusing to give him such an education, the son was likewise set aside, and for ever excluded from that succession. The famous Queen Christina, daughter to the Great Gustavus, who was so sensible of those troubles which would accrue both to herself and her people, should she avow the Roman Catholic religion while she was upon the throne of Sweden; that she did not make an open profession of that faith, till she had resigned her crown, and was actually upon her journey to Rome.

In short, if there be any political maxim, which may be depended upon as sure and infallible, this is one: That it is im possible for a nation to be happy, where a people of the reformed religion are governed by a king that is a papist. Were he, indeed, only a nominal Roman Catholic, there might be a possibility of peace and quiet under such a reign; but if he is sincere in the principles of his church, he must treat heretical subjects as that church directs him, and knows very well, that he ceases to be religious, when he ceases to be a persecutor.

---

## NO. 44. MONDAY, MAY 21.

Multaque præterea variarum monstra ferarum
Centauri in foribus stabulant, scyllæque biformes,
Et centum-geminus Briareus, ac bellua Lernæ
Horrendum stridens, flammisque armata Chimæra,
Gorgones, Harpyiæque, et forma tricorporis umbræ.
Corripit hic subita trepidus formidine ferrum
Æneas, strictamque aciem venientibus offert.
Et, ni docta comes tenues sine corpore vitas
Admoneat volitare cava sub imagine formæ,
Irruat, et frustra ferro diverberet umbras.—VIRG.

As I was last Friday taking a walk in the park, I saw a country gentleman at the side of Rosamond's pond, pulling a handful of oats out of his pocket, and with a great deal of pleasure, gathering the ducks about him. Upon my coming up to him, who should it be but my friend the fox-hunter, whom I gave some account of in my twenty-second paper! I immediately joined him, and partook of his diversion, till he had not an oat left in his pocket. We then made the tour of the park together, when, after having entertained me with the description of a decoy-pond that lay near his seat in the country, and of a meeting-house that was going to be rebuilt in a neighbouring market-town, he gave me an account of some very odd adventures which he had met with that morning; and which I shall lay together in a short and faithful history, as well as my memory will give me leave.

My friend, who has a natural aversion to London, would never have come up, had not he been subpœnaed to it, as he told me, in order to give his testimony for one of the rebels, whom he knew to be a very fair sportsman. Having travelled all night, to avoid the inconvenience of dust and heat, he arrived with his guide, a little after break of day, at Charing-cross; where, to his great surprise, he saw a running footman carried in a chair, followed by a waterman in the same kind of vehicle. He was wondering at the extravagance of their masters, that furnished them with such dresses and accommodations, when, on a sudden, he beheld a chimney-sweeper conveyed after the same manner, with three footmen running before him. During his progress through the Strand, he met with several other figures no less wonderful and surprising. Seeing a great many in rich morning-gowns, he was amazed to find that persons of quality were up so early: and was no less astonished to see many lawyers in their bar-gowns, when he knew by his almanac the term was ended. As he was extremely puzzled and confounded in himself what all this should mean, a hackney-coach chancing to pass by him, four batts[a] popped out their heads all at once, which very much frighted both him and his horse. My friend, who always takes care to cure his horse of such starting fits, spurred him up to the very side of the coach, to the no small diversion of the batts; who, seeing him with his long whip, horse-hair periwig, jockey belt, and coat without sleeves, fancied him to be one of the masqueraders on horseback, and received him with a loud peal of laughter. His mind being full of idle stories, which are spread up and down the nation by the disaf-

[a] *Batts.* A sort of *maskers,* so called from their resemblance to these night-birds.

fected, he immediately concluded that all the persons he saw in these strange habits were foreigners, and conceived a great indignation against them, for pretending to laugh at an English country-gentleman. But he soon recovered out of his error, by hearing the voices of several of them, and particularly of a shepherdess quarrelling with her coachman, and threatening to break his bones, in very intelligible English, though with a masculine tone. His astonishment still increased upon him, to see a continued procession of harlequins, scaramouches, punchinellos, and a thousand other merry dresses, by which people of quality distinguish their wit from that of the vulgar.

Being now advanced as far as Somerset-house, and observing it to be the great hive whence these chimeras issued forth, from time to time, my friend took his station among a cluster of mob, who were making themselves merry with their betters. The first that came out was a very venerable matron, with a nose and chin that were within a very little of touching one another. My friend, at the first view fancying her to be an old woman of quality, out of his good breeding put off his hat to her, when the person pulling off her mask, to his great surprise, appeared a smock-faced young fellow. His attention was soon taken off from this object, and turned to another that had very hollow eyes, and a wrinkled face, which flourished in all the bloom of fifteen. The whiteness of the lily was blended in it with the blush of the rose. He mistook it for a very whimsical kind of mask; but, upon a nearer view, he found that she held her vizard in her hand, and that what he saw was only her natural countenance, touched up with the usual improvements of an aged coquette.

The next who shewed herself was a female quaker, so very pretty, that he could not forbear licking his lips, and saying to the mob about him, 'It is ten thousand pities she is not a churchwoman.' The quaker was followed by half a dozen nuns, who filed off one after another up Catharine-street, to their respective convents in Drury-lane.

The 'squire, observing the preciseness of their dress, began now to imagine, after all, that this was a nest of sectaries; for he had often heard that the town was full of them. He was confirmed in this opinion upon seeing a conjurer, whom he guessed to be the holder-forth. However, to satisfy himself, he asked a porter, who stood next him, what religion these people were of? The porter replied, 'They are of no religion; it is a masquerade.' 'Upon that, (says my friend,) I began to smoke that they were a parcel of mummers;' and being himself one of the quorum in his own county, could not but wonder that none of the Middlesex justices took care to lay some of them by the heels. He was the more provoked in the spirit of magistracy, upon discovering two very unseemly objects: the first was a judge, who rapped out a great oath at his footman; and the other a big-bellied woman, who, upon taking a leap into the coach, miscarried of a cushion. What still gave him greater offence, was a drunken bishop, who reeled from one side of the court to the other, and was very sweet upon an Indian queen. But his worship, in the midst of his austerity, was mollified at the sight of a very lovely milk-maid, whom he began to regard with an eye of mercy, and conceived a particular affection for her, until he found, to his great amazement, that the standers-by suspected her to be a duchess.

I must not conclude this narrative, without mentioning one disaster which happened to my friend on this occasion. Having for his better convenience dismounted, and mixed among the crowd, he found, upon his arrival at the inn, that he had lost his purse and his almanac. And though it is no wonder such a trick should be played him by some of the curious spectators, he can not beat it out of his head, but that it was a cardinal who picked his pocket, and that this cardinal was a Presbyterian in disguise.

---

## No. 45. FRIDAY, MAY 25.

Nimium nisus pretium est si probitatis impendio constat.—QUINTIL.

I HAVE lately read, with much pleasure, the Essays upon several Subjects, published by Sir Richard Blackmore; and though I agree with him in many of his excellent observations I cannot but take that reasonable freedom, which he himself makes use of with regard to other writers, to dissent from him in some few particulars. In his reflections upon works of wit and humour, he observes how unequal they are to combat vice and folly; and seems to think, that the finest raillery and satire, though directed by these generous views, never reclaimed one vicious man, or made one fool depart from his folly.[a]

This is a position very hard to be contradicted, because no author knows the number or names of his converts. As for the Tatlers and Spectators, in particular, which are obliged to this ingenious and useful author for the character he has given of them, they were so generally dispersed in single sheets, and have since been printed in so great numbers, that it is to be hoped they have made some proselytes to the interests, if not to the practice of wisdom and virtue, among such a multitude of readers.

I need not remind this learned gentleman, that Socrates, who was the greatest propagator of morality in the heathen world, and a martyr for the unity of the godhead, was so famous for

[a] I incline to Sir Richard Blackmore's opinion. But such writings may *prevent* vice and folly, which is better than reclaiming them.

the exercise of this talent among the politest people of antiquity, that he gained the name of (ὁ Ἔιρων) *the Droll.*

There are very good effects which visibly arose from the above-mentioned performances, and others of the like nature; as, in the first place, they diverted raillery from improper objects, and gave a new turn to ridicule, which, for many years, had been exerted on persons and things of a sacred and serious nature. They endeavoured to make mirth instructive; and, if they failed in this great end, they must be allowed, at least, to have made it innocent. If wit and humour begin again to relapse into their former licentiousness, they can never hope for approbation from those who know that raillery is useless when it has no moral under it, and pernicious when it attacks any thing that is either unblameable or praise-worthy. To this we may add, what has been commonly observed, that it is not difficult to be merry on the side of vice, as serious objects are the most capable of ridicule; as the party, which naturally favours such a mirth, is the most numerous: and as there are the most standing jests and patterns for imitation in this kind of writing.

In the next place, such productions of wit and humour, as have a tendency to expose vice and folly, furnish useful diversions to all kinds of readers. The good or prudent man may, by these means, be diverted, without prejudice to his discretion or morality. Raillery, under such regulations, unbends the mind from serious studies, and severer contemplations, without throwing it off from its proper bias. It carries on the same design that is promoted by authors of a graver turn, and only does it in another manner. It also awakens reflection in those who are the most indifferent in the cause of virtue or knowledge, by setting before them the absurdity of such practices as are generally unobserved, by reason of their being common or fashionable; nay, it sometimes catches the dissolute and abandoned before they are aware of it who are often betrayed to laugh at themselves, and, upon reflection, find, that they are merry at their own expence. I might farther take notice, that by entertainments of this kind a man may be cheerful in solitude, and not be forced to seek for company every time he has a mind to be merry.

The last advantage I shall mention from compositions of this nature, when thus restrained, is that they shew wisdom and virtue are far from being inconsistent with politeness and good humour. They make morality appear amiable to people of gay dispositions, and refute the common objection against religion, which represents it as only fit for gloomy and melancholy tempers. It was the motto of a bishop, very eminent for his piety and good works, in King Charles the second's reign, *Inservi Deo et lætare*, 'Serve God and be chearful.' Those, therefore, who supply the world with such entertainments of mirth as are instructive, or at least harmless, may be thought to deserve well of mankind; to which I shall only add, that they retrieve the honour of polite learning, and answer those sour enthusiasts who affect to stigmatize the finest and most elegant authors, both ancient and modern, (which they have never read) as dangerous to religion, and destructive of all sound and saving knowledge.

Our nation are such lovers of mirth and humour, that it is impossible for detached papers, which come out on stated days, either to have a general run, or long continuance, if they are not diversified, and enlivened from time to time, with subjects and thoughts accommodated to this taste, which so prevails among our countrymen. No periodical author, who always maintains his gravity, and does not sometimes sacrifice to the graces, must expect to keep in vogue for any considerable time. Political speculations in particular, however just and important, are of so dry and austere a nature, that they will not go down with the public without frequent seasonings of this kind. The work may be well performed, but will never take, if it is not set off with proper scenes and decorations. A mere politician is but a dull companion, and, if he is always wise, is in great danger of being tiresome or ridiculous. Besides, papers of entertainment are necessary to increase the number of readers, especially among those of different notions and principles; who, by this means, may be betrayed to give you a fair hearing, and to know what you have to say for yourself. I might likewise observe, that in all political writings there is something that grates upon the mind of the most candid reader, in opinions which are not conformable to his own way of thinking; and that the harshness of reasoning is not a little softened and smoothed by the infusions of mirth and pleasantry.

Political speculations do likewise furnish us with several objects that may very innocently be ridiculed, and which are regarded as such by men of sense in all parties; of this kind are the passions of our stateswomen, and the reasonings of our fox-hunters.

A writer who makes fame the chief end of his endeavours, and would be more desirous of pleasing than of improving his readers, might find an inexhaustible fund of mirth in politics. Scandal and satire are never-failing gratifications to the public. Detraction and obloquy are received with as much eagerness as wit and humour. Should a writer single out particular persons, or point his raillery at any order of men, who, by their profession ought to be exempt from it; should he slander the innocent, or satirize the miserable; or should he, even on the proper subjects of derision, give the full play to his mirth, without regard to decency and good manners; he might be sure of pleasing a great part of his readers, but must be a very ill man, if by such a proceeding he could please himself.

## No. 46. MONDAY, MAY 28.

——————male nominatis
Parcite verbis:
Hic dies, vere mihi festus, atras
Eximet curas; ego nec tumultum
Nec mori per vim metuam, tenente
Cæsare terras. Hor.

The usual salutation to a man upon his birth-day among the ancient Romans was, *Multos et fœlices;* in which they wished him many happy returns of it. When Augustus celebrated the secular year, which was kept but once in a century, and received the congratulations of his people on that account, an eminent court-wit saluted him in the birth-day form (*Multos et fœlices*) which is recorded as a beautiful turn of compliment, expressing a desire that he might enjoy a happy life of many hundreds of years. This salutation cannot be taxed with flattery, since it was directed to a prince, of whom it is said by a great historian, 'It had been happy for Rome, if he had never been born, or if he had never died.' Had he never been born, Rome would, in all probability have recovered its former liberty: had he never died, it would have been more happy under his government, than it could have been in the possession of its ancient freedom.

It is our good fortune that our sovereign, whose nativity is celebrated on this day, gives us a prospect, which the Romans wanted under the reign of their Augustus, of his being succeeded by an heir, both to his virtues and his dominions. In the mean time it happens very luckily, for the establishment of a new race of kings upon the British throne, that the first of this royal line has all those high qualifications which are necessary to fix the crown upon his own head, and to transmit it to his posterity. We may, indeed, observe, that every series of kings who have kept up the succession in their respective families, in spite of all pretensions and oppositions formed against them, has been headed by princes famous for valour and wisdom. I need only mention the names of William the Conqueror, Henry the second, Henry the fourth, Edward the fourth, and Henry the seventh. As for King James the first, the founder of the Stuart race, had he been as well turned for the camp as the cabinet, and not confined all his views[a] to the peace and tranquillity of his own reign, his son had not been involved in such fatal troubles and confusions

Were an honest Briton to wish for a sovereign, who, in the present situation of affairs, would be most capable of advancing our national happiness, what could he desire more than a prince mature in wisdom and experience; renowned for his valour and resolution; successful and fortunate in his undertakings; zealous for the reformed religion; related or allied to all the most considerable Protestant powers of Europe; and blessed with a numerous issue! A failure in any one of these particulars has been the cause of infinite calamities to the British nation; but when they all thus happily concur in the same person, they are as much as can be suggested, even by our wishes, for making us a happy people, so far as the qualifications of a monarch can contribute to it.

I shall not attempt a character of his present Majesty, having already given an imperfect sketch of it in my second paper; but shall chuse rather to observe that cruel treatment which this excellent prince has met with from the tongues and pens of some of his disaffected subjects. The baseness, ingratitude, and injustice of which practice will appear to us, if we consider,

First, that it reflects highly upon the good sense of the British nation, who do not know how to set a just value upon a prince,

[a] Had he *been* as well *turned* for the camp as the cabinet, and *not confined* all his views, &c This way of coupling a passive, and active verb together is not accurate.

whose virtues have gained him the universal esteem of foreign countries. Those potentates who, as some may suppose, do not wish well to his affairs, have shewn the greatest respect to his personal character, and testified their readiness to enter into such friendships and alliances as may be advantageous to his people. The northern kings solicit him with impatience to come among them, as the only person capable of settling the several claims and pretensions, which have produced such unspeakable calamities in that part of the world. Two of the most remote and formidable powers of Europe have entertained thoughts of submitting their disputes to his arbitration. Every one knows his ancient subjects had such a long experience of his sovereign virtues, that at his departure from them his whole people were in tears; which were answered with all those sentiments of humanity, that arise in the heart of a good prince on so moving an occasion. What a figure, therefore, must we make among mankind, if we are the only people of Europe who derogate from his merit, that may be made happy by it; and if, in a kingdom which is grown glorious by the reputation of such a sovereign, there are multitudes who would endeavour to lessen and undervalue it.

In the next place: such a treatment from any part of our fellow-subjects, is by no means answerable to what we receive from his Majesty. His love and regard for our constitution is so remarkable, that, as we are told by those whose office it is to lay the business of the nation before him, it is his first question, upon any matter of the least doubt or difficulty, whether it be in every point according to the laws of the land? He is easy of access to those who desire it, and is so gracious in his behaviour and condescension on such occasions, that none of his subjects retire from his presence without the greatest idea of his wisdom and goodness. His continued application to such public affairs as may conduce to the benefit of his kingdoms, diverts him from those pleasures and entertainments which may be indulged by persons in a lower station, and are pursued with eagerness by princes who have not the care of the public so much at heart. The least return, which we can make to such a sovereign, is that tribute which is always paid by honest men, and is always acceptable to great minds, the praise and approbation that are due to a virtuous and noble character. Common decency forbids opprobrious language, even to a bad prince; and common justice will exact from us, towards a good prince, the same benevolence and humanity with which he treats his subjects. Those who are influenced by duty and gratitude, will rise much higher in all the expressions of affection and respect, and think they can never do too much to advance the glory of a sovereign, who takes so much pains to advance their happiness.

When we have a king, who has gained the reputation of the most unblemished probity and honour, and has been famed, through the whole course of his life, for an inviolable adherence to his promises, we may acquiesce (after his many solemn declarations) in all those measures which it is impossible for us to judge rightly of, unless we were let into such schemes of council and intelligence as produce them; and therefore we should rather turn our thoughts upon the reasonableness of his proceedings, than busy ourselves to form objections against them. The consideration of his Majesty's character should at all times suppress our censure of his conduct: and since we have never yet seen, or heard of any false steps in his behaviour, we ought in justice to think, that he governs himself by his usual rules of wisdom and honour, until we discover something to the contrary.

These considerations ought to reconcile to his Majesty the hearts and tongues of all his people: but as for those who are the obstinate, irreclaimable, professed enemies to our present establishment, we must expect their calumnies will not only con tinue, but rise against him in proportion as he pursues such measures as are likely to prove successful, and ought to recommend him to his people.

---

## No. 47, FRIDAY, JUNE 1.

———cessit furor, et rabida ora quierunt.—VIRG.

I QUESTION not but most of my readers will be very well pleased to hear, that my friend the fox-hunter, of whose arrival in town I gave notice in my forty-fourth paper, is become a convert to the present establishment, and a good subject to King George. The motives to his conversion shall be the subject of this paper, as they may be of use to other persons who labour under those prejudices and prepossessions, which hung so long upon the mind of my worthy friend. These I had an opportunity of learning the other day, when, at his request, we took a ramble together, to see the curiosities of this great town.

The first circumstance, as he ingenuously confessed to me (while we were in the coach together), which helped to disabuse him, was seeing King Charles I. on horseback, at Charing-Cross; for he was sure that prince could never have kept his seat there, had the stories been true he had heard in the country, that forty one was come about again.

He owned to me that he looked with horror on the new church that is half built in the Strand, as taking it, at first sight, to be half demolished: but upon inquiring of the workmen, was agreeably surprised to find, that instead of pulling it down, they were building it up; and that fifty more were raising[a] in other parts of the town.

[a] *Were raising.* The verb, *to raise*, is always used transitively; the participle, therefore, cannot be intransitive. It should be—*were rising.*

To these I must add a third circumstance, which I find had no small share in my friend's conversion. Since his coming to town, he chanced to look into the church of St. Paul, about the middle of sermon-time, where, having first examined the dome, to see if it stood safe, (for the screw-plot still ran in his head) he observed, that the Lord-mayor, Aldermen, and city-sword, were a part of the congregation. This sight had the more weight with him, as, by good luck, not above two of that venerable body were fallen a-sleep.

This discourse held us till we came to the Tower; for our first visit was to the lions. My friend, who had a great deal of talk with their keeper, inquired very much after their health, and whether none of them had fallen sick upon the taking of Perth, and the flight of the Pretender? and hearing they were never better in their lives, I found he was extremely startled: for he had learned from his cradle, that the lions in the Tower were the best judges of the title of our British kings, and always sympathized with our sovereigns.

After having here satiated our curiosity, we repaired to the Monument, where my fellow-traveller, being a well-breathed man, mounted the ascent with much speed and activity. I was forced to halt so often in this perpendicular march, that, upon my joining him on the top of the pillar, I found he had counted all the steeples and towers which were discernible from this advantageous situation, and was endeavouring to compute the number of acres they stood upon. We were both of us very well pleased with this part of the prospect; but I found he cast an evil eye upon several warehouses, and other buildings, that looked like barns, and seemed capable of receiving great multitudes of people. His heart misgave him that these were so many meeting-houses, but, upon communicating his suspicions to me, I soon made him easy in this particular.

We then turned our eyes upon the river, which gave me an occasion to inspire him with some favourable thoughts of trade and merchandise, that had filled the Thames with such crowds of ships, and covered the shore with such swarms of people.

We descended very leisurely, my friend being careful to count the steps, which he registered in a blank leaf of his new almanac. Upon our coming to the bottom, observing an English inscription upon the basis, he read it over several times, and told me he could scarce believe his own eyes, for that he had often heard from an old attorney, who lived near him in the country, that it was the Presbyterians who burned down the city; whereas, says he, this pillar positively affirms in so many words, that 'the burning of this ancient city was begun and carried on by the treachery and malice of the popish faction, in order to the carrying on their horrid plot for extirpating the Protestant religion, and old English liberty, and introducing popery and slavery.' This account, which he looked upon to be more authentic, than if it had been in print, I found, made a very great impression upon him.

We now took coach again, and made the best of our way for the Royal Exchange, though I found he did not much care to venture himself into the throng of that place; for he told me he had heard they were, generally speaking, republicans, and was afraid of having his pocket picked amongst them. But he soon conceived a better opinion of them, when he spied the statue of King Charles II. standing up in the middle of the crowd, and most of the kings in Baker's Chronicle ranged in order over their heads; from whence he very justly concluded, that an antimonarchical assembly could never chuse such a place to meet in once a day.

To continue this good disposition in my friend, after a short stay at Stock's Market, we drove away directly for the Mews, where he was not a little edified with the sight of those fine sets of horses which have been brought over from Hanover, and with the care that is taken of them. He made many good remarks upon this occasion, and was so pleased with his company, that I had much ado to get him out of the stable.

In our progress to St. James's Park (for that was the end of our journey) he took notice, with great satisfaction, that, contrary to his intelligence in the country, the shops were all open and full of business; that the soldiers walked civilly in the streets; that clergymen, instead of being affronted, had generally the wall given them; and that he had heard the bells ring to prayers from morning to night, in some part of the town or another.[a]

As he was full of these honest reflections, it happened very luckily for us, that one of the king's coaches passed by with the three young princesses in it, whom by an accidental stop we had an opportunity of surveying for some time; my friend was ravished with the beauty, innocence, and sweetness, that appeared in all their faces. He declared several times, that they were the finest children he had ever seen in all his life; and assured me that, before this sight, if any one had told him it had been possible for three such pretty children to have been born out of England, he should never have believed them.

We were now walking together in the Park, and as it is usual for men who are naturally warm and heady, to be transported with the greatest flush of good nature when they are once sweetened; he owned to me very frankly, he had been much imposed upon by those false accounts of things he had heard in the coun-

[a] *In some part of the town or another.* We say—in *some* part or *other*,—and, in *one* part or *another*. The reason seems to be, that the adjective, *some*, is less definitive than *one*, and conveys in it a confused idea of *plurality*, even though the noun to which it is joined, be singular. As here, *some part* is nearly equivalent to *some parts;* the correlative, therefore, is, *other*, that is, *other parts;* while the correlative to *one* part is necessarily *another*, or *one* other. When, *some*, in this form of expression, is followed by *another*, the extent of that adjective is limited by the addition of *one:* as, when we say, *in some one* part of the town, or *another*

try; and that he would make it his business, upon his return thither, to set his neighbours right, and give them a more just notion of the present state of affairs.

What confirmed my friend in this excellent temper of mind, and gave him an inexpressible satisfaction, was a message he received, as we were walking together, from the prisoner for whom he had given his testimony in his late trial. This person having been condemned for his part in the late rebellion, sent him word that his Majesty had been graciously pleased to reprieve him, with several of his friends, in order, as it was thought, to give them their lives; and that he hoped before he went out of town they should have a cheerful meeting, and drink health and prosperity to King George.

---

## No. 48. MONDAY, JUNE 4.

Tu tamen, si habes aliquam spem de Republica, sive desperas: ea para, meditare, cogita, quæ esse in eo cive ac viro debent, qui sit Rempublicam afflictam et oppressam miseris temporibus ac perditis moribus in veterem dignitatem ac libertatem vindicaturus.

CICER.

THE condition of a minister of state is only suited to persons who, out of love to their king and country, desire rather to be useful to the public than easy to themselves. When a man is posted[a] in such a station, whatever his behaviour may be, he is sure, beside the natural fatigue and trouble of it, to incur the envy of some, and the displeasure of others; as he will have many rivals, whose ambition he cannot satisfy, and many dependants whose wants he cannot provide for. These are misfortunes inseparable from such public employments, in all countries; but there are several others which hang upon this condition of life in

[a] *Posted.* A vulgar and unauthorized word. He might have said — *placed in*, or, *advanced to*, such a station

our British government, more than any other sovereignty in Europe ; as, in the first place, there is no other nation which is so equally divided into two opposite parties, whom it is impossible to please at the same time. Our notions of the public good, with relation both to ourselves and foreigners, are of so different a nature, that those measures which are extolled by one half of the kingdom, are naturally decryed by the other. Besides, that in a British administration, many acts of government are absolutely necessary, in which one of the parties must be favoured and obliged, in opposition to their antagonists. So that the most perfect administration, conducted by the most consummate wisdom and probity, must unavoidably produce opposition, enmity, and defamation, from multitudes who are made happy by it.

Farther, it is peculiarly observed of our nation, that almost every man in it is a politician, and hath a scheme of his own, which he thinks preferable to that of any other person. Whether this may proceed from that spirit of liberty which reigns among us, or from those great numbers of all ranks and conditions, who from time to time are concerned in the British legislature, and by that means are let into the business of the nation, I shall not take upon me to determine. But for this reason it is certain, that a British ministry must expect to meet with many censurers, even in their own party, and ought to be satisfied, if, allowing to every particular man that his private scheme is wisest, they can persuade him that next to his own plan that of the government is the most eligible.

Besides, we have a set of very honest and well meaning gentlemen in England, not to be met with in other countries, who take it for granted they can never be in the wrong, so long as they oppose ministers of state. Those whom they have admired through the whole course of their lives for their honour and integrity, though they still persist to act in their former character and change nothing but their stations, appear to them in a disadvantageous light, as soon as they are placed upon state eminences. Many of these gentlemen have been used to think there is a kind of slavery in concurring with the measures of great men, and that the good of the country is inconsistent with the inclinations of the court: by the strength of these prejudices, they are apt to fancy a man loses his honesty, from the very moment that he is made the most capable of being useful to the public; and will not consider that it is every whit as honourable to assist a good minister as to oppose a bad one.

In the last place, we may observe, that there are greater numbers of persons who solicit for places, and perhaps are fit for them, in our own country, than in any other. To which we must add that, by the nature of our constitution, it is in the power of more particular persons in this kingdom, than in any other, to distress the government when they are disobliged. A British minister must, therefore, expect to see many of those friends and dependants fall off from him, whom he cannot gratify in their demands upon him; since to use the phrase of a late statesman, who knew very well how to form a party, 'the pasture is not large enough.'

Upon the whole: the condition of a British minister labours under so many difficulties, that we find in almost every reign since the conquest, the chief ministers have been new men, or such as have raised themselves to the greatest posts in the government, from the state of private gentlemen. Several of them neither rose from any conspicuous family, nor left any behind them, being of that class of eminent persons, whom Sir Francis Bacon speaks of, who, like comets or blazing stars, draw upon them the whole attention of the age in which they appear, though nobody knows whence they came, nor where they are lost. Persons of hereditary wealth and title have not been over-forward to engage in so great a scene of cares and perplexities, nor to run all the risks of so dangerous a situation. Nay, many whose greatness and fortune were not made to their hands, and had sufficient qualifications and opportunities of rising to these high posts of trust and honour, have been deterred from such pursuits by the difficulties that attend them, and chose rather to be easy than powerful: or, if I may use the expression, to be carried in the chariot than to drive it.

As the condition of a minister of state in general is subject to many burdens and vexations; and as that of a British minister in particular is involved in several hazards and difficulties peculiar to our own country; so is this high station exposed more than ordinary to such inconveniences in the present juncture of affairs; first, as it is the beginning of a new establishment among us; and, secondly, as this establishment hath been disturbed by a dangerous rebellion.

If we look back into our English history, we shall always find the first monarch of a new line received with the greatest opposition, and reconciling to himself, by degrees, the duty and affection of his people. The government, on such occasions, is always shaken before it settles. The inveteracy of the people's prejudices, and the artifices of domestic enemies, compelled their rulers to make use of all means for reducing them to their allegiance, which perhaps, after all, was brought about rather by time than by policy. When commotions and disturbances are of an extraordinary and unusual nature, the proceedings of the government must be so too. The remedy must be suited to the evil, and I know no juncture more difficult to a minister of state, than such as requires uncommon methods to be made use of, when, at the same time, no other can be made use of than what are prescribed by the known laws of our constitution. Several measures may be absolutely necessary in such a juncture, which may be represented as hard and severe, and would not be proper in a time of public peace and tranquillity. In this case Virgil's excuse, which he puts in the mouth of a fictitious sovereign, upon a complaint of this nature, hath the utmost force of reason and justice on its side.—*Res dura et regni novitas me talia cogunt.* 'The difficulties that I meet with in the beginning of my reign make such a proceeding necessary.'

In the next place, as this establishment has been disturbed by a dangerous rebellion, the ministry has been involved in many additional and supernumerary difficulties. It is a common remark, that English ministers never fare so well as in a time of war with a foreign power, which diverts the private feuds and animosities of the nation, and turns their efforts upon the common enemy. As a foreign war is favourable to a ministry, a rebellion is no less dangerous; if it succeeds, they are the first persons who must fall a sacrifice to it; if it is defeated, they naturally become odious to all the secret favourers and abettors of it. Every method they make use of for preventing or suppressing it, and for deterring others from the like practices for the future, must be unacceptable and displeasing to the friends, relations, and accomplices of the guilty. In cases where it is thought necessary to make examples, it is the humour of the multitude to forget the crime, and remember the punishment. However, we have already seen, and still hope to see, so many instances of mercy in his Majesty's government, that our chief ministers have more to fear from the murmurs of their too violent friends than from the reproaches of their enemies.

## No. 49. FRIDAY, JUNE 8.

——jam nunc sollennes ducere pompas
Ad delubra juvat—— —VIRG.

YESTERDAY was set apart as a day of public thanksgiving for the late extraordinary successes, which have secured to us every thing that can be esteemed, and delivered us from every thing that can be apprehended, by a Protestant and a free people. I cannot but observe, upon this occasion, the natural tendency in such a national devotion, to inspire men with sentiments of religious gratitude, and to swell their hearts with inward transports of joy and exultation.

When instances of divine favour are great in themselves, when they are fresh upon the memory, when they are peculiar to a certain country, and commemorated by them in large and solemn assemblies; a man must be of a very cold or degenerate temper, whose heart doth not burn within him in the midst of that praise and adoration, which arises at the same hour in all the different parts of the nation, and from the many thousands of the people.

It is impossible to read of extraordinary and national acts of worship, without being warmed with the description, and feeling some degree of that divine enthusiasm, which spreads itself among a joyful and religious multitude. A part of that exuberant devotion, with which the whole assembly raised and animated one another, catches a reader at the greatest distance of time, and makes him a kind of sharer in it.

Among all the public solemnities of this nature, there is none in history so glorious as that under the reign of King Solomon, at the dedication of the Temple. Besides the great officers of state, and the inhabitants of Jerusalem, all the elders and heads of tribes, with the whole body of the people ranged under them, from one end of the kingdom to the other, were summoned to assist in it. We may guess at the prodigious number of this assembly from the sacrifice on which they feasted, consisting of a hundred and twenty thousand sheep, and two hundred and twenty hecatombs of oxen. When this vast congregation was formed into a regular procession to attend the ark of the covenant, the king marched at the head of his people, with hymns and dances, to the new temple, which he had erected for its reception. Josephus tells us, that the Levites sprinkled the way as they passed with the blood of sacrifices, and burned the holy incense in such quantities as refreshed the whole multitude with its odours, and filled all the region about them with perfume. When the ark was deposited under the wings of the cherubims in the holy place, the great consort of praise began. It was enlivened with a hundred and twenty trumpets, assisted with a proportionable number of other kinds of musical instruments, and accompanied with innumerable voices of all the singers of Israel, who were instructed and set apart to religious performances of this kind. As this mighty chorus was extolling their Maker, and exciting the whole nation thus assembled, to the praise of his never-ceasing goodness and mercy, the Shekinah descended: or, to tell it in the more emphatical words of holy writ, 'It came to pass, as the trumpets and singers were as one, to make one sound to be heard in praising and thanking the Lord, and when they lift up their voice with the trumpets and cymbals, and instruments of music, and praised the Lord, saying, For he is good, for his mercy endureth for ever; that then the house was filled with a cloud.' The priests themselves, not able to bear the awfulness of the appearance, retired into the court of the temple, where the king being placed upon a brazen scaffold, so as to be seen by the whole multitude, blessed the congregation of Israel, and afterwards, spreading forth his hands to Heaven, offered up that divine prayer which is twice recorded at length in Scripture, and has always been looked upon as a composition fit to have proceeded from the wisest of men. He had no sooner finished his prayer, when a flash of fire fell from Heaven and burned up the sacrifice which lay ready upon the altar. The people, whose hearts were gradually moved by the solemnity of the whole proceeding, having been exalted by the religious strains of music, and awed by the appearance of that glory which filled the temple, seeing now the miraculous consumption of the sacrifice, and observing the piety of their king, who lay prostrate before his Maker, 'bowed themselves with their faces to the ground upon the pavement and worshipped and praised the Lord, saying, For he is good, for his mercy endureth for ever.'

What happiness might not such a kingdom promise to itself where the same elevated spirit of religion ran through the prince, the priests, and the people! But I shall quit this head, to observe that such an uncommon fervour of devotion shewed itself among our own countrymen, and in the persons of three princes who were the greatest conquerors in our English history. These are Edward the third, his son the Black Prince, and Henry the fifth. As for the first, we are told that, before the famous battle of Cressy, he spent the greatest part of the night in prayer, and in the morning received the sacrament with his son, the chief of his officers, and nobility. The night of that glorious day was no less piously distinguished by the orders, which he gave out to his army, that they should forbear all insulting of their enemies, or boasting of their own valour, and employ their time in returning thanks to the Great Giver of the victory. The Black Prince, before the battle of Poictiers, declared, that his whole confidence was in the Divine assistance; and after that great victory, behaved himself in all particulars like a truly Christian conqueror. Eight days successively were appointed by his father in England, for a solemn and public thanksgiving; and when the young prince returned in triumph with the king of France as his prisoner, the pomp of the day consisted chiefly in extraordinary processions, and acts of devotion. The behaviour of the Black Prince, after a battle in Spain, whereby he restored the king of Castile to his dominions, was no less remarkable. When that king, transported with his success, flung himself upon his knees to thank him, the generous prince ran to him, and, taking him by the hand, told him it was not he who could lay any claim to his gratitude, but desired they might go to the altar together, and jointly return their thanks to whom only it was due.[a]

Henry the fifth, (who, at the beginning of his reign, made a public prayer in the presence of his Lords and Commons, that he might be cut off by an immediate death, if Providence foresaw he would not prove a just and good governor, and promote the welfare of his people) manifestly derived his courage from his piety, and was scrupulously careful not to ascribe the success of it to himself. When he came within sight of that prodigious army, which offered him battle at Agincourt, he ordered all his cavalry to dismount, and, with the rest of his forces, to implore upon their knees a blessing on their undertaking. In a noble speech, which he made to his soldiers immediately before the first onset, he took notice of a very remarkable circumstance, namely, that this very day of battle was the day appointed in his own kingdom, to offer up public devotions for the prosperity of his arms; and therefore bid them not doubt of victory, since, at the same time they were fighting in the field, all the people of England were lifting up their hands to heaven for their success. Upon the close of that memorable day, in which the king had performed wonders with his own hand, he ordered the hundred and fifteenth

[a] *To whom only it was due.* Certainly better than—*to* him *to* whom it was due—the sense is clear enough, and the ellipsis fully justified by the ear.

Psalm to be repeated in the midst of his victorious army, and at the words, 'Not unto us, not unto us, but unto thy name be the praise,' he himself, with his whole host, fell to the earth upon their faces, ascribing to Omnipotence the whole glory of so great an action.

I shall conclude this paper with a reflection, which naturally rises out of it. As there is nothing more beautiful in the sight of God and man, than a king and his people concurring in such extraordinary acts of devotion, one cannot suppose a greater contradiction and absurdity in a government, than where the king is of one religion and the people of another. What harmony or correspondence can be expected between a sovereign and his subjects, when they cannot join together in the most joyful, the most solemn, and most laudable action of reasonable creatures; in a word, where the prince considers his people as heretics, and the people look upon their prince as an idolater!

---

## No. 50. MONDAY, JUNE 11.

O quisquis volet impias
  Cædes, et rabiem tollere civicam:
Si quæret pater urbium
  Subscribi statuis; indomitam audeat
Refrænare licentiam
  Clarus postgenitis—— —— HOR.

WHEN Mahomet had for many years endeavoured to propagate his imposture among his fellow-citizens, and, instead of gaining any number of proselytes, found his ambition frustrated, and his notions ridiculed; he forbad his followers the use of argument and disputation in the advancing of his doctrines, and to rely only[a] upon the cimeter for their success. Christianity,

[a] *He forbad his followers the use of argument—and to rely only*, &c.

he observed, had made its way by reason and miracles, but he professed it was his design to save men by the sword. From that time he began to knock down his fellow-citizens with a great deal of zeal, to plunder caravans with a most exemplary sanctity, and to fill all Arabia with an unnatural medley of religion and bloodshed.

The enemies of our happy establishment seem at present to copy out the piety of this seditious prophet, and to have recourse to his laudable method of club-law, when they find all other means of enforcing the absurdity of their opinions to be ineffectual. It was usual among the ancient Romans, for those, who had saved the life of a citizen, to be dressed in an oaken garland; but among us, this has been a mark of such well-intentioned persons, as would betray their country if they were able, and beat out the brains of their fellow-subjects. Nay, the leaders of this poor unthinking rabble, to shew their wit, have lately decked them out of their kitchen gardens in a most insipid pun, very well suited to the capacity of such followers.

This manner of proceeding has had an effect quite contrary to the intention of these ingenious demagogues; for by setting such an unfortunate mark on their followers, they have exposed them to innumerable drubs and contusions. They have been cudgelled most unmercifully in every part of London and Westminster; and over all the nation have avowed their principles, to the unspeakable damage of their bones. In short, if we may believe our accounts both from town and country, the noses and ears of the party are very much diminished, since they have appeared under this unhappy distinction.

The truth of it is, there is such an unaccountable frenzy and

Perspicuity and grammar, both call upon us to reform this sentence, thus—*he forbad his followers the use of argument, and* [required them] *to rely only*, &c.

licentiousness spread through the basest of the people, of all parties and denominations, that if their skirmishes did not proceed to too great an extremity, one would not be sorry to see them bestowing so liberally upon one another, a chastisement which they so richly deserve. Their thumps and bruises might turn to account, and save the government a great deal of trouble, if they could beat each other into good manners.

Were not advice thrown away on such a thoughtless rabble, one would recommend to their serious consideration what is suspected, and indeed known, to be the cause of these popular tumults and commotions in this great city. They are the Popish missionaries, that lie concealed under many disguises in all quarters of the town, who mix themselves in these dark scuffles, and animate the mob to such mutual outrages and insults. This profligate species of modern apostles divert themselves at the expence of a government which is opposite to their interests, and are pleased to see the broken heads of heretics, in what party soever they have listed themselves. Their treatment of our silly countrymen, puts me in mind of an account in Tavernier's Travels through the East Indies. This author tells us, there is a great wood in those parts very plentifully stocked with monkies; that a large highway runs through the middle of this wood; and that the monkies who live on the one side of this highway, are declared enemies to those who live on the other. When the inhabitants of that country have a mind to give themselves a diversion, it is usual for them to set these poor animals together by the ears; which they do after this manner: They place several pots of rice in the middle of the road, with great heaps of cudgels in the neighbourhood of every pot. The monkies, on the first discovery of these provisions, descend from the trees on either side in prodigious numbers, take up the arms, with which their good friends have furnished them, and belabour one another with a storm of thwacks, to the no small mirth and entertainment of the beholders. This mob of monkies act, however, so far reasonably in this point, as the victorious side of the wood find, upon the repulse of their enemies, a considerable booty on the field of battle; whereas our party mobs are betrayed into the fray without any prospect of the feast.

If our common people have not virtue enough left among them, to lay aside this wicked and unnatural hatred, which is crept into their hearts against one another, nor sense enough to resist the artifice of those incendiaries, who would animate them to the destruction of their country; it is high time for the government to exert itself in the repressing of such seditious tumults and commotions. If that extraordinary lenity and forbearance which has been hitherto shewn on those occasions, proves ineffectual to that purpose, these miscreants of the community ought to be made sensible, that our constitution is armed with a sufficient force for the reformation of such disorders, and the settlement of the public peace.

There cannot be a greater affront to religion, than such a tumultuous rising of the people, who distinguish the times set apart for the national devotions by the most brutal scenes of violence, clamour, and intemperance. The day begins with a thanksgiving, and ends in a riot. Instead of the voice of mutual joy and gladness, there is nothing heard in our streets, but opprobrious language, ribaldry, and contention.

As such a practice is scandalous to our religion, so it is no less a reproach to our government. We are become a by-word among the nations for our ridiculous feuds and animosities, and fill all the public prints of Europe with the accounts of our midnight brawls and confusions.

The mischiefs arising to private persons from these vile disturbers of the commonwealth are too many to be enumerated.

The great and innocent are insulted by the scum and refuse of the people. Several poor wretches, who have engaged in these commotions, have been disabled for their lives, from doing any good to their families and dependants; nay, several of them have fallen a sacrifice to their own inexcusable folly and madness. Should the government be wearied out of its present patience and forbearance, and forced to execute all those powers with which it is invested for the preservation of the public peace; what is to be expected by such heaps of turbulent and seditious men!

These and the like considerations, though they may have no influence on the headstrong unruly multitude, ought to sink into the minds of those who are their abettors, and who, if they escape the punishment here due to them, must very well know that these several mischiefs will be one day laid to their charge.

---

## NO. 51. FRIDAY, JUNE 15.

Quod si in hoc erro, libenter erro; nec mihi hunc errorem, quo delector, dum vivo, extorqueri volo. CICER.

As there is nothing which more improves the mind of man, than the reading of ancient authors, when it is done with judgment and discretion; so there is nothing which gives a more unlucky turn to the thoughts of a reader, when he wants discernment, and loves and admires the characters and actions of men in a wrong place. Alexander the Great was so inflamed with false notions of glory, by reading the story of Achilles, in the Iliad, that after having taken a town, he ordered the governor, who had made a gallant defence, to be bound by the feet to his chariot, and afterwards dragged the brave man round the city because Hector had been treated in the same barbarous manner by his admired hero.

Many Englishmen have proved very pernicious to their own country, by following blindly the examples of persons to be met with in Greek and Roman history, who acted in conformity with their own governments, after a quite different manner, than they would have acted in a constitution like that of ours. Such a method of proceeding is as unreasonable in a politician, as it would be in a husbandman to make use of Virgil's precepts of agriculture, in managing the soil of our country, that lies in a quite different climate, and under the influence of almost another sun.

Our regicides, in the commission of the most execrable murder, used to justify themselves from the conduct of Brutus, not considering that Cæsar, from the condition of a fellow-citizen, had risen by the most indirect methods, and broken through all the laws of the community, to place himself at the head of the government, and enslave his country. On the other side, several of our English readers, having observed that a passive and unlimited obedience was paid to Roman emperors, who were possessed of the whole legislative, as well as executive power, have formerly endeavoured to inculcate the same kind of obedience, where there is not the same kind of authority.

Instructions, therefore to be learned from histories of this nature, are only such as arise from particulars agreeablu to all communities, or from such as are common to our own constitution, and to that of which we read. A tenacious adherence to the rights and liberties transmitted from a wise and virtuous ancestry, public spirit, and a love of one's country, submission to established laws, impartial administrations of justice, a strict regard to national faith, with several other duties, which are the supports and ornaments of government in general, cannot be too much admired among the states of Greece and Rome, nor too much imitated by our own community.

But there is nothing more absurd, than for men who are conversant in these ancient authors, to contract such a prejudice in favour of Greeks and Romans, as to fancy we are in the wrong in every circumstance whereby we deviate from their moral or political conduct. Yet nothing hath been more usual, than for men of warm heads to refine themselves up into this kind of state-pedantry: like the country school-master, who, being used for many years to admire Jupiter, Mars, Bacchus, and Apollo, that appear with so much advantage in classic authors, made an attempt to revive the worship of the heathen gods. In short, we find many worthy gentlemen, whose brains have been as much turned by this kind of reading, as the grave knight's of Mancha were by his unwearied application to books of knight-errantry.

To prevent such mischiefs from arising out of studies, which, when rightly conducted, may turn very much to our advantage, I shall venture to assert, that in our perusal of Greek or Roman authors, it is impossible to find a religious or civil constitution, any way comparable to that which we enjoy in our own country. Had not our religion been infinitely preferable to that of the ancient heathens, it would never have made its way through Paganism, with that amazing progress and activity. Its victories were the victories of reason, unassisted by the force of human power, and as gentle as the triumphs of light over darkness. The sudden reformation which it made among mankind, and which was so justly and frequently boasted of by the first apologists for Christianity, shews how infinitely preferable it is to any system of religion that prevailed in the world before its appearance. The pre-eminence of Christianity to any other general religious scheme which preceded it appears likewise from this particular, that the most eminent and the most enlightened among the Pagan philosophers disclaimed many of those superstitious follies, which are condemned by revealed religion, and preached up several of those doctrines which are some of the most essential parts of it.

And here I cannot but take notice of that strange motive which is made use of in the history of free-thinking, to incline us to depart from the revealed doctrines of Christianity, as adhered to by the people of Great Britain, because Socrates, with several other eminent Greeks, and Cicero, with many other learned Romans, did in the like manner depart from the religious notions of their own countrymen. Now this author should have considered, that those very points, in which these wise men disagreed from the bulk of the people, are points in which they agreed with the received doctrines of our nation. Their free-thinking consisted in asserting the unity and immateriality of the Godhead, the immortality of the soul, a state of future rewards and punishments, and the necessity of virtue, exclusive of all silly and superstitious practices, to procure the happiness of a separate state. They were, therefore, only free-thinkers, so far forth as they approached to the doctrines of Christianity, that is, to those very doctrines which this kind of authors would persuade us, as free-thinkers, to doubt the truth of. Now I would appeal to any reasonable person, whether these great men should not have been proposed to our imitation, rather as they embraced these divine truths, than only upon the account of their breaking loose from the common notions of their fellow-citizens. But this would disappoint the general tendency of such writings.

I shall only add under this head, that as Christianity recovered the law of nature out of all those errors and corruptions, with which it is overgrown in the times of Paganism,[a] our national religion has restored Christianity itself to that purity and

[a] It is overgrown in *the times* of Paganism, *i. e.* in times *past:* he should, therefore, have said—it *was* overgrown.

simplicity in which it appeared, before it was gradually disguised and lost among the vanities and superstitions of the Romish church.

That our civil constitution is preferable to any among the Greeks or Romans, may appear from this single consideration; that the greatest theorists in matters of this nature, among those very people, have given the preference to such a form of government, as that which obtains in this kingdom, above any other form whatsoever. I shall mention Aristotle, Polybius, and Cicero, that is, the greatest philosopher, the most impartial historian, and the most consummate statesman of all antiquity. These famous authors give the pre-eminence to a mixed government, consisting of three branches, the regal, the noble, and the popular. It would be very easy to prove, not only the reasonableness of this position, but to shew, that there was never any constitution among the Greeks or Romans, in which these three branches were so well distinguished from each other, invested with such suitable proportions of power, and concurred together in the legislature, that is, in the most sovereign acts of government, with such a necessary consent and harmony, as are to be met with in the constitution of this kingdom. But I have observed, in a foregoing paper, how defective the Roman commonwealth was in this particular, when compared with our own form of government, and it will not be difficult for the reader, upon singling out any other ancient state, to find how far it will suffer in the parallel.

## No. 52. MONDAY, JUNE 18.

An tu populum Romanum esse illum putas qui constat ex iis, qui mercede conducuntur? qui impelluntur, ut vim afferant magistratibus? ut obsideant senatum? optent quotidie cædem, incendia, rapinas? quem tu tamen populum nisi tabernis clausis, frequentare non poteras: cui populo duces Ventidios, Lollios, Sergios, præfeceras. O speciem, dignitatemque populi Romani, quam Reges, quam nationes exteræ, quam gentes ultimæ pertimescunt; multitudinem hominum ex servis conductis, ex facinorosis, ex egentibus congregatam!—CICER.

THERE is in all governments a certain temper of mind, natural to the patriots and lovers of their constitution, which may be called state-jealousy. It is this which makes them apprehensive of every tendency in the people, or in any particular member of the community, to endanger or disturb that form of rule, which is established by the laws and customs of their country. This political jealousy is absolutely requisite in some degree for the preservation of a government, and very reasonable in persons who are persuaded of the excellency of their constitution, and believe that they derive from it the most valuable blessings of society.

This public-spirited passion is more strong and active under some governments than others. The commonwealth of Venice, which hath subsisted by it for near fourteen hundred years, is so jealous of all its members, that it keeps continual spies upon their actions; and if any one of them presume to censure the established plan of that republic, or touch upon any of its fundamentals, he is brought before a secret council of state, tried in a most rigorous manner, and put to death without mercy. The usual way of proceeding with persons who discover themselves unsatisfied with the title of their sovereign in despotic governments, is to confine the malecontent, if his crimes are not capital, to some castle or dungeon for life. There is, indeed, no constitution so tame and careless of their own defence, where any person dares to give the least sign or intimation of being a traitor in his heart.[a] Our English history furnishes us with many examples of great severities during the disputes between the houses of York and Lancaster, inflicted on such persons as shewed their disaffection to the prince who was on the throne. Every one knows, that a factious inn-keeper, in the reign of Henry the seventh, was hanged, drawn, and quartered, for a saucy pun, which reflected, in a very dark and distant manner, upon the title of that prince to the crown. I do not mention the practice of other governments, as what should be imitated in ours, which, God be thanked, affords us all the reasonable liberty of speech and action, suited to a free people; nor do I take notice of this last instance of severity in our own country, to justify such a proceeding, but only to display the mildness and forbearance made use of under the reign of his present Majesty. It may, however, turn to the advantage of those, who have been instrumental in stirring up the late tumults and seditions among the people, to consider the treatment which such a lawless ungoverned rabble would have met with in any other country, and under any other sovereign.

These incendiaries have had the art to work up into the most unnatural ferments, the most heavy and stupid part of the community; and, if I may use a fine saying of Terence upon another occasion, 'to convert fools into madmen.' This frenzy hath been raised among them to such a degree, that it has lately discovered itself in a sedition which is without a parallel. They have had the fool-hardiness to set a mark upon themselves on the Pretender's birth-day, as the declared friends to his cause, and professed enemies to their king and country. How fatal would such a distinction, of which every one knew the meaning, have proved in

[a] This whole sentence is expressed very inaccurately. It might have been given thus—*There is, indeed, no constitution so tame and careless of its defence, as to permit that any person should dare to give*, &c.

former reigns, when many a circumstance of less significancy has been construed into an overt act of high treason! This unexampled piece of insolence will appear under its just aggravations, if we consider in the first place, that it was aimed personally at the king.

I do not remember among any of our popular commotions, when marks of this nature have been in fashion, that either side were so void of common sense, as to intimate by them an aversion to their sovereign. His person was still held as sacred by both parties. The contention was not who should be the monarch over them, but whose scheme of policy should take place in his administration. This was the conduct of whigs and tories under King Charles the second's reign, when men hung out their principles in different coloured ribbons. Nay, in the times of the great rebellion, the avowed disaffection of the people always terminated in evil counsellors. Such an open outrage upon Majesty, such an ostentation of disloyalty, was reserved for that infamous rabble of Englishmen, who may be justly looked upon as the scandal of the present age, and the most shameless and abandoned race of men that our nation has yet produced.

In the next place. It is very peculiar to this mob of malecontents, that they did not only distinguish themselves against their king, but against a king possessed of all the power of the nation, and one who had so very lately crushed all those of the same principles, that had bravery enough to avow them in the field of battle. Whenever was there an instance of a king who was not contemptible for his weakness, and want of power to resent, insulted by a few of his unarmed dastard subjects.

It is plain, from this single consideration, that such a base ungenerous race of men could rely upon nothing for their safety in this affront to his Majesty, but the known gentleness and lenity of his government. Instead of being deterred by knowing that he had in his hands the power to punish them, they were encouraged by knowing that he had not the inclination. In a word, they presumed upon that mercy, which in all their conversations they endeavour to depreciate and misrepresent.

It is a very sensible concern to every one, who has a true and unfeigned respect of our national religion, to hear these vile miscreants calling themselves sons of the church of England, amidst such impious tumults and disorders; and joining in the cry of high-church, at the same time that they bear a badge, which implies their inclination to destroy the reformed religion. Their concern for the church always rises highest, when they are acting in direct opposition to its doctrines. Our streets are filled at the same time with zeal and drunkenness, riots and religion. We must confess, if noise and clamour, slander and calumny, treason and perjury, were articles of their communion, there would be none living more punctual in the performance of their duties; but if a peaceable behaviour, a love of truth, and a submission to superiors, are the genuine marks of our profession, we ought to be very heartily ashamed of such a profligate brotherhood. Or if we will still think and own these men to be true sons of the church of England, I dare say there is no church in Europe which will envy her the glory of such disciples. But it is to be hoped we are not so fond of party, as to look upon a man, because he is a bad Christian, to be a good church of England man.

## No. 53. FRIDAY, JUNE 22.

———Bellua Centiceps.—Hor.

There is scarce any man in England, of what denomination soever, that is not a free thinker in politics, and hath not some particular notions of his own, by which he distinguishes himself from the rest of the community. Our island, which was formerly called a nation of saints, may now be called a nation of statesmen. Almost every age, profession, and sex among us, has its favourite set of ministers, and scheme of government.

Our children are initiated into factions before they know their right hand from their left. They no sooner begin to speak, but whig and tory are the first words they learn. They are taught in their infancy to hate one half of the nation; and contract all the virulence and passion of a party, before they come to the use of their reason.

As for our nobility, they are politicians by birth; and though the commons of the nation delegate their power in the community to certain representatives, every one reserves to himself a private jurisdiction, or privilege, of censuring their conduct, and rectifying the legislature. There is scarce a fresh man in either university, who is not able to mend the constitution in several particulars. We see 'squires and yeomen coming up to town every day, so full of politics, that, to use the thought of an ingenious gentleman, we are frequently put in mind of Roman dictators, who were called from the plough. I have often heard of a senior alderman in Buckinghamshire, who, at all public meetings, grows drunk in praise of aristocracy, and is as often encountered by an old justice of the peace who lives in the neighbourhood, and will talk you from morning till night on the Gothic balance. Who hath not observed several parish clerks, that have ransacked Hopkins and Sternhold for staves in favour of the race of Jacob; after the example of their politic predecessors in Oliver's days, who, on every Sabbath were for binding kings in chains, and nobles in links of iron! You can scarce see a bench of porters without two or three casuists in it, that will settle you the right of princes, and state the bounds of the civil and ecclesiastical power, in the drinking of a pot of ale. What is more usual than on a rejoicing night to meet with a drunken cobler bawling out for the church, and perhaps knocked down a little after, by an enemy in his own profession, who is a lover of moderation!

We have taken notice in former papers of this political ferment being got into the female sex, and of the wild work it makes among them. We have had a late most remarkable instance of it in a contest between a sister of the white rose, and a beautiful and loyal young lady, who, to shew her zeal for revolution-principles, had adorned her pretty bosom with a sweet-william. The rabble of the sex have not been ashamed very lately to gather about bonfires, and scream out their principles in the public streets. In short, there is hardly a female in this our metropolis, who is not a competent judge of our highest controversies in church and state. We have several oyster-women that hold the unlawfulness of episcopacy; and cinder wenches that are great sticklers for indefeasible right.

Of all the ways and means by which this political humour hath been propagated among the people of Great Britain, I cannot single out any so prevalent and universal, as the late constant application of the press to the publishing of state-matters. We hear of several that are newly erected in the country, and set apart for this particular use. For, it seems, the people of Exeter, Salisbury, and other large towns, are resolved[a] to be as

[a] What was only then *resolved* in one or two of our chief cities, is now executed in almost every great town of the kingdom. I write this in 1770

great politicians as the inhabitants of London and Westminster and deal out such news of their own printing, as is best suited to the genius of the market-people, and the taste of the county.

One cannot but be sorry, for the sake of these places, that such a pernicious machine is erected among them; for it is very well known here, that the making of the politician is the breaking of the tradesman. When a citizen turns a Machiavel, he grows too cunning to mind his own business; and I have heard a curious observation, that the woollen manufacture has of late years decayed in proportion as the paper manufacture has increased. Whether the one may not properly be looked upon as the occasion of the other, I shall leave to the judgment of persons more profound in political inquiries.

As our news writers record many facts which, to use their own phrase, 'afford great matter of speculation,' their readers speculate accordingly, and by their variety of conjectures, in a few years become consummate statesmen; besides, as their papers are filled with a different party-spirit, they naturally divide the people into different sentiments, who generally consider rather the principles, than the truth of the news-writer. This humour prevails to such a degree, that there are several well-meaning persons in the nation, who have been so misled by their favourite authors of this kind, that in the present contention between the Turk and the emperor, they are gone over insensibly from the interests of Christianity, and become well-wishers to the Mahometan cause. In a word, almost every news-writer has his sect, which (considering the natural genius of our countrymen to mix, vary, or refine, in notions of state) furnishes every man, by degrees, with a particular system of policy. For, however any one may concur in the general scheme of his party, it is still with certain reserves and deviations, and with a salvo to his own private judgment.

Among this innumerable herd of politicians, I cannot but take notice of one set, who do not seem to play fair with the rest of the fraternity, and make a very considerable class of men. These are such as we may call the Afterwise, who, when any project fails, or hath not had its desired effect, foresaw all the inconveniences that would arise from it, though they kept their thoughts to themselves till they discovered the issue. Nay, there is nothing more usual than for some of these wise men, who applauded public measures, before they were put in execution, to condemn them upon their proving unsuccessful. The dictators in coffee-houses are generally of this rank, who often give shrewd intimations that things would have taken another turn, had they been members of the cabinet.

How difficult must it be for any form of government to continue undisturbed, or any ruler to be uncensured, where every one of the community is thus qualified for modelling the constitution, and is so good a judge in matters of state! A famous French wit, to shew how the monarch of that nation, who has no partners in his sovereignty, is better able to make his way through all the difficulties of government, than an emperor of Germany, who acts in concert with many inferior fellow-sovereigns; compares the first to a serpent with many tails to one head; and the other to a serpent with one tail to many heads: and puts the question, which of them is like to glide with most ease and activity through a thicket? The same comparison will hold in the business of a nation conducted by a ministry, or a whole kingdom of politicians.

## No. 54. MONDAY, JUNE 25.

> ———————Tu, nisi ventis
> Debes ludibrium, cave.
> Nuper solicitum quæ mihi tædium,
> Nunc desiderium, curaque non levis. Hor.

The general division of the British nation is into whigs and tories, there being very few, if any, who stand neuters in the dispute, without ranging themselves under one of these denominations. One would, therefore, be apt to think, that every member of the community, who embraces with vehemence the principles of either of these parties, had thoroughly sifted and examined them, and was secretly convinced of their preference to those of that party which he rejects. And yet it is certain, that most of our fellow-subjects are guided in this particular, either by the prejudice of education, private interest, personal friendships, or a deference to the judgment of those, who perhaps, in their own hearts, disapprove the opinions which they industriously spread among the multitude. Nay, there is nothing more undoubtedly true, than that great numbers of one side concur in reality with the notions of those whom they oppose, were they able to explain their implict sentiments, and to tell their own meaning.

However, as it becomes every reasonable man to examine those principles by which he acts, I shall in this paper select some considerations, out of many, that might be insisted on, to shew the preference of what is generally called the whig-scheme, to that which is espoused by the tories.

This will appear in the first place, if we reflect upon the tendency of their respective principles, supposing them carried to their utmost extremity. For if, in this case, the worst consequences of the one are more eligible than the worst consequences of the other, it is a plain argument, that those principles are the most eligible of the two, whose effects are the least pernicious

Now the tendency of these two different sets of principles, as they are charged upon each party by its antagonists, is as follows. The stories tell us, that the whig-scheme would end in Presbyterianism and a commonwealth. The whigs tell us, on the other side, that the tory-scheme would terminate in Popery and arbitrary government. Were these reproaches mutually true; which would be most preferable[a] to any man of common sense, Presbyterianism and a republican form of government, or Popery and tyranny? Both extremes are indeed dreadful, but not equally so; both to be regarded with the utmost aversion by the friends of our constitution, and lovers of our country: but if one of them were inevitable, who would not rather chuse to live under a state of excessive liberty, than of slavery, and not prefer a religion that differs from our own in the circumstantials, before one that differs from it in the essentials of Christianity!

Secondly, let us look into the history of England, and see under which of these two schemes the nation has enjoyed most honour and prosperity. If we observe the reigns of Queen Elizabeth and King James the first[b] (which an impudent Frenchman calls the reigns of King Elizabeth and Queen James) we find the whig-scheme took place under the first, and the tory-scheme under the latter. The first, in whom the whigs have always gloried, opposed and humbled the most powerful among the Roman Catholic princes; raised and supported the Dutch; assisted the French Protestants; and made the reformed religion an overbalance for Popery through all Europe. On the contrary, her successor aggrandized the Catholic King; alienated himself from the Dutch; suffered the French power to increase,

[a] *Most preferable. Preferable* is equivalent to the comparative degree. So that *most preferable* is a solecism, and the same thing as—*most welcomer.*

[b] The author is pleasant in making a whig of Queen Elizabeth. But he thought it allowable, in so good a cause, to make use of a little sophistry.

till it was too late to remedy it; and abandoned the interests of the king of Bohemia, grand-father to his present Majesty, which might have spread the reformed religion through all Germany. I need not describe to the reader the different state of the kingdom as to its reputation, trade, and wealth, under these two reigns. We might, after this, compare the figure in which these kingdoms, and the whole Protestant interest of Europe, were placed by the conduct of King Charles the second, and that of King William;[a] and every one knows which of the schemes prevailed in each of those reigns. I shall not impute to any tory-scheme the administration of King James the second, on condition that they do not reproach the whigs with the usurpation of Oliver; as being satisfied that the principles of those governments are respectively disclaimed and abhorred by all the men of sense and virtue in both parties, as they now stand. But we have a fresh instance which will be remembered with grief by the present age and all our posterity, of the influence both of whig and tory principles in the late reign. Was England ever so glorious in the eyes of Europe, as in that part of it when the first prevailed? or was it ever more contemptible than when the last took place?

I shall add, under this head, the preference of the whig-scheme with regard to foreigners. All the Protestant states of Europe, who may be considered as neutral judges between both parties and are well-wishers to us in general, as to a Protestant people, rejoice upon the success of a whig-scheme; whilst all of the church of Rome, who contemn, hate, and detest us as the great bulwark of heresy, are as much pleased when the opposite party triumphs in its turn. And here let any impartial man put this question to his own heart, whether that party doth not act reasonably, who look upon the Dutch as their genuine friends and

[a] This instance is to the purpose.

allies, considering that they are of the reformed religion, that they have assisted us in the greatest times of necessity, and that they can never entertain a thought of reducing us under their power. Or, on the other hand, let him consider whether that party acts with more reason, who are the avowed friends of a nation, that are of the Roman Catholic religion, that have cruelly persecuted our brethren of the reformation, that have made attempts in all ages to conquer this island, and supported the interest of that prince, who abdicated the throne, and had endeavoured to subvert our civil and religious liberties.

Thirdly, Let us compare these two schemes from the effects they produce among ourselves within our own island; and these we may consider, first with regard to the king, and secondly with regard to the people.

First, With regard to the king. The whigs have always professed and practised an obedience which they conceive agreeable to the constitution; whereas the tories have concurred with the whigs in their practice, though they differ from them in their professions; and have avowed a principle of passive-obedience to the temptation, and afterwards to the destruction, of those who have relied upon it. Nor must I here omit to take notice of that firm and zealous adherence which the whig-party have shewn to the Protestant succession, and to the cause of his present Majesty. I have never heard of any in this principle, who was either guilty or suspected of measures to defeat this establishment, or to overturn it, since it has taken effect. A consideration, which, it is hoped, may put to silence those who upbraid the whig-schemes of government, with an inclination to a commonwealth, or a disaffection to kings.

Secondly, With regard to the people. Every one must own, that those laws which have most conduced to the ease and happiness of the subject, have always passed in those parliaments, which their enemies branded with the name of whig, and during the time of a whig-ministry. And, what is very remarkable, the tories are now forced to have recourse to those laws for shelter and protection: by which they tacitly do honour to the whig-scheme, and own it more accommodated to the happiness of the people, than that which they espouse.

I hope I need not qualify these remarks with a supposition which I have gone upon through the whole course of my papers, that I am far from considering a great part of those who call themselves tories, as enemies to the present establishment; and that by the whigs I always mean those who are friends to our constitution both in church and state. As we may look upon these to be, in the main, true lovers of their religion and country, they seem rather to be divided by accidental friendships and circumstances, than by any essential distinction.

---

## No. 55. FRIDAY, JUNE 29.

——— cæstus artemque repono.—Virg.

A rising of parliament being a kind of cessation from politics, the Freeholder cannot let his paper drop at a more proper juncture. I would not be accessary to the continuing of our political ferment, when occasions of dispute are not administered to us by matters depending before the legislature; and when debates without doors naturally fall with those in the two houses of parliament. At the same time a British Freeholder would very ill discharge his part, if he did not acknowledge, with becoming duty and gratitude, the excellency and seasonableness of those laws, by which the representatives of men in his rank have recovered their country in a great measure out of its confusions, and provided for its future peace and happiness under the present establishment. Their unanimous and regular proceeding, under the conduct of that honourable person who fills their chair with the most consummate abilities, and hath justly gained the esteem of all sides by the impartiality of his behaviour; the absolute necessity of some acts which they have passed, and their dis-inclination to extend them any longer,[a] than that necessity required; their manifest aversion to enter upon schemes, which the enemies of our peace had insinuated to have been[b] their design; together with that temper so suitable to the dignity of such an assembly, at a juncture when it might have been expected that very unusual heats would have arisen[c] in a House of Commons, so zealous for their king and country; will be sufficient to quiet those groundless jealousies and suspicions, which have been industriously propagated by the ill-wishers to our constitution.

The undertaking, which I am now laying down, was entered upon in the very crisis of the late rebellion, when it was the duty of every Briton to contribute his utmost assistance to the government, in a manner suitable to his station and abilities. All services, which had a tendency to this end, had a degree of merit in them, in proportion as the event of that cause which they espoused was then doubtful. But at present they might be regarded, not as duties of private men to their endangered country, but as insults of the successful over their defeated enemies.

Our nation indeed continues to be agitated with confusions and tumults; but, God be thanked, these are only the impotent

[a] *Extend longer.* He should either have said—*extend them any farther*, or *continue them any longer.*

[b] *Had insinuated to have been*, rather, *had insinuated to be.* But, the expression, at best, is somewhat awkward. I should have said, "*which the enemies of our peace had charged them with projecting.*"

[c] *It might have been expected* that very unusual heats *would have arisen.* Certainly, *would arise.*

remains of an unnatural rebellion, and are no more than the after-tossings of a sea when the storm is laid. The enemies of his present Majesty, instead of seeing him driven from his throne, as they vainly hoped, find him in a condition to visit his dominions in Germany, without any danger to himself or to the public; whilst his dutiful subjects would be in no ordinary concern upon this occasion, had they not the consolation to find themselves left under the protection of a prince, who makes it his ambition to copy out his royal father's example; and who, by his duty to his Majesty, and affection to his people, is so well qualified to be the guardian of the realm.

It would not be difficult to continue a paper of this kind, if one were disposed to resume the same subjects, and weary out the reader with the same thoughts in a different phrase, or to ramble through the cause of whig and tory, without any certain aim or method, in every particular discourse. Such a practice in political writers, is like that of some preachers taken notice of by Dr. South, who being prepared only upon two or three points of doctrine, run the same round with their audience from one end of the year to the other, and are always forced to tell them, by way of preface, These are particulars of so great importance, that they cannot be sufficiently inculcated. To avoid this method of tautology, I have endeavoured to make every paper a distinct essay upon some particular subject, without deviating into points foreign to the tenor of each discourse. They are, indeed, most of them essays upon government, but with a view to the present situation of affairs in Great Britain; so that if they have the good fortune[a] to live longer than works of this

[a] They have had, and will continue to have, *this good fortune;* not so much for their own intrinsic merit (though it be considerable) as for the high reputation which the author of them had so justly acquired to himself, by his other works. It follows, that if a writer would *live,* he should only, or chiefly, treat subjects of a general concern.

nature generally do, future readers may see in them the complexion of the times in which they were written. However, as there is no employment so irksome, as that of transcribing out of one's self, next to that of transcribing out of others, I shall let drop the work, since there do not occur to me any material points arising from our present situation, which I have not already touched upon.

As to the reasonings in these several papers, I must leave them to the judgment of others. I have taken particular care that they should be conformable to our constitution, and free from that mixture of violence and passion, which so often creeps into the works of political writers. A good cause doth not want any bitterness to support it, as a bad one cannot subsist without it. It is indeed observable, that an author is scurrilous in proportion as he is dull; and seems rather to be in a passion, because he cannot find out what to say for his own opinion, than because he has discovered any pernicious absurdities in that of his antagonists. A man satirized by writers of this class, is like one burnt in the hand with a cold iron: there may be ignominious terms and words of infamy in the stamp, but they leave no impression behind them.

It would indeed have been an unpardonable insolence for a fellow-subject to treat in a vindictive and cruel style, those persons whom his Majesty has endeavoured to reduce to obedience by gentle methods, which he has declared from the throne to be most agreeable to his inclinations. May we not hope that all of this kind, who have the least sentiments of honour or gratitude, will be won over to their duty by so many instances of royal clemency, in the midst of so many repeated provocations! May we not expect that Cicero's words to Cæsar, in which he speaks of those who were Cæsar's enemies, and of his conduct towards them, may be applied to his majesty; Omnes enim qui fuerunt, aut suâ pertinaciâ vitam amiserunt, aut tuâ misericordiâ retinuerunt; ut aut nulli supersint de inimicis, aut qui superfuerunt, amicissimi sint.—Quare gaude tuo isto tam excellenti bono, et fruere cum fortunâ, et gloriâ, tum etiam naturâ, et moribus tuis. Ex quo quidem maximus est fructus, jucunditasque sapienti—Nihil habet nec fortuna tua majus, quam ut possis, nec natura tua melius, quam ut velis, quamplurimos conservare.

As for those papers of a gayer turn, which may be met with in this collection, my reader will of himself, consider, how requisite they are to gain and keep up an audience to matters of this nature; and will perhaps be the more indulgent to them, if he observes, that they are none of them without a moral, nor contain any thing but what is consistent with decency and good manners.

It is obvious that the design of the whole work, has been to free the people's minds from those prejudices conveyed into them, by the enemies to the present establishment, against the king and royal family, by opening and explaining their real characters; to set forth his Majesty's proceedings, which have been very grossly misrepresented, in a fair and impartial light; to shew the reasonableness and necessity of our opposing the Pretender to his dominions, if we have any regard to our religion and liberties: and, in a word, to incline the minds of the people to the desire and enjoyment of their own happiness. There is no question, humanly speaking, but these great ends will be brought about insensibly, as men will grow weary of a fruitless opposition; and be convinced by experience, of a necessity to acquiesce under a government which daily gathers strength, and is able to disappoint the utmost efforts of its enemies. In the meanwhile, I would recommend to our malecontents, the advice given by a great moralist to his friend upon another occasion; that he would shew it was in the power of wisdom to compose his passions; and let that be the work of reason which would certainly be the effect of time.

I shall only add, that if any writer shall do this paper so much honour, as to inscribe[a] the title of it to others, which may be published upon the laying down of this work; the whole praise or dispraise of such a performance, will belong to some other author; this fifty-fifth being the last paper that will come from the hand of the Freeholder.

[a] *Inscribe to*—We say—*ascribe to*—but, *inscribe on*.

## NOTES ON ADDISON'S FREEHOLDER.

"THE Freeholder, it must be remembered, was a kind of political Spectator, published periodically, with the purpose of reconciling the people of England to the accession of the House of Hanover. These papers, while they exhibit the exquisite humour and solid sense peculiar to the author, shew also, even amid the strength of party, that philanthropy and gentleness of nature, which were equally his distinguishing attributes. None of these qualities would have conciliated his great opponent Swift, had the field of combat yet remained open to him. But as he withdrew from it in sullen indignation, he seems to have thrown out the following flashes of satire, as brief examples of what he would have done had the hour of answer been yet current."—SCOTT.

---

The following MS. Notes were transcribed from the original, in Swift's own hand, in Addison's Freeholder, which belonged to Dr. Bernard, late Bishop of Limerick.

### FREEHOLDER, No. 2.—*Character of George I.*

"IT was by this (this firmness of mind) that he surmounted those many difficulties which lay in the way to his succession."—What difficulties were those, or what methods did he take to surmount them? Swift.

"It is observed by Sir William Temple, that the English are particularly fond of a king who is valiant: upon which account his majesty has a title to all the esteem that can be paid to a most warlike prince; though, at the same time, for the good of his subjects, he studies to decline all occasions of military glory."—This seems to be a discovery. S.

"I might here take notice of his majesty's more private virtues, but have rather chosen to remind my countrymen of the public parts of his character."—This is prudent. S.

"But the most remarkable interpositions of Providence in favour of him, have appeared in removing those seemingly invincible obstacles to his succession; in taking away, at so critical a juncture, the person who might have proved a dangerous enemy, &c."—False, groundless, invidious, and ungrateful. Was that person the queen? S.

No. 3.—*Ludicrous Account of the Principles of the Northumberland Insurgents, and the Causes of their taking Arms.*—Could this author, or his party, offer as good reasons for their infamous treatment of our blessed queen's person, government, and majesty? S.

The same. "Having been joined by a considerable reinforcement of Roman Catholics, whom we could rely upon, as knowing them to be the best Tories in the nation, and avowed enemies to Presbyterianism."—By this irony, the best Whigs are professed friends to fanatics. S.

The same. "But before we could give the word, the trainbands, taking advantage of our delay, fled first."—An argument for a standing army. S.

No. 6.—*On the Oath of Allegiance.*—"Though I should be unwilling to pronounce the man who is indolent or indifferent in the cause of his prince, to be absolutely perjured, I may venture to affirm, that he falls very short of that allegiance to which he is obliged by oath."—Suppose a king grows a beast, or a tyrant, after I have taken an oath: a 'prentice takes an oath; but, if his master useth him barbarously, the lad may be excused if he wishes for a better. S.

No. 7. "If we may credit common report, there are several remote parts of the nation in which it is firmly believed, that all the churches in London are shut up, and that if any clergyman walks the streets in his habit, it is ten to one but he is knocked down by some sturdy schismatic."—No—but treated like a dog. S.

No. 8.—*Exhortation to the Ladies to be loyal to George I.*—"It is to be hoped that every fine woman will make this laudable use of her charms; and that she may not want to be frequently reminded of this great duty, I will only desire her to think of her country every time she looks in her glass."—By no means, for if she loves her country, she will not be pleased with a man the sight. S.

"Every wife ought to answer for her man. If the husband be engaged in a seditious club, or drinks mysterious healths, let her look to him," &c.—Will they hang a man for that? S.

No. 9.—*Declaration of the Freeholders, in Answer to that of the Pretender.*—"Can you in conscience think us to be such fools as to rebel against the king—for having removed a general, (*the Duke of Ormond*,) who is now actually in arms against him?"—Driven out by tyranny, malice, and faction. S.

"The next grievance which you have a mighty mind to redress among us, is, the Parliament of Great Britain, against whom you bring a stale accusation, which has been used by every minority in the memory of man; namely, that it was procured by unwarrantable influences and corruptions."—The freeholders will never sign this paragraph. S.

"How comes it to pass that the Electorate of Hanover is become all of a sudden one of the most considerable provinces of the empire?"—It is indeed grown considerable by draining o' England. S.

No. 12.—*On Rebellions.*—"The present rebellion (1715) is

formed against a king, who has not been charged with one illegal proceeding."—Are you serious? S.

No. 13. "In such a juncture, (a rebellion,) though a man may be innocent of the great breach which is made upon government, he is highly culpable, if he does not use all the means that are suitable to his station for reducing the community into its former state of peace and good order."—He speaks at his ease, but those who are ill used will be apt to apply what the boy said to his mother, who told him the enemy was approaching. S.

"The law (in Athens) made it necessary for every citizen to take his party, because it was highly probable the majority would espouse that cause, which was most agreeable to the public weal." —No—for, in England, a faction that governs a weak, or honours a wicked prince, will carry all against a majority in the kingdom, as we have seen by sad experience. S.

No. 14.—*The Tory's Creed.*—"Article 13. That there is an unwarrantable faction in this island, consisting of King, Lords, and Commons."—This article is too true, with a little alteration.

The same. "Article 15. That an act of parliament to empower the king to secure suspected persons in times of rebellion, is the means to establish the sovereign on the throne, and consequently a great infringement of the liberties of the subject."—No—but to destroy liberty. S.

No. 21.—*On the Princess of Wales.*—"When this excellent princess was in her father's court, she was so celebrated for the beauty of her person," &c.—I have bad eyes. S.

"There is no part of her royal highness's character which we observe with greater pleasure, than that behaviour by which she has so much endeared herself to his majesty."—What would he say now? S.*

* The prince and his father, Georg I. were now at variance.

No. 24. "To this, we may add, that submissive deference of his royal highness, both from duty and inclination, to all the measures of his royal father."—Which still continues. S.

"There is no question but his majesty will be as generally valued and beloved in his British, as he is in his German dominions, when he shall have time to make his royal virtues equally known among us."—How long time does he require? S.

"Several inconveniencies which those must undergo who have not yet surrendered to the government."—Would he pimp for the court? S.

No. 29. "Those of our fellow-subjects who are sensible of the happiness they enjoy in his majesty's accession to the throne, are obliged, by all the duties of gratitude, to adore that Providence which has so signally interposed in our behalf, by clearing a way to the Protestant succession through such difficulties as seemed insuperable."—I wish he had told us any one of those difficulties. S.

"It is the duty of an honest and prudent man to sacrifice a doubtful opinion to the concurring judgment of those whom he believes to be well intentioned to their country, and who have better opportunities of looking into all its most complicated interests."—A motion to make men go every length with their party. I am sorry to see such a principle in this author. S.

No. 31.—*On the Treatment of the Persons concerned in the Rebellion, in Answer to a Pamphlet, entitled* "*An Argument to prove the Affections of the People of England to be the best Security of the Government,*" *&c.*—"This middle method (of tempering justice with mercy) has hitherto been made use of by our sovereign."—In trifles. S.

"Would it be possible to imagine, that of the several thousands openly taken in arms, and liable to death by the laws of their country, not above forty have yet suffered?"—A trifle! S.

"Has not his majesty then shewn the least appearance of grace in that generous forgiveness which he has already extended to such great numbers of his rebellious subjects, who must have died by the laws of their country, had not his mercy interposed in their behalf?"—Prodigious clemency, not to hang all the common soldiers who followed their leaders! S.

"Those who are pardoned would not have known the value of grace, if none had felt the effects of justice."—And only hanging the lords and gentlemen, and some of the rabble. S.

"Their (the last ministry's) friends have ever since made use of the most base methods to infuse those groundless discontents into the minds of the common people," &c.—Hath experience shewn those discontents groundless? S.

"If the removal of these persons from their posts has produced such popular commotions, the continuance of them might have produced something much more fatal to their king and country."—Very false reasoning. S.

"No man would make such a parallel, (between the treatment of the rebels and that of the Catalans under King Philip,) unless his mind be so blinded with passion and prejudice, as to assert, in the language of this pamphlet, 'that no instances can be produced of the least lenity under the present administration, from the hour of its commencement to this day.'"—Nor to this, 1727. S.

"God be thanked, we have a king who punishes with reluctance."—A great comfort to the sufferers! S.

"It would be well if those who—are clamorous at the proceedings of his present majesty, would remember, that notwithstanding that rebellion, (the Duke of Monmouth's)—had no tendency to destroy the national religion," &c.—To introduce fanaticism, and destroy monarchy. S.

"No prince has ever given a greater instance of his inclina

tion to rule without a standing army."—We find this true by experience. S.

"What greater instances could his majesty have given of his love to the Church of England, than those he has exhibited by his most solemn declarations, by his daily example, and by his promotions of the most eminent among the clergy to such vacancies as have happened in his reign?"—Most undeniable truth, as any in Rabelais. S.

No. 44.—*The fox-hunter in London.*—"What still gave him greater offence, was a drunken bishop, who reeled from one side of the court to another, and was very sweet upon an Indian Queen."—Then, that story is true? S.

No. 45. "I have lately read, with much pleasure, the Essays upon several Subjects, published by Sir Richard Blackmore."—I admire to see such praises from this author to so insipid a scoundrel, whom I know he despised. S.

No 51. "History of Freethinking."—Writ by Collins. S.

"The greatest theorists among those very people, (the Greeks and Romans,) have given the preference to such a form of government as that which obtains in this kingdom."—Yet, this we see is liable to be wholly corrupted. S.

No. 52.—*On the Adherents to the Pretender.*—"It is plain, that such a base ungenerous race of men could rely upon nothing for their safety in this affront to his majesty, (wearing a mark on the Pretender's birth-day,) but the known gentleness and lenity of his government."—Then the devil was in them. S.

No. 54. "The Whigs tell us,—that the Tory scheme would terminate in Popery and arbitrary government."—But Tories never writ or spoke so gently and favourably of Popery, as Whigs do of Presbytery. Witness a thousand pamphlets on both sides.

"I shall not impute to any Tory scheme the administration

of King James the Second, on condition that they do not reproach the Whigs with the usurpation of Oliver."—I will not accept that condition, nor did I ever see so unfair a one offered. S.

No. 55. "The enemies of his majesty—find him in a condition to visit his dominions in Germany, without any danger to himself or to the public; whilst his dutiful subjects would be in no ordinary concern on this occasion, had they not the consolation to find themselves left under the protection of a prince, who makes it his ambition to copy out his royal father's example."—Then, why was he never trusted a second time?

"It would, indeed, have been an unpardonable insolence for a fellow-subject to treat in a vindictive and cruel style, those persons whom his majesty has endeavoured to reduce to obedience by gentle methods, which he has declared from the throne to be most agreeable to his inclinations."—And is that enough?

"May we not hope, that all of this kind, who have the least sentiments of honour or gratitude, will be won over to their duty by so many instances of royal clemency?"—Not one instance produced. S.

# THE PLEBEIAN,[a]

BY SIR RICHARD STEELE.

"Quisquis erit vitæ scribam color."—HOR. 2 Sat. i. 60.
I still must write, whatever be my doom.—DUNCOMBE.

# WITH THE OLD WHIG,[b]

BY MR. ADDISON.

---

## INTRODUCTORY REMARKS.

THE Plebeian and Old Whig have given rise to such contradictory and exaggerated statements, that it has been thought best to publish them together. That there was a coolness between Addison and Steele towards the close of Addison's life cannot be doubted: but Steele lived to mourn the friend of his boyhood, and bear the same unreserved testimony to his genius and virtue after his death, that he had invariably done during his life. Macaulay has corrected one of the current errors upon this subject, but has fallen into another scarcely less pardonable, and his account of the Plebeian and Old Whig is far from doing justice to Steele. The first accusation came from Addison (v. Old Whig. p. 299 *ad conflandam invidiam*), who in his second number has played off his satire as sharply upon his old friend, as he had ever done upon the Tories themselves in the Whig Examiner. I give the general history of the controversy in the words of Johnson:

*** "In 1718–19, a controversy was agitated, with great vehemence, between those friends of long continuance, ADDISON and STEELE. It may be asked, in the language of Homer, what power or what cause could set them

a Originally printed in quarto, price 6d. each number; and published by S. Popping, at the Black Raven, in Paternoster-Row, where Letters directed for the Plebeian were taken in.

b Originally published in quarto, price 6d. each number, by J. Roberts, in Warwick-Lane; and A. Dodd, at the Peacock, without Temple-Bar.

at variance. The subject of their dispute was of great importance. The earl of Sunderland proposed an act called the PEERAGE BILL, by which the number of peers should be fixed, and the king restrained from any new creation of nobility, unless when an old family should be extinct. To this the lords would naturally agree; and the king, who was yet little acquainted with his own prerogative, and, as is now well known, almost indifferent to the possessions of the crown, had been persuaded to consent. The only difficulty was found among the commons, who were not likely to approve the perpetual exclusion of themselves and their posterity. The bill therefore was eagerly opposed, and among others by Sir Robert Walpole, whose speech was published. The lords might think their dignity diminished by improper advancements, and particularly by the introduction of twelve new peers at once, to produce a majority of Tories in the last reign; an act of authority violent enough, yet certainly legal, and by no means to be compared with that contempt of national right, with which some time afterwards, by the instigation of Whiggism, the commons, chosen by the people for three years, chose themselves for seven. But, whatever might be the disposition of the lords, the people had no wish to increase their power. The tendency of the bill, as STEELE observed in a letter to the earl of Oxford, was to introduce an Aristocracy, for a majority in the house of lords, so limited, would have been despotic and irresistible. To prevent this subversion of the ancient establishment, STEELE, whose pen readily seconded his political passions, endeavoured to alarm the nation by a pamphlet called the PLEBEIAN. To this an answer was published by ADDISON under the title of the OLD WHIG, in which it is not discovered that STEELE was then known to be the advocate for the Commons. STEELE replied by a second PLEBEIAN; and, whether by ignorance or by courtesy, confined himself to his question, without any personal notice of his opponent. Nothing hitherto was committed against the laws of friendship, or proprieties of decency; but controvertists cannot long retain their kindness for each other. The OLD WHIG answered the PLEBEIAN, and could not forbear some contempt of *Little Dicky, whose trade it was to write pamphlets. Dicky* however did not lose his settled veneration for his friend; but contented himself with quoting some lines of Cato, which were at once detection and reproof. The bill was laid aside during that Session; and Addison died before the next, in which its commitment was rejected by two hundred sixty-five to one hundred seventy-seven. Every reader surely must regret that these two illustrious friends, after so many years past in confidence and endearment, in unity of interest, conformity of opinion, and fellowship of study, should finally part in acrimonious opposition. Such a controversy was *Bellum plusquam civile*, as Lucan expresses it. Why could not faction find other advocates? But, among the uncertainties of the human state, we are doomed to number the instability of friendship.

Of this dispute I have little knowledge but from the *Biographia Britannica.* The *Old Whig* is not inserted in Addison's works, nor is it mentioned by Tickell in his Life. Why it was omitted the biographers doubtless give the true reason: the fact was too recent, and those who had been heated in the contention were not yet cool.

In the text and notes the edition of 1789 by Nichols, which contains the original advertisements, has been followed, as giving the most faithful idea of the appearance of the original work, which has never before been included in the editions of Addison's writings.—G

# THE PLEBEIAN,

**BY A MEMBER OF THE HOUSE OF COMMONS.**

---

## No. 1. SATURDAY, MARCH 14, 1718–19.

CONSIDERATIONS UPON THE REPORTS RELATING TO THE PEERAGE.

"—Hoc miseræ Plebi—commune Sepulchrum."
HOR. I. Sat. viii. 10.

In this detested ground
A common tomb the vulgar found. FRANCIS.

ALL men in high stations have their enemies, who are ready to suggest on every occasion whatever may tend to lessen their credit, and make them odious to the public. The persons at present in great authority have been pursued by this Evil Spirit; but it would be unjust to give too easy belief to the insinuations of malicious people. At the beginning of this session it was reported with much assurance, that a wonderful discovery was made, that all the charters of England were forfeited into the hands of the Crown; and this happy incident, as they called it, was to afford an opportunity of introducing a law much for the public service. But this was so far from being true, that the bill which came down from the house of Peers was a confirmation of the charters, without so much as a declaration of any forfeiture. Perhaps it might have been true, that some little lawyer had found out some mean chicane in law, worthy enough of the pursuit of such a person, in a private corporation-squabble; but such a project in order to a universal forfeiture, could never have weight with any judicious man whatever. Nobody could be so very a novice in business, or so extravagant in politics, as to put his Majesty upon an undertaking, which contributed more towards the ruin of king James, than any one thing, or perhaps than every thing else besides. When this report was blown over, the next thing insinuated to the public was a design of making a jest of what justice has been accidently done to the nation, by repealing the attainder of one of the greatest offenders of the late reign. It is very certain no such attempt will be now made. There has been a just indignation shewn already at the bare mention of it, and it is unfair to charge any particular person with having had any such intention; much less should a scandalous discourse gain credit, that any great officer belonging to his Majesty would correspond abroad with an attainted fugitive, intercede for him at home, and even prostitute the character of an ambassador so low, as to become the messenger of a traitor. These two unjust accusations were laid at the door of some great people at the beginning, and towards the middle of this session; and now at the end of it, the public is alarmed at the report of another design of a more dangerous nature than either of those already mentioned. But as those former reports have not proved true, so I doubt not but this will likewise vanish in the same manner. However, as I was ready to have appeared in public on either of the former occasions, if there had been a necessity for it; so, if I am a little more forward in the present affair, I hope the importance of it will justify me: and if I should lose my labour, I shall however shew that good intention for the service of my Sovereign and my fellow-subjects with which I have always exposed myself at a dangerous crisis.

It is affirmed by some people, that a bill will be offered to the House of Commons, in which the present 16 Peers of Scotland are to be made hereditary, to the exclusion of their electors, and 9 more added upon the same foot; and 6 more are to be added to the number of English peers; and then the Crown is to be restrained from making any new Lords but upon the extinction of families.

At first sight, this proposal must appear very shocking; it carries with it so great an alteration of the constitution; it implies so direct a breach of the Union, and of natural justice; and encroaches so much upon the prerogative of the Crown.

As to what relates to the Scottish Peerage, I must confess I am at a loss to say any thing to it. If the most solemn contract betwixt two Nations is to be violated; if persons are to be deprived of their right without being heard, and without any pretence of forfeiture; if those, who have a power intrusted to them by their principals only for a few years, can seize it to themselves and their posterity for ever; what use will be made of power so acquired, I leave every one to judge.

The shutting up the door of the House of Lords, in the manner talked of, cannot but prove a great discouragement to virtuous actions, to learning and industry, and very detrimental to the House of Peers itself, by preventing such frequent supplies from going into it as the nature of such a body requires; for want of which it may in time become corrupt and offensive, like a stagnated pool, which hitherto has been preserved wholesome and pure by the fresh streams that pass continually into it.

I am not unaware that it will be said, *That the frequent extinctions of families will salve this inconvenience, and make room for the rewarding of Merit.* But this expedient, I fear, is not much to be depended on; for the uncertainty of the time when the Crown will have any such power, will make it much the same as if it was never to have it at all. Besides it is to be considered, that the patrons of this proposal argue vehemently for it, *on account, that this will be a means to ease the Crown from the great importunity of Pretenders to Peerage.* If so, it is certain in what manner they will proceed in all vacancies, which will be by filling them up instantly; or else the inconvenience would be increased as to importunity, and not diminished. This being the case, it is very evident by what sort of people those vacancies will be supplied; undoubtedly by the creatures and relations of those Peers who have at that time the greatest influence in the House, and whose requests to the Throne will very much resemble *demands;* and this honour, in all probability, will only be thought proper for their own families. An instance of this we have in the distinction of the Garter. At the first institution of that order, and till of late years, several Commoners had the honour (as the reward of merit) to be of that noble body; but at present it would be looked upon as a high presumption in any Commoner to pretend to it, let his services be never so great.

But another consequence, of a much higher nature, attending the limitation of the number of Peers, is the danger there will be of changing the Constitution by this means into an Aristocracy; and this may at any time in such case be effected by the confederacy of two or three great families, which would form such a body amongst the Lords as the Crown would not be able to controul. That this kind of government is one of the worst sorts of slavery, is too well known to be disputed. In a Democracy a great many different persons may come to have a share of power by several incidents; but in the other state it is birth only that entitles to superiority; and the milk such Nobles are nursed up with, is hatred and contempt for every human creature but those of their own imaginary dignity.

These being some of the inconveniences and hazards which naturally occur upon this proposal, let us see what are the advantages which on the other hand, it is said, will flow from it.

*First,* "That this will be a bar upon the Crown, and prevent the King upon the throne from flinging-in a great number of Lords on a sudden, only to answer a present purpose, as the late Queen once did."

*Secondly,* "That it will be a means to keep property or great estates in the House of Commons, from whence they are generally drawn out into the House of Peers."

These are said to be such plain whig-points, as no whig can oppose.

Whiggism, if I understand it aright, is a desire of liberty, and a spirit of opposition to all exorbitant power in any part of the constitution. Formerly the danger on this account was from the crown; but since the Habeas Corpus Act, and the many restraints laid upon the crown in King William's time, and the great and numerous limitations of the Succession Acts, the prerogative of the crown is reduced so low, that it is not at all dangerous to the Commons. Besides, the Crown has frequent occasions for the assistance of the Commons; but the Lords never. The Lords are judges of the property of the Commons in the last resort; and even in cases where they themselves are concerned, they have their actions *de Scandalis Magnatum*, and exercise a power of imprisoning, not confined within any very certain boundaries. And therefore the chief circumspection of the Commons ought to be employed at present, that those who have so much power already do not get more than the Commons will be able to withstand in any manner. I confess the making a great number of Lords on a sudden has one inconvenience: it may prevent some good to the public, but cannot do any great hurt, and is more grievous in its consequences to the Crown than to the People. The increasing the number of Peers is always to be wished for by the Commons, because the greater their number, the less considerable they become, and the less within the influence of Court favours; by which means alone ministers are kept in awe, and remain in a situation of being called to account for their actions. Were it otherwise, they would be out of the reach of any accusation. They would know exactly by whom they were to be tried, and their Judges might be their accomplices. And should this once come to be the case, what might they not attempt with impunity?

On the other hand, if their Lordships complain of the great number of Peers as a grievance to themselves, why are they desirous any more should be made? If twelve at once was so bad a precedent, what is fifteen, taking it in one light? what is thirty-one, if you take it in another?

If, at the Union, sixteen Scottish Noblemen were found to be a just proportion to represent their whole Nobility, what has happened since, to give reason to increase their number to twenty-five? Why may they not as well a few years hence, especially if the head of a clan is to be taken in, who may not like the set of Nobles at that time, demand to be made fifty, to give his followers the majority; and so from time to time continue to play the game into each other's hands, as long as there is one Nobleman left in Scotland, or any Civil List in England? If the Commoners of England are to be excluded from the House of Lords, why are they not excluded forthwith? It cannot be supposed that titles *in petto* are kept on purpose to bribe persons of consequence in the house of Commons, to drive such a bill through that part of the Legislature.

Upon the foot the Constitution has subsisted many years, the Crown, in all great emergencies relating immediately to itself, has been able to fence against the Lords by adding to their number, and against the Commons by dissolutions; and in like manner in cases of difference betwixt the two Houses. But if such a law as is mentioned above should be made, and any difference happen hereafter betwixt the Crown and the House of Peers, or betwixt the Two Houses of Parliament, the Crown may not have it in its power to influence the Lords in relation to the Commons. And therefore it must be the inevitable consequence of such a misfortune, that both the Crown and the Commons must submit to the Lords. In former times, the greatest art and care of the Crown and Ministers used to be the preventing of jealousies and differences betwixt the two Houses. This proposal, I fear, would be raising an implacable animosity and hatred, scarce ever to be reconciled.

The great advantage that the number of their body cannot be increased, is at present the most valuable privilege of the Commons, and the only thing that makes them considerable. The Lords are possessed of many great privileges that they will not permit the Commons to share with them; and therefore the Commons would be highly wanting to themselves, if they should add this advantage likewise to the Lords, which is the only one that they enjoy distinct from them.

It has been used as an argument, by some people, for the increasing the number of the Lords, "That the Crown formerly increased the number of the Commons, in particular in Queen Elizabeth's reign." But I desire it may be understood, that the sending members to Parliament at that time was not desired as a favour, but imposed as a burden. Queen Elizabeth erected several new corporations; but then the reason for it was, she relieved several ancient and decayed ones from sending any Members at all. And how little this resembles the present case is easily perceived.

The other advantage, which it is said will accrue from this proposal, is, "That it will be a means to keep property amongst the Commons."

I cannot see that there is occasion for so extraordinary a step as this, and accompanied with so many evils, to procure us this assurance. Property or wealth in every age flows faster back to the Commons by the extinction of families, but much more by the want of economy in the Peers, than it is drawn from them by the promotions of the Crown. Besides, we see estates are often extinct before families; and property is very rarely increased in the House of Peers. Indeed, if a restraining bill should pass, I do not doubt but it would soon be followed with a bill to prevent Lords from alienating their estates, for which many plausible reasons are to be produced; and then, without all dispute, the balance of property would be soon turned on the side of their Lordships.

These are all the arguments I have heard for this supposed bill; which is neither a Whig nor a Tory point, but would be a scheme that might hereafter set up some Nobles above the Crown and the Commons both. For as to what is commonly said, That the Lords would get nothing, no new power would be added to them by this means; I beg leave to state this matter in a proper light. Suppose the balance to be now *even* betwixt the Lords and the Crown, as it certainly is, or else the Constitution would not subsist in quiet; is it not plain to the most common capacity, that when two scales are upon an equal poise, if you take any weight out of one of them, you give the advantage to the other, without putting any thing into it?

How dangerous it may prove to vary the balance of power in a limited Monarchy, we may learn from the ruin of one of the best-founded Governments among the Antients. The original power, the Ephori, in the Lacedæmonian state, were invested with, besides that of being part of the Legislature, was chiefly the determining law matters relating to private contracts, and such like business. In the absence of their Kings they composed the Regency: "Regum absentum vicarii erant," is the expression made use of by Crags, de Rep. Lac. p. 76. But afterwards, upon the diminution of the Regal authority (which indeed was voluntarily complied with by their King, as I shall shew by and by), their power grew immense, "Eorum potestas in immensum aucta est." Crags, ibid.

They administered every thing of consequence: they disposed of the public treasure: they influenced the assembly of the people, and made them vote for peace or war, as they thought fit; "Concionem populi regebant; bellum pacemque concionis suffragiis sciscebant.' Ubbo Emius, de Rebus Græcis, p. 293. They made or broke treaties; they raised or disbanded the army. In fine, they had or usurped the right of rewarding or punishing whom and when they pleased. At last they took upon them to dethrone, or imprison, or execute their Kings themselves. Theopompus, King of Sparta, was advised against giving way to the diminution of the royal dignity, by which the power of those Magistrates grew so great: but he declared he did it, to settle the government by that means upon a more lasting foundation; "ut diuturniorem potestatem relinqueret." Crags, p. 74.

This unwary step proved fatal both to the Crown and the People, and ended in the ruin of the Constitution. Theopompus was one of the most virtuous, most moderate, and most gracious Princes amongst all the Spartan Kings. It appeared evidently by this very instance of his willingness to part with the power of the Crown for the good of his People: but for that very reason the People should not have suffered the authority of the Crown to have been weakened; but should rather have added to it, since power could not be lodged any where else so much for their safety and advantage. When the Prince had no longer force enough to restrain the many-headed Sovereignty, it bore down all that stood in its way, as we have heard; and in the end grew so insupportable, that the People, to be delivered from so vile a slavery, submitted to the usurpation of a private person, who, to the satisfaction of revenging them upon their oppressors, added this single act of grace: he wiped off all the public debts at once, "ut plebem demulseret, æs alienum universum delevit." Emmius, p. 349. "Et respublica in Tyrannidem conversa est." Crags, p. 72.

Those who are desirous to consult the Author himself, whom I have chiefly quoted on this occasion, must have recourse to his book of the Lacedemonian government, printed 1593, apud Petrum Santandreanum. It appears by the dedication of this treatise, that he was a follower of the first minister of the Court of Denmark, upon whom he solely depended to make his fortune, "tuo patrocinio salus mea constituta," Ep. Ded. The character Ubbo Emmius (a great Lawyer of that age, who was a sort of rival to my Author) gives of Crags, is, That he was a person of great boldness and industry, "ausu & industriâ," Pref. to De Reb. Græc. but not so happy in his judgment. But, begging pardon for this digression, which is only intended for the curious, and to return to my subject. There are other and more modern instances, and living Historians of our own, who can satisfy us, that too great a power in the hands of the Nobility has brought on the ruin of many free nations. This was the case of Sweden a few years ago, as appears plainly from the very ingenious labours of a venerable Prelate * of the present house of Peers. This was the case of Denmark, of which a very accurate account has been given by a noble Lord † of a neighbouring kingdom, a member of the House of Commons. Nothing can be better writ, or more instructive to any one that values liberty, than the narrative of that tragedy in that excellent treatise. I wish gentlemen would see there, how Commoners were treated by the Nobility when they had the power over them. This noble Lord will inform them, that "they laid heavy impositions on the Commons at pleasure;

* Dr. John Robinson, at that time Bishop of London, had in his younger days been a considerable time Envoy at the Court of Sweden; and published "The History of Livonia" in 1706. See further particulars of him in "Bishop ATTERBURY's Epistolary Correspondence, 1789," vol. I. p. 436.

† Robert Lord Viscount Molesworth was sent Envoy extraordinary to Denmark by King William in 1692. After a residence of three years, some particulars in his conduct disobliging his Danish Majesty, he was forbid the Court. Pretending business in Flanders, he retired thither without any audience of leave, and came from thence home: where he was no sooner arrived, than he drew up "an Account of Denmark;" in which he represented the government of that country to be arbitrary and tyrannical. This piece was greatly resented by Prince George of Denmark, consort to the Princess, afterwards Queen Anne; and Scheel, the Danish Envoy, first presented a memorial to King William, complaining of it, and then furnished materials for an answer, which was executed by Dr. William King of the Commons. From King's account it appears, that Molesworth's offence in Denmark was, his boldly pretending to some privileges, which, by the custom of the country, are denied to every body but the King; as travelling the King's road, and hunting the King's game: which being done, as is represented, in defiance of opposition, occasioned the rupture between the Envoy and that Court. In the mean time his book was well received by the publick, and translated into several languages.

which weight they themselves would not touch with one of their fingers." And when the Commons presumed to complain, though they were just come "from saving, from a foreign yoke, not only the capital city of their country, but the whole kingdom, the Royal Family, nay those very Nobles that dealt so hardly by them:" I say, when the Commons ventured to complain, let any Englishman but hear the answer that was given them: "A principal Senator," says his Lordship, "stood up, and in great anger told the President of the city, that the Commons neither understood nor considered the privileges of the Nobility, nor the true condition of themselves, who were no other than slaves." The Commons, fired with indignation at this treatment, and resolving, if they were to be slaves, to be slaves to their Prince, rather than slaves to their fellow-subjects, instantly surrendered all their liberties to their King; and the Lords were forced to follow their example with so much haste, that "in four days time that kingdom was changed," says my noble and honest Author, "to as absolute a Monarchy as any in the whole world."

In short, it has been for our ancient Constitution that we have struggled with so much vigour for many years together: it is for that we have poured out a river of English blood, and a treasure unheard-of in any former age. This Constitution may have its imperfections; but, faulty as it is, our ancestors have conveyed down Liberty to us through that channel: and we ought to continue it on, as well as we can, to our posterity, and not give way to the new-modelling schemes of every extraordinary genius. It would certainly be new-modelling the Constitution in a great measure, to take a considerable part of what power is left to the Crown from the Crown, and by that means add very much to the power of the Lords.

Besides, it is to be remembered, that the evil, which may be brought upon the Commons by this means, will be irretrievable. Those persons deceive themselves, who think, that if such a law should prove destructive, it may be annulled, nothing being more usual than for one Parliament to repeal the acts of another. This is true in common cases, because almost all laws relate to every part of the Legislature, and any inconvenience is felt in some measure by each of them: but this will be a law which will relate chiefly, nay solely, to the Lords; and, whatever injury the Crown or the Commons may receive by it, their Lordships will be very sensible of the advantage of it to themselves: and nothing can be more vain, than to imagine that the Commons will be ever able to shake off any exorbitant power that the Lords shall be once possessed of, unless it be by an universal destruction, like those just mentioned, which will swallow Lords and Commons and all Estates together. For which reasons, this project, if it should ever be offered to the Commons, is not only to be opposed with all the zeal imaginable, but every step, every attempt towards it, is to be detested. He that gives the power of blood, is a murderer; and he that gives the power of tyranny, is a tyrant. I shall add but one word more. The greatest traytor to civil society that ever yet appeared, will be the man, if such a one can be found, who shall contend for such a bill, should it be proposed amongst the Commons, with the assurance in his pocket of being a Peer as soon as the bill passes: and should he succeed (which God forbid!) that honour, which is to be the reward of so base a treachery, will be a lasting mark of infamy to the family that bears it, whilst any notion of honesty remains amongst mankind.

# THE OLD WHIG.

## No. 1. THURSDAY, MARCH 19, 1718-19.

### ON THE STATE OF THE PEERAGE.

WITH REMARKS UPON THE PLEBEIAN

"—— quod optanti Divûm promittere nemo
Auderet, volvendo dies en attulit ultro."—VIRG. ÆN. IX. 7.

What none of all the Gods could grant thy vows,
That, Turnus, this auspicious day bestows.—DRYDEN.

I FIND that men, who have turned their thoughts to what IS now the great subject, not only of our parliamentary debates, but of our private conversation, are apt to complain, it is a matter of such a preplext nature, and admits of so many arguments on either side, that they are rather bewildered than instructed, by what they have heard in discourse, or seen in print, upon this occasion. But, as I think this perplexity does not arise in men's minds from the nature of the thing itself, so much as from the way of handling it, I shall endeavour to draw out the whole state of this affair with such brevity and method, as may neither tire nor puzzle the reader; but carry his thoughts through a series of observations and arguments, that will regularly grow out of one another, and set this matter in its full light.[a]

[a] Among the pamphlets occasioned by the Peerage Bill, we may reckon, "The Thoughts of a Member of the Lower House, in relation to a project

1. Those who are thought the best writers upon Government, both Antients and Moderns, have unanimously agreed in opinion, that the most perfect and reasonable form is a mixt Government, in opposition to that of any single person, or any single order of men. For whether the Supreme, that is, the Legislative Power, be lodged entirely in a Prince, or in an Aristocracy, or in a Democracy, it is still looked upon as Tyrannical, and not properly calculated for the happiness of the whole community.

2. It is also established as a maxim among Political Writers, that the division of the Supreme or Legislative Power is most perfect, when it is distributed into three branches. If it all centers in one man, or in a body of men of the same quality, it is that form of Government which is called Tyrannical. If it be thrown into two branches, it wants a Casting Power, and is under

for restraining and limiting the power of the Crown, in the future creation of Peers. Printed for J. Roberts, price 3*d.*"

"Si violandum jus, regnandi causa violandum
Better to reign in Hell, than serve in Heaven.
DEVIL'S SPEECH IN MILTON'S PARADISE LOST."

Published March 17, 1718–19. [This was written by Mr. Asgill.]

"Some considerations relating to the Peerage of Great Britain; wherein the arguments for the reasonableness and expediency of a Bill said to be depending are stated pro and con. Printed for Bez. Creake. Price 6*d.*" March 18.

"A Letter from a Member of the House of Commons to a gentleman without doors, relating to the Bill of Peerage lately brought into the House of Lords; together with two Speeches, for and against the Bill, supposed to be spoke in the House of Commons. Printed for J. Roberts, price 1*s.*" March 19.

"Considerations concerning the Nature and Consequences of the Bill now depending in Parliament, relating to the Peerage of Great Britain. In a Letter from one Member of the House to another. Printed for J. Roberts, Price 4*d.*" March 19.

"The OLD WHIG," March 19. [Two numbers only; both here preserved.]

"Some Reflections upon a Pamphlet called the OLD WHIG. By the Author of the Thoughts of a Member of the Lower House.

"The Evils that I have done cannot be safe
But by attempting greater; and I find
A Spirit within me chides my sluggish hands,
And says, go on."—Vid. CATILINE'S CONSPIRACY.

"Flectere si nequeo superos, Acheronta movebo.

"Printed for J. Roberts, Price 6*d.*" March 2*d.*

such a divided authority as would often draw two different ways, and produce some time or other such a discord as would expose the weaker to that which had most strength in it, and by degrees end in a single authority. If it consist of four Branches, it wants likewise a Casting Power, and is liable to the same inconveniences as when it is composed of Two. And if it be divided into five or more parts, it necessarily runs into confusion, and will not long retain either the form or the name of Government. For this reason, three branches in a Legislature have been always fixed upon as the proper number; because it affords a Casting Power, and may moderate any heats in any two contending branches, and overpower the third in case it should prove unreasonable, or refuse to come into measures apparently necessary for the good and preservation of the Community.

3. The most natural and equitable division of these three branches of the Legislature is the Regal, the Noble, and the Plebian;' because the whole Community is cast under these

"Two Lists. shewing the alterations that have been made in the House of Commons, from the beginning of the Reign of King Henry VIII. to the end of that of King James I. And in the House of Peers, from the accession of King James I. to this time. Printed for J. Roberts, price 6*d.*' March 20.

"An exact list of the Peers of Scotland at the time of the Union. Printed for J. Morphew, price 2*d.*" March 21. [This and the preceding article are preserved in the "Political State, 1719." vol. XVII.]

"Some considerations humbly offered relating to the Peerage of Great Britain. By a Gentleman.

> "Res Italas armis tuteris, moribus ornes,
> Legibus emendes."—HOR. EP. AD. AUGUSTUM. VER. 2.

"Printed for Bez. Creake, price 6*d.*" March 21.

"The PATRICIAN. To be continued Weekly. No. 1. Being Considerations on the Peerage. In answer to the PLEBEIAN

> ———that sins against his Reason,
> Calls sawcy loud Sedition Public Zeal,
> And Mutiny the Dictates of his Spirit."—OTWAY'S ORPHAN.

"By one who is neither a Knight, nor a Member of the House of Commons. Printed for J. Roberts. Price 3*d.*" March 21.

Three other Numbers of this Work appeared, which will all be duly noticed as they arise in order of time.

several heads, and has not in it a single Member who is without his Representative in the Legislature of such a Constitution.

4. In the next place it is necessary that these three branches should be entirely separate and distinct from each other, so that no one of them may lie too much under the influence and controul of either of the collateral Branches. For if one part of the Legislature may any ways be invested with a power to force either of the other Two to concur with it, the Legislative Power is in reality, whatever it may pretend to, divided into no more than Two Branches.

5. It is the usual boast of Englishmen, that our Government is fixed upon this triple basis, which has been allowed even in speculation, and that by persons who could have no eye to our Constitution, a form the most accommodated to the happiness of a Community, and the most likely to stand secure in its own strength. But if upon examination one branch of its Legislature is liable on any occasion to be entirely mastered and controled by one of the other, it is certain that nothing can be more desirable than such an improvement in our Constitution as may remove out of it this visible imperfection. If a King has power, when he pleases, to add what number he shall think fit to a body of Nobles who have a vote in the Legislature, it is plain he may secure his point in that branch of the Legislature, and by that means command two votes out of three. This has made many assert, and I wish I could hear a satisfactory answer to it, that there are not properly more than two branches in our Legislature, notwithstanding we flatter ourselves that they are three.

6. In this case, a precarious power of Nobles, so far subject to the Regal Power in their legislative capacity, might sometimes be more pernicious to the public than if the power of both the Branches were confessedly united in the Sovereign; because we might well suppose a bad King would scarce venture upon some

things, were the whole odium of them to turn upon himself; whereas a body of Peerage, should they only be created in an emergency to carry any unjustifiable design, would serve to divert or silence the murmurs of the publick.

7. It is a known saying of the late British King, "That if his friends could gain him a House of Commons, he would throw his troop of guards into the House of Lords, rather than miscarry in his measures." And whether it is possible for a Court to gain a House of Commons of what complection they please, and what would be the consequences at some time or other of their success in such an attempt, whilst the Crown is possest of a certain means, by virtue of its prerogative, of filling the House of Lords with its own creatures, are points too evident in themselves to be insisted upon.

8. The foregoing reflections are like first principles that have scarce been ever called into dispute, and have not only been the avowed maxims of those who have been distinguished by the name of Whigs, but have furnished matter of complaint to every party in its turn. This power of the Prerogative has always occasioned murmurs, when either side has found it exerted to their prejudice. We have often wished for a redress of it, and have now an opportunity of coming at it, which if we do not lay hold of, is not likely to offer itself again so long as we are a people.

9. It is proposed, to prevent those many inconveniences which may arise from an arbitrary creation of Peers, in what proportion and at what time the Sovereign shall please, to restrain the Peers to a certain number. It is evident that such a law would remedy those many evils that may proceed from such sudden and numerous additions which have been made to the House of Lords in the most critical conjunctures. But I find there are objections

made to this expedient, from the consequences it would have upon the Crown.

10. It is represented, that it will be the cutting off a branch from the Prerogative. But if this be only the cutting off a branch which is pernicious to the publick, it is certainly a very good argument for doing it, when we can; and that this Power is of such a nature, can scarce admit of a dispute. Besides, that the Crown, far from being lessened by it, will receive a greater lustre, by parting with a Prerogative that has so often given offence, and may some time turn to the destruction of the subject.

11. The Crown, as a branch of the Legislature, cannot desire a greater Prerogative than that of a Negative in the passing of a law; and as it ought not to influence either House in their debates, what can a good King desire more than the power of approving or rejecting any such bill as cannot pass into a law without the Royal Assent?

12. The Crown will have still all the power in it of doing good to the people, in which the Prerogative of our British Kings will be still unlimited. In short, it neither touches the executive nor the legislative power of the Crown, nor takes away the Prerogative of creating Peers, but only of doing it in such a manner as seems repugnant to reason and justice. The British King will still be the source of Nobility, and hold in himself the principle of Peerage, though it is not to be lavished away on multitudes, or given occasionally to the detriment of the publick.

13. Besides, what does the Crown do more in parting with a branch of its Prerogative, than what the two other parts of the Legislature have frequently done, with regard to their respective bodies, when they have found any of their rights or privileges prejudicial to the Community? All such self-denying acts are of a popular nature, and have been passed with the good-liking and applause of their fellow-subjects. Nay the Crown has never

more recommended itself to the affection of the people, than when it has retrenched itself in any exorbitance of Power that did not seem consistent with their liberty; as in passing the bill of Habeas Corpus, and that for establishing Triennial Parliaments.

14. Indeed, were this a point extorted from the Crown in its necessities, it might be generous at such a juncture to appear in the defence of the Prerogative; but this is not our case: we are only disputing whether we shall accept of a voluntary concession made by the Sovereign himself, who out of his unparalleled goodness has shown, by this instance, that he places the true dignity of a British Monarch, where it always ought to be placed, in the liberty of his people.

15. Having considered this alteration proposed to be made in our Constitution with relation to the Crown, let us now consider it with regard first to the House of Commons, and in the next place to the whole body of the English commonalty; and if we find that it will prove advantageous in its consequences under both these views, it is undoubtedly an alteration very much to be wished for.

16. The number of Peers is in a few reigns increased from 59 to near 220; and there is no question but that in as few succeeding reigns their present number will be doubled; nor will posterity be able to see an end of them, unless it be timely prevented. Nay, we have all the reason in the world to apprehend that their number will hereafter swell in greater proportions than it has done hitherto. It is a general remark, that since the act has passed for triennial elections, Commoners of great estates are more desirous than ever of gaining a place in the Upper House, which will exempt them from such a constant dependance on their electors, and the frequent returns of trouble and expense in their elections. At least it is natural to suppose that every

King will make such additions as will give his friends a majority; nay, if we may conclude from experience, every Minister who differs in his politics from his predecessor, will bring to his assistance a sufficient number to turn the balance in his favor. And it is obvious to every one how quick is the succession of Ministers in this country.

17. The first good consequence, therefore, of the proposed alteration to the House of Commons will be this, That it will fill that House with men of the largest fortunes, and the greatest abilities; for we may well suppose that such men will set themselves forward to be elected into such a seat, when it is the highest honour they can have immediately in view. By this means, those will be the Representatives of the people, who have the greatest stake among them. Those will have the giving of money in their power, who have the most of it in their possession. But, above all, the influence of the House of Commons, and consequently of all the Commons of England, will preserve itself in its due strength; for, of all maxims, none is more uncontested than that power follows property. But what additional strength would this give the House of Lords, if the richest Members of the House of Commons may be draughted out of it in such numbers as the present frame of our Constitution permits? Nor would the inconvenience be less with respect to men of great parliamentary abilities, if, instead of continuing to add weight and authority to the Lower House, they may be called up at any time to employ the same abilities in aggrandizing the figure of another House.

18. And as the proposed alteration will be a proper means to give a figure to the House of Commons, so will it likewise be an expedient to preserve their integrity, as it will take off one method, and indeed the most effectual method, of bribing men of over-grown fortunes. When a Peerage dangles before the eyes of the most wealthy Commoner, it may have charms in it to

one, who would have a contempt for any offers of another kind. A man's ambition is as susceptible of bribes as his avarice, and it should be the care of a Legislature to cut off all temptations to corruption in the one as well as the other. It is true, the alteration proposed would not utterly remove the influence of such a motive; but it would certainly very much weaken it, and render it infinitely more ineffectual than what it is at present.

19. If this method restrains men of the greatest figure of the Lower House from making their way so easily to the Upper, it will evidently tend to the bringing a greater number of places of the highest trust, honour, or profit, into the hands of the most able and wealthy Commoners. Men so accomplished will have a diffusive influence both in their own house, and in their respective counties; and it will be necessary for all Governments to find out proper rewards and gratifications for such men; and gratifications of this kind no Commoner will envy them, since they enable them to be beneficial to the body of people whom they represent, and do not in their nature deprive us of their strength and assistance in that branch of the Legislature to which we belong.

20. However, the proposed restraint on the number of Peers is far from being an exclusion of such Commoners who are recommended by their fortunes, or their abilities. According to the calculation generally received, there may happen two extinctions or vacancies, taking one year with another, in the body of Peers, as fixed and ascertained by the new scheme, in case it should obtain. And surely the Commons of England will think it sufficient to lose annually two of their most considerable members, whatever may be the opinion of particular persons, who are in haste to leave their company.

21. A restraint upon the number of the Lords will necessarily restrain the influence of that body in the election of Members to

serve in the Lower House. It is very well known, that few Members of the House of Commons are advanced to Peerage, who have not one or more Corporations under their direction; nay, that very often this is one reason for their promotion. If, therefore, this perpetually increasing body of Lords continues on the foot it is now, in proportion as their number is augmented, their influence in elections will grow more general, till at length, as the Upper House are the creature of the Crown, the Lower House may be in a great measure the creature of the Lords. And it is worth while to consider whether in process of time, unless seasonably prevented, the House of Commons may not be filled with the stewards and bailiffs of our Peers.

22. In the next place, let us see what would be the consequences from such an alteration upon the whole bulk of the English commonalty, which should always find the first place in the thoughts of their Representatives. If they should gain only this single advantage, I think it is a very considerable one, that it will hinder the nation from being overrun with Lords. We know that, in the sale of an estate, it is no small recommendation to the buyer, that there is no Lord within so many miles of it, and the distance of such a borderer is often looked upon as an equivalent to a year's purchase. But who can be secure from such a neighbour, whilst the species is so apt to increase and multiply? I shall not insist upon paying of debts, which is looked upon as a moral duty, among Commoners, who cannot but be sorry to see any additions to an order of men that are sheltered by privileges from the demands of their honest and industrious creditors. To which many considerations of the like nature may be added, were they not obvious to the private reflection of every reader.

23. But the great point, and which ought to carry the chief weight with us in this case is, that the alteration now proposed

will give such a mighty power to the bulk of the English Commons, as can be never counterbalanced by the body of the Nobility. Should we suppose 235 Peers possest, one with another, of £5000 *per annum*, this would amount to no more than £1,175,000 *per annum;* and what is such a property, and the power arising out of it, compared with the power arising out of the property of those many millions possest by the Commons? Besides, that the great accessions of wealth yearly made in the body of the Commons would give it continually an increase of property and power, which would accrue to the body of the Nobles, in case their door was always open to men of overflowing fortunes, who might find no great difficulty in procuring an entrance.

24. I shall now offer two fair questions to any man, who impartially weighs these matters.

First, If two schemes of government were proposed to him, in both of which the Legislature should consist of three branches, whether he would prefer that scheme, in which one of the branches might be increased at pleasure by another of them; or that scheme in which every branch should be limited to a certain stated number: Nay, if the two schemes were placed in parallel with one another, and considered in their respective consequences, whether the first would not appear a most wild and indigested project?

In the second place, I would propose this question. If the Lords had been limited to a certain number by our constitution, whether it would not have been thought unpardonable in any one who should have proposed to have taken off that limitation, and left it to the pleasure of the Crown arbitrarily to add to them any number at any time.

Nobody can be at a loss to determine himself in these questions, who considers this subject by those plain lights which are already exhibited in this discourse, and which may be strengthened by many other considerations.

25. This subject naturally engages me in one talk more, which is, to examine the objections that have been started against this alteration proposed to be made in the Constitution of the House of Peers. And here I cannot discover any inconvenience which can be said to follow from such an alteration, that does not now subsist, or is not answered by some much greater inconvenience in the present state of the Peerage. But, that I may not follow the example of those who have appeared in print on the other side of this debate, in putting weak arguments into the mouth of their antagonists, I shall answer such objections as have been the most approved by those who declare themselves against this bill, as they are laid together in a pamphlet, intitled, THE PLEBEIAN.

26. As for the introduction, the digression upon the Ephori, and the concluding paragraph, they are only arguments *ad conflandam invidiam*, and such as are not to be answered by reason, but by the same angry strain in which they are written, and which would discredit a cause that is able to support itself without such an assistance.

27. "At first sight," says the PLEBEIAN, "this proposal must appear very shocking; it carries with it so great an alteration of the Constitution." This is the first general objection, and I wish it had been pursued regularly; but because it is dropt and resumed in the following part of the discourse, I must be forced to collect those scattered passages on this head, as I find them in different parts of the book. This great objection will be sufficiently answered, if this alteration of the Constitution is from worse to better; which I think has been fully proved. As every thing is formed into perfection by degrees, the wisdom of all Legislatures has embraced every opportunity of making such changes in

their government, as have been advantageous to those who live under it. This Author himself gives us an eminent instance of a great alteration of our Constitution in the Lower House, under the reign of Queen Elizabeth, "when the Crown erected several new Corporations, and relieved several ancient and decayed ones from sending any Members at all." I do not make use of this increase in the number of the Commons, as an argument for an increase of the number of the Lords, which the Author produces as the reasoning of some people who are for the bill. Such people, if any there are, must talk inconsistently with themselves, since it is the purport of the bill to prevent the House of Lords from growing too numerous. But it is an unanswerable argument to show, that there has been as great an alteration in one branch of our Legislature, as is now proposed to be made in another; and that such an alteration should be introduced into our form of government, when there are good reasons for it; on which account our Author himself justifies the above-mentioned alteration in the House of Commons. Our Author furnishes us with another very good argument in this particular against himself. "Whiggism," says he, "if I understand it aright, is a desire of Liberty, and a spirit of opposition to all exorbitant Power in any part of the Constitution. Formerly the danger on this account was from the Crown; but since the Habeas Corpus Act, and the many restraints laid upon the Crown in King William's time, and the great and numerous limitations of the Succession Acts, the Prerogative of the Crown is reduced so low, that it is not at all dangerous to the Commons." As we have the Author's confession in the aforementioned instance of an alteration in the Plebeian, he has here given us an account of as remarkable changes in the Regal branch of our government. The Prerogative was retrenched in those several instances, because without such retrenchment the power of it appeared exorbitant and dan gerous to the Commons. If therefore there still inheres in the Crown a power that is exorbitant and dangerous to the Commons, there is the same reason why the Commons should lay hold of the present opportunity to retrench it. This is the matter in debate betwixt us; but, be that as it will, the argument which the Author here makes use of against the bill in question, "that it carries in it too great an alteration of the Constitution," would have been as good an argument against the Habeas Corpus Act, or any other of those above-mentioned. What is further said upon this subject in p. 271, would make a handsome sentence in a popular speech, but will never stand the test of a strict examination in a discourse addrest to the reasons and not the passions of men. "In short, it has been for our ancient Constitution," says the Author, "that we have struggled with so much vigour for many years together: it is for that we have poured out a river of English blood, and a treasure unheard of in any former age. This Constitution may have its imperfections; but, faulty as it is, our ancestors have conveyed down Liberty to us through that channel: and we ought to continue it on, as well as we can, to our posterity, and not give way to the new-modelling schemes of every extraordinary genius." This is not arguing, but declaiming. Our Ancestors remedied several imperfections from time to time, and we are obliged to them for having conveyed Liberty down to us through the channel which they had so often altered and reformed. And will not our posterity be as thankful to us, if we transmit to them their Liberty through the same channel, when it shall be only altered for the better conveyance of it?

28 Having taken off the force of this main objection, I shall follow others as the Author leads me. He tells us that "the shutting up the door of the House of Lords, in the manner talked of, cannot but prove a great discouragement to virtuous actions

to learning and industry, and very detrimental to the House of Peers itself, by preventing such frequent supplies from going into it, as the nature of such a body requires; for want of which, it may in time become corrupt and offensive, like a stagnated pool, which hitherto has been preserved wholesome and pure by the fresh streams that pass continually into it.* " This consideration, if it has any force, cuts down all the other arguments drawn from the new accessions of figure and power, which he supposes would accrue to the House of Lords, by the passing of the bill so much talked of. Can it be detrimental to the House of Lords, and at the same time throw into their hands all the places and honours that the Crown can confer upon them? Will that body of men, which would become mean and despicable, and offensive as a stagnated pool, by the means of this alteration, be raised by the same means to be the most formidable, and the most honoured part in our Constitution? Or could the same body degenerate into a public nuisance, as our Author represents it, and at the same time be able to overawe both King and People? Can two such contrary effects be produced from one and the same cause? But could we suppose that this body of men might thus degenerate; would they be able, without numerous recruits of wealth, learning and industry, to oppose any thing for the good of the Community, in contradiction to the King and People? But more of this hereafter.

29. Our Author adds, "I am not unaware, it will be said, that the frequent extinctions of [noble] families will salve this inconvenience, and make room for the rewarding of Merit. But," says he, "this expedient, I fear, is not much to be depended on; for the uncertainty of the time when the Crown will have any such power will make it much the same as if it were never to have it at all;" which is as much as to say, that unless the Crown has power of making what number of Lords it pleases

and at what time it pleases, and to serve what turn it pleases, it had as good have no power at all of making Peers, which the Author supposes is the only adequate power it has of rewarding merit. Not to ask the Author whether it be generally virtuous actions, learning, or industry, that recommend Commoners to the Peerage, or of what other kind the merit is which has been often thus rewarded; I shall only ask him, whether any man has so crying a merit as immediately requires a Peerage for its reward? or whether the extinction of two titles in a year will not leave room enough for the Crown to reward those extraordinary persons, whose merits give them such a demand upon it? As for another argument which the Author puts into the mouth of those whom he calls patrons of the Bill proposed, "that it will ease the Crown of importunities," as I think it has no great weight in it, I am not concerned to urge any thing in its defence against the PLEBEIAN's answer to it.

30. We come now to the most considerable paragraph of the whole book, which I shall therefore transcribe at length. "But another consequence, of a much higher nature, attending the limitation of the number of Peers, is the danger there will be of changing the Constitution by this means into an Aristocracy. And this may at any time in such case be effected by the confederacy of two or three great families, which would form such a body in the House of Lords, as the Crown would not be able to controul. That this kind of government is one of the worst sorts of slavery, is too well known to be disputed. In a Democracy, a great many different persons may come to have a share of power by several incidents, but in the other case it is birth only that intitles to superiority: And the milk such Nobles are nursed up with, is hatred and contempt for every human creature but those of their own imaginary dignity." The question to be stated here is, Whether the House of Lords under their present Con

stitution is not as likely to run into an Aristocracy, as it would be in case their number should be limited. It appears very plain to me, that a body of Peers perpetually increasing, and capable of additions, has in it a natural tendency to an Aristocracy. Supposing that the House of Lords from 60 members is now swelled to 200: These, if increased by the same proportion, would in the same number of years amount to 666, to which we may presume there would be still the like proportionable additions. By this means they would in time receive such vast accessions of property, as might encourage them not only to entertain so ambitious a design, but in a great measure to render it effectual; especially when any men could be admitted into their own order, with their great abilities in Parliament, or their great influence among the people, who might be most capable of opposing their incroachments upon the Commons. I do allow that such additions would be prejudicial to the Crown; but this is no reason why they would not be made, as it has not prevented the additions that have been made in our own memory. For though the Crown in general would be a sufferer by this method; yet it would naturally have recourse to it, as it has formerly, when it labours under any present exigency, that can only be removed by such an expedient. This danger of an Aristocracy, every one must confess, would be very much abated, and, I think, utterly removed, by the limitation of the Lords to such a number as is now proposed. In such a case, their property would be so very inconsiderable, when compared with that of the Commons (as I have before showed to a demonstration) that it would render such a design in them the most chimerical, and the most impracticable. And since it is impossible that the whole body of Lords in their united strength could be able to establish themselves into an Aristocracy, the Author's imagination vanishes, that "this may at any time, in such a case, be effected by the confederacy of two or three great families, which would form such a body among the Lords as the Crown would not be able to controul." If the Author means in this place, by the Crown not being able to controul the Lords, that it would be restrained from pouring in such a number as would always sway them to its inclinations, it is what ought to be wished for. If he means that this want of power in the Crown would enable them to erect an Aristocracy, it is certainly a wrong consequence, because not only the Crown, but the people would have a superior Power in them to the body of Nobles, and are equally concerned to preserve their stations in the government. The Author after this brings an argument to prove, that an Aristocracy is a bad form of government, and that a Democracy is preferable to it, in which I entirely agree with him; but must add, that a mixt government made out of Aristocracy, Democracy, and Monarchy, is better than either of them. The Author subjoins, that "the milk which Nobles are nursed up with is hatred and contempt of every humane creature, but those of their own imaginary dignity." If so, the fewer of them the better. What Commoner would not desire to put a stop to the increase of them?

31. The next objection I meet with is from the great privileges the Lords are already possessed of, with relation to actions *de Scandalis Magnatum*, &c., which is likewise a very good reason why we should hinder the increase of persons invested with these privileges; and as for the judicial power, with that of imprisoning, they are such as subsist in their body as it is now constituted, and therefore cannot be objected to the proposed alteration, which would only leave them as they are.

32. "The increasing the number of Peers," says the Author, "is always to be wished for by the Commons." We have seen sufficient reasons why it should not. "Because the greater their number, the less considerable they become;" the contrary of

which has been evidently proved; "and the less within the influence of Court favours." What! when by this very power of increasing them at will, it can secure any point among them that it pleases? "By which means alone Ministers are kept in awe, and remain in a situation of being called to account for their actions. Were it otherwise, they would be out of the reach of any accusation. They would know exactly by whom they were to be tried, and their judges might be their accomplices. And should this once come to be the case, what might they not attempt with impunity?" Is this inconvenience better prevented in a House of Peers on the bottom it now stands? Can any who has been a good Minister be secure, if the Crown should add a sufficient number of his enemies to those who sit in judgement upon him? Or is a bad Minister in any danger, when he may be sheltered by the addition of a sufficient number of his friends?

33. I must not pass over another remarkable paragraph of the Author upon the same argument for increasing the Lords at pleasure. "The great advantage," says he, "that the number of their body cannot be increased, is at present the most valuable privilege of the House of Commons, and the only thing that makes them considerable." This is indeed a very poor advantage, to found upon it the grandeur of a House of Commons. Is not the power of giving money and raising taxes confined to that body, and which can never fail to give them the greatest weight in the Legislature? Will not this be always the most valuable privilege of the Commons? and what other privilege can make them more considerable? He goes on, "The Lords are possessed of many great privileges that they will not permit the Commons to share with them; and therefore the Commons would be highly wanting to themselves, if they should add this advantage likewise to the Lords, which is the only one that they can enjoy distinct from them." Our Author, as it may turn to

his account, sometimes considers the Lords in their personal Privileges as they are individuals, and sometimes as they are a body of men in the Legislature. If he here means their Privileges in the former view, I do allow they are very great ones, and therefore certainly every Commoner cannot desire an increase of such individuals. But if he here means their Privileges as a Legislative Body, it is certain that all their Privileges together are not equal to that One, of commanding the purse of the Community. So that it is wonderful how he could advance, that the number of the House of Commons not being subject to an increase, " is the only advantage that they enjoy distinct from the House of Lords."

34. Our Author next proceeds to speak of the proportion of Property between the two Houses of Lords and Commons, which is a point already so fully discussed, that I shall not trouble the Reader with any repetitions; but cannot omit what the Author asserts as an indisputable point, and which in itself is the greatest paradox I ever heard advanced. His words are, " Indeed, if a restraining bill should pass, I do not doubt but it would be soon followed with a bill to prevent Lords from alienating their estates, for which many plausible reasons are to be produced; and then, without all dispute, the balance of property will be soon turned on the side of their Lordships." Which is as much as to say, in plain English, that the Lords will have as much wealth amongst them as the whole body of the British Commons, or that one million will be a balance against a hundred millions. Indeed the House of Lords in their present Constitution may be always approaching to a balance in property with the Commons, from whence they are continually receiving into their body such large supplies; but if their number be once limited, you cut off their recruits, and lay them under an impossibility of

ever rivaling the other branch of the Legislature in this particular.

35. Our Author's argument, that a new Power would arise to the House of Lords from the alteration so much talked of, is founded upon a fact which every one denies at first sight. His words are these: "For as to what is commonly said, that the Lords would get nothing, no new power would be added to them by this means; I beg leave to state this matter in a proper light. Suppose the balance to be now even betwixt the Lords and the Crown, as it certainly is, or else the Constitution would not subsist in quiet: Is it not plain to the most common capacity, that when two scales are upon an equal poise, if you take any weight out of one of them, you give the advantage to the other without putting any thing into it?" The Author here supposes that the balance between the two parts of the Legislature should be even; and so far I concur with him, that being the chief end which this alteration has in view. But I can by no means suppose with him that they are even, because it is contrary to matter of fact. For we plainly see that the Sovereign has it always in his power to make what division of party or opinion he pleases prevail in that House. As for the reason of their present supposed equality, "that otherwise they could not subsist in quiet," it has no force in it, because we see very ill-constituted governments will subsist in quiet for many ages, not that they are preserved by a rightly tempered Constitution, which would give them the greatest strength, but by other accidental causes. The ill consequences of such an inequality may be frequently felt and complained of, though they may not shake the tranquillity of the publick.

36. I have now gone through every thing that carries the face of an argument for the Constitution of the House of Lords, as it now stands, or of an objection against the alteration propos

ed to be made; having only avoided saying any thing in this case as it affects the Scottish Nobility, because I have here considered it only as an English Commoner, and because I have thoughts of prosecuting the subject, as it relates to Scotland, in another pamphlet, being unwilling to swell this to a greater bulk.

37. Since the writing of the foregoing Discourse, I have perused a pamphlet, intituled, "The Thoughts of a Member of the Lower House," &c.* in which the Author first approves our Constitution as divided into its Three branches, and through the whole course of his Book contends in effect that it should consist of no more than Two; for he supposes the House of Lords instituted only as guardians and ornaments to the Throne, and to be augmented by the Crown in such a proportion, as may strengthen it in opposition to the House of Commons. The Reader may see his scheme in the following words: "There is not," says this Writer, "a more certain maxim in politicks, than that a Monarchy must subsist by an Army, or Nobility. The first makes it despotic, and the latter a free government. I presume none of those nobler personages themselves, who have the honour to make up that illustrious body, do believe they are so distinguished and advanced above their fellow-subjects for their own sakes: They know they are intended the Guardians, as well as Ornaments of the Monarchy, an essential prerogative of which it must be to add to and augment their number in such proportion, as to render them a proper balance against the Democratical part of our Constitution, without being formidable to the Monarchy itself, the support of which is the reason of their institution." This is a most extraordinary notion of government, that one branch of a Legislature should be instituted, only to be subservient to the strength and support of another, but it is on this bottom that he founds his whole discourse; and as for his objections to the pre-

* By Mr. Asgill.

posed alteration, I find they are such as I have already obviated in the course of this pamphlet. If any thing remains in them unanswered, it will fall under the last objection against the matter in debate, which I should not take notice of, did not I find that it makes an impression upon some people's minds.

38. Suppose, says the objection, there should be an inflexible obstinacy in a House of Peers, what method would there be left to bring them to a concurrence with the two other branches of the Legislature, when it will not be in the power of the King to bring them over to reason, by flinging in sufficient numbers among them? To this I answer, That if the Lords are obstinate in a point that is *Reasonable* and *Beneficial* to the Community, it will be happy for their country that they should be invested with the proper power of a Legislative branch, not to be overruled to wrong measures. This may sometimes be of great advantage to the publick, if we can possibly suppose that the two other branches may concur in any thing that is not consistent with justice, or the national interest If the Peers are thus inflexibly obstinate in any methods that are *Dishonourable*, *Unjust*, or *Pernicious* to their country; can we imagine they could not be influenced into a compliance by the anthority of the two sharing branches in the Legislature? Or can we think they would persist in measures which would draw upon them the displeasure of the Crown, and the resentments of the whole Commons of Great Britain? Every body of men takes as much care as possible to preserve their credit, and to render themselves popular; and we cannot think that any branch of a Legislature would be made up of madmen, or pursue such measures as must necessarily end in their infamy, or their destruction; especially when they are infinitely weaker than either of the other constituent parts of our Legislature. Could any person apprehend such a behaviour from them, I am sure the same person cannot in his heart apprehend

their growing up into an Aristocracy. The Peers are so little a match for the Crown in power, or the Commons in property, much less able to cope with the united force of both; that it is wildness to suppose them guilty of such an unjust and unreasonable obstinacy, as they know might endanger their very being in the British Constitution. And now I shall only propose it to every one's thoughts, whether an expedient, which will remedy the greatest inconvenience that may arise to us, from one of the branches of the Legislature, and of which we have had experience, as has been already sufficiently explained, should prevail with us to lay it aside, out of a groundless fear, that it should expose us to an inconvenience from another branch of the Legislature, which must suppose them destitute of common sense, void of honour and equity, and regardless of self-preservation, before it can possibly befall us. To this I shall only add, that whatever objections are made against this alteration in the Constitution, may be made against every form of government, in which the Legislature consists of three distinct branches, and that is, against such a form as has been pronounced the most perfect by those who have been the most skilful politicians, and the most famous for their observations on the nature of government.

*** A letter in the "Weekly Medley, March 28, 1719, pays some merited compliments to an ingenious Artisan, Mr. Price, of St. Andrew's, Holbourn, "for restoring the ancient beautiful art of Staining and Painting Glass to perfection; an art now so long lost, its loss so lamented, and its re-invention so much coveted. Too luminous a Church is too gay for the business that is done there; it shews in too clear a point of sight, too many objects for distraction; but that which pervades and penetrates the coloured glass, strikes one with a Religious awe, a spirit of recollection and meditation, and has in it, something I do not know what of solemn and sacred. Besides, it draws frequently the eye off from the book of Prayer in a Church; and then, while the eye is looking through the window towards the Heavens, the passages represented on the glass, being taken out of Holy Writ, lift and elevate the mind, as they do the eye, to Heaven. A better pattern of this old art (and that is great to say) is not to be found in any old Church, than is now to be seen in the East window of St. Andrew's, Holbourn, where the Passion of our Saviour, whose Divinity some would be permitted to deny, and yet to enter that Church, is represented in a lively manner. And the red part of the colour is so beautifully strong, that it would cast a blush upon any guilty wretch, that standing opposite to it should say, that the Saviour, whose Passion it represents, had not the Divinity joined with the Humanity."

††† "At the Blue Leg in Bow-Lane, near Watling-street, are sold LOTTERY TICKETS, and SHARES, Whole Tickets at the same price as upon the Exchange; and, for the conveniency of such as cannot purchase whole tickets, or would extend their chances to a larger latitude, they may have half tickets, quarter tickets, fifth parts, tenth parts, or twentieth parts of tickets; a person for 4*s.* may have the 20th part of one ticket, for 8*s.* a share in two tickets, for 20*s*, a share of five tickets, for 40*s.* a share of ten tickets, for 4*l.* a share of 20 tickets, for 10*l.* a share of 50 tickets, for 20*l*, a share of 100 tickets, all several numbers; and in the same proportion to any other number. There are but 5 blanks to one prize; the lowest is 10*l.* and the highest 20,000*l.* There are but a small number left, therefore those who intend to have any must be expeditious."

# THE PLEBEIAN.

## No. II. MONDAY, MARCH 23, 1718–19.

CONSIDERATIONS UPON THE REPORTS RELATING TO THE PEERAGE CONTINUED; AND REMARKS UPON THE PAMPHLETS THAT HAVE BEEN WRIT FOR THE SUPPOSED BILL. BY A MEMBER OF THE HOUSE OF COMMONS.

> "Quis enim jam non intelligat Artes
> Patricias?" * * * * *—JUV. SAT. IV. 101.
>
> Who sees not now through the Lords thin disguise?—DRYDEN.

THOSE who are not particularly acquainted with the vocation of Pamphlet writing, have very much wondered that a matter of so great consequence, as the affair of the PEERAGE, and espoused by such persons as are very well known to be its patrons, could have been so long a while upon the stage, and no champion appear for it; but others, who are more versed in this kind of business, know, there could not be wanting persons enough to make their court, by producing their lucubrations on this head. But as it is a subject that will not very well bear debating, their masters, without doubt, were of opinion, that the best way was, to let all manner of writing alone, and keep all that could be said on the subject for the time and place where it was absolutely necessary to say something.

The agitators for the bill assured themselves, that nobody would be so bold as to attack first; and consequently judged themselves out of all danger. But the PLEBEIAN starting forth unexpectedly, they were forced, like people in a surprize, or on an invasion, to march immediately any troops they had; and indeed these are some of the most tattered I ever saw.

The first Champion that appeared for this bill, was a person who exhibited himself in the St. James's-Post, of Wednesday, March 18, in this advertisement: "Some Considerations relating to the Peerage of Great Britain Wherein the arguments *for* the reasonableness and expediency of a bill, said to be depending, are stated *Pro* and *Con.*"

This performance I have not been able to venture upon; for He that can state arguments *for* the bill, both *Pro* and *Con*, is too slippery a person for any body to lay hold of.

The next that entered the lists, on the same side of the question, having been more fortunate than to *discover himself beforehand*, I have perused his labours. The account he gives of himself, is, "That he is a Member of the House of Commons, who has a friend with whom he uses to talk over in *private* all arguments and considerations which concern any thing of moment, as far as they could collect and remember them: and they having both agreed that this was a matter of a very extraordinary nature, the one entreated the other to put his thoughts about it in writing, that he might be better able to judge of them all together, And in order to continue the privacy of this correspondence, those thoughts came out, printed for J. Roberts in Warwick-Lane."

This notable introduction was very near having the same effect upon me, as to this pamphlet, as the advertisement just mentioned had to the former; but with much ado I went through the performance. All I can learn from it is, That this Gentleman was present at the debates of the House of Lords; where he does not seem to have been mightily enlightened as to the true state of the case, the debate having in all probability run pretty much one way.

The next that follows these two combatants for this bill, is somebody or other that is used to masquerading, as I suppose; and indeed he is so well disguised, that it is impossible to know him. When I first read the title, *The Old Whig*, I expected no less than the utmost wrath and indignation against the House of Lords. I could not help thinking but he would have been for *Voting them useless* at least, as his ancestors did formerly: but I was extremely surprized to find just the contrary; that he is for giving them such a power, as would make the *House of Commons useless;* and therefore he might as well have taken any other title in the world, as *The Old Whig*. I am afraid he is so *old a Whig*, that he has quite *forgot his Principles.*

But I shall shew now more plainly, what is said in the former PLEBEIAN, that this is neither a *Whig* nor a *Tory* point, but is a jumble, a hodge-podge, a confusion of all parties and all persons together; and must inevitably in its consequences destroy first *Whig* and *Tory*, and afterwards *Crown* and *People.* As all sorts of people unite for it, so ought all sorts, and of every denomination, that have any value for their Constitution, to unite against it.

This Pamphlet, by the marks it appears with, being in all probability the best performance that is to come from that quarter, the PLEBEIAN will consider it thoroughly; and in order to proceed more methodically, for this Author's satisfaction?

*First*, I will answer the objections made to the last PLEBEIAN.

*Secondly,* I will consider the argument, as the *Old Whig* states it himself.

The first objection the Author of the Remarks makes to the PLEBEIAN, is page 299, where he says, "That the *Introduction,* the Digression upon the *Ephori,* and the *Conclusion,* are all arguments *ad con flandam invidiam.*" He who says that arguments drawn from History, which can only shew what has happened in former times, are arguments *ad conflandam invidiam,* gives up the matter in dispute, and lets the world know, by passing them so slightly over, that he feels their force: for it is a tacit admission, that in all probability the like disasters will happen from the alterations now projected in our Constitution; which, history informs us, were the real consequences of alterations of the like nature in other countries; otherwise those arguments could not now contribute to make persons invidious. Besides, I always thought that bringing examples from history was looked upon as the most impartial and unexceptionable method of arguing, as it is abstracted from the passions and interests of the present times: for what is Learning and History, if it be not to draw inferences of what may happen, from what has happened?

As to the digression upon the *Ephori,* the PLEBEIAN was very careful to avoid giving offence. Amongst the many extraordinary Powers exercised by those magistrates, there was one of a very uncommon nature; which was, that as they took upon themselves the sole inspection of the youth, they were particularly curious of the persons of the *Boys.* They employed every tenth day in examining the youths of about fifteen, stark-naked, *Oportebat Ephebos decimo quoque dieEphoris se sistere sine veste,* Ubbo Em mius, de Rep. Lac. p. 235, with whom *Crags* agrees almost in the same words, in the Treatise mentioned in the former PLEBEIAN, p. 284. What an ill use was made of this power, we may see in *Emmius,* p. 236, where speaking of the manner how the *Ephori* lived with those young men they liked best, he says, *Iis* (Ephebis) *assiduo fere adhærebant.* Which words, for fear of offending the PLEBEIAN Ladies, I am not at liberty to translate. However, it is very plain all this was omitted to avoid the least appearance of personal reflection.

The first argument of the PLEBEIAN, which the *Old Whig* objects to, is, p. 299. "That though the PLEBEIAN declares against the proposed bill, because it will make so great an alteration in our Constitution, yet he produces an eminent instance of a great alteration of our Constitution in the Lower House under the reign of Queen Elizabeth, when the Crown erected several new Corporations, and relieved several ancient decayed ones from sending any Members at all."

This, the Remarker says, was as great an alteration in one branch of our Legislature, as is now proposed to be made in another. The Remarker quite mistakes this point; for, instead of being an alteration of so great consequence to the Constitution of the Commons, as this new proposal is of that of the Lords, it was an alteration of no consequence at all. Suppose the towns of Watchet and Dunster, two sea-ports in Somersetshire, to have been destroyed in the wars with Ireland in Queen Elizabeth's time. The inhabitants, on account of poverty, apply to the Crown to be exempted from the charge of paying four Members to represent them in Parliament. The Crown some time after grants Charters to two neighbouring towns in flourishing circumstances, and directs the writs at a following summons of a Parliament to be sent to Tiverton and Honiton, instead of Watchet and Dunster. Let any body judge if this alteration can be of any consequence to the House of Commons. Here is nothing else but the places changed; and four Members from Tiverton and Honiton are the same thing as four from Watchet and Dunster. But to state this matter with nicety would require much more labour and time than I am able to allow it.

Another argument, which the Remarker says the PLEBEIAN furnishes against himself, is, "That he owns the Prerogative has been retrenched in several instances; because without such retrenchment the Power of it appeared exorbitant and dangerous to the Commons." But these retrenchments being now made, the question at present is, Whether the Commons ought to go on stripping the Crown of every jewel, till it becomes less resplendent than a Doge of Venice's coronet, or less comfortable than the Sword-bearer's Cap of Maintenance; and, what is of the greatest moment to the Commons, less able to protect them against the Power of a House of Lords, if ever their Lordships should be disposed to claim a larger share of authority than belongs to them?

As to the complaint the Remarker makes, That the PLEBEIAN *applies to mens Passions, and not their Reasons; and declaims instead of arguing;* what must be said in answer to this is, That people must make use of what arm they have. On the one side, it is evident there can be nothing but arguing and reasoning, and declaiming and exemplifying; but on the other, the PLEBEIAN is afraid there are more irresistible arts of applying to the *Passions*, rather than to the *Reasons* of men, or else he would not have one minute's pain for the issue of this question.

The manner in which the *Remarker* states the PLEBEIAN's argument, relating to the *shutting up the door of the House of Lords,* shews he either wilfully or ignorantly mistakes that part of the Controversy: "For, after having cited the words of the PLEBEIAN, he asks, if it can be detrimental to the House of Lords, and at the same time throw into their hands all the places and honours that the Crown can confer upon them? Will that body of men, which would become mean and despicable, and offensive as a stagnated pool, by the means of this alteration, be raised by the same means to be the most formidable and most honoured part of the Constitution? Or would they be able, without numerous recruits of wealth, learning, and industry, to oppose any thing for the good of the Community?" To this

I answer, It will not be detrimental to them in point of Power, but will be detrimental on account of those talents that ought to accompany Power; the want of which the Commons will feel in their *Judicature*, and in many more particulars. They will be *offensive* to others, but not perceive it themselves; they will be *formidable*, but not *honoured*. These are natural *Effects* that all *Exorbitant Power produces*. As to wealth, they will take it, it is to be feared, where they can find it; and learning and industry will be as useless baubles to their Lordships, as *Dangling Peerages* (as my Author describes them excellently well) are to men of sense amongst the Commons.

The next objection of the *Old Whig* to the PLEBEIAN is, "That he avers the uncertainty of the extinction of families will leave so little opportunity for the Crown to reward merit by PATRICIAN Honours, that it will be much the same thing as if the Crown were never to have any such Power at all." *Whereas* (says he) *there will be two Titles extinct every year, according to the Calculation generally received.*

By the *Calculation generally received*, I suppose the *Remarker* means the List published by way of prelude to this project. Whether it be true or false, if some Heralds know any thing of this matter, would take more time to examine into, than, I dare say, the Constitution it is intended to introduce would subsist. But supposing, for argument sake, that that Calculation is right, and that in one hundred and sixteen years there have been one hundred and fifty-four extinctions, there will be found wanting seventy-eight to make up his number of two a year; so that the extinctions have not been during that term quite so many as after the rate of one *Lord and a half* per annum. But besides this error in Arithmetic, there is another error of an *odd nature* in this *Computation*; which, unless some method is proposed to ascertain it, will reduce the extinctions to fewer than even one a year. And if so, those who expect to have their services rewarded by reversions so uncertainly computed, may have time enough to try all their patience, and at last find that, instead of advancing themselves to dignity, they have been forging their own chains. In the *Computations of the Titles extinct*, all those are comprehended who have been extinguished by *the edge of the Law, for Treason, Rebellion, and other capital offences:* and who, without the Spirit of Prophecy, can foretell what *Vacancies* may happen by such means for the future? But if, in favour of this *scheme*, it be admitted that in all probability there may be as many and as great *Criminals* hereafter in that Noble Body as there have been for the time past, is it not to be feared that the *Path to justice may be more difficult, after this narrowing the way up to the House of Peers, than it has been formerly.*

As to what the *Remarker* has objected to the arguments of the PLEBEIAN, which prove, "That the Limitation of the number of the Lords will run the Constitution into an Aristocracy;" this matter shall be fully con sidered presently, when I come to examine the *Old Whig's* state of the case.

In a following paragraph, where the *Remarker* takes notice of what the PLEBEIAN urges on the side of the King and Commons, *viz.*, "That an ill Minister might be skreened against them both, if this Law should take place, by reason that in such case he would know exactly his judges (who might likewise be his accomplices), and so act with impunity; the *Remarker* argues, That if this bill does not pass, an innocent Minister cannot be secure, nor a guilty one punished, if the Crown should add to the House of Peers a sufficient number of the enemies of the one, or of the friends of the other." In either of which cases the utmost iniquity must be supposed in the Crown, which, I confess, I cannot bring myself to do, and therefore my argument remains entire. And it would grieve me to the heart, if I could think there were any *innocent Ministers*, who ought to be emboldened by the consciousness of their integrity, and yet should have greater apprehensions from honest actions, than have been hitherto shown by men of the most guilty consciences, through the many ages that this Constitution has subsisted, without the alteration now desired.

The *Remarker* thinks it wonderful how the PLEBEIAN could advance, "That the number of the House of Commons not being subject to an increase, is the only advantage that they enjoy distinct from the House of Lords; and alledges, that *all their Lordships Privileges together are not equal to that one of commanding the purse of the community.* Were it true, that the Commoners enjoyed this privilege of *commanding the purse of the Community*, distinct from the House of Lords, they would be very easy as to the increasing, or diminishing, or fixing their number, or as to any thing else that might belong to that Noble Assembly. But, alas! this is not the case; for their Lordship's concurrence is as necessary to a money-bill, as to any other bill: nay, whether a money-bill may not originally take its rise in their House, is a point never yet clearly given up by their Lordships, if I am not very much misinformed; and whether they may not be more inclinable to dispute this matter, if ever their door comes to be shut in the manner now proposed, may deserve very serious reflection.

Thus having answered every objection made to the former PLEBEIAN by the *Old Whig*, except such as will occur in considering this argument, as he states it himself; I shall now proceed to that point which I proposed at first setting out.

I agree with our Author, "That the best kind of Government is that which is composed of these three branches, the *Regal*, the *Noble*, and the *Plebeian*." This is at present our happy Constitution: "But then," says this Author, "we have one imperfection or defect in it, which wants to be remedied; and that is, the Crown has too great a power over one branch of this Constitution, namely, the *Noble;* in that the Crown can, whenever it pleases, add so many to their number as to influence their actions

And this Author likewise assures us, p. 4. "That the Crown has power enough also to gain a House of Commons of what complexion it pleases." From whence I observe, first, That if it be a fault in the Constitution, that the Crown has so great power over one branch of the Constitution, the *Noble*, as this Author affirms, it is as great an imperfection that the Crown has so great a Power, as he also affirms it has, over the PLEBEIAN. And therefore this Author should have proposed some method to have remedied this defect in the latter, as well as in the former branch; or else that perfection in the Constitution, he seems to be desirous of, cannot be arrived at. He contends, that it is absolutely necessary the *Lords should be entirely independent of the Crown.* An impartial friend to the *whole body of the people,* and to sound reason, would have said as much for the Commons. Then these two Estates would have been upon a level. But even by such an alteration, which is the only equal one, our Constitution would not be mended, but made much worse; for if both Lords and Commons were as independent of the Crown as this Author desires the Lords may be, the unhappy consequence that must ensue would be, that if any discord should arise betwixt them, and each remain inflexibly resolved, here the constitution would certainly want a casting power; and the only way of ending the dispute must be like a *Polish* Dyet, *by getting up on horseback.* And therefore this Power now in the Crown, and which has been in it for so many ages, is necessary for the good of the whole Community, to prevent the greatest confusion, which might otherwise arise from the passions of men.

The Crown once parted with this Power out of its hands to the Commons; and that concession produced the ruin of the Monarchy, and of the Peerage. If the Crown should part with the Power now to the Lords, that it has over them, why may it not be very reasonably apprehended, that the same fatal consequence may ensue to the King and the Commons?

If it be necessary, as it has been plainly shewn, that the Power now in the Crown should remain there, for the good of the people in general; it is as necessary for the defence and advantage of the Crown itself. The Lords (by the Power the Crown has of adding to their number) are a fluctuating uncertain body. This is all that gives the Crown any influence over them, and prevents combinations, cabals, and factions against the Crown. But if the door comes once to be shut, so that the Crown cannot make any considerable addition to their number in any exigencies whatever, what a door is opened at the same time to form a Power superior to that of the Crown, and superior to all human controul! Then they will become a fixed certain body: and should three or four ambitious bold men combine together hereafter, of the greatest families, and the greatest estates, where would the difficulty be of getting a majority of two hundred thirty-five? and, if once obtained, what remedy could be provided in so desperate a case? Whilst they act in the common methods of governmen.

they would command all *favours;* and, should they ever act in an *arbitrary* manner, necessity and self-defence would make the union amongst them the stronger.

I will now examine what the Author of the *Old Whig* calls the *Great Point,* and which ought to carry the chief weight with us in this case: which is, "That the Alteration now proposed will give such a mighty Power to the bulk of the *English* Commons, as can never be counterbalanced by the body of the Nobility. Should we suppose two hundred thirty-five Peers possessed one with another of 5000*l.* *per annum,* this would amount to no more than 1,175,000*l.* *per annum.* And what is such a property, and the Power arising out of it, compared with the Power arising out of the property of those many millions possessed by the Commons?"

By this state of the case, we are to suppose on the one hand a certain, limited, fixed, hereditary body, of two hundred thirty-five Peers, enjoying great privileges above the Commons, and possessed of an annual revenue amounting to 1,175,000*l.* which they have entirely in their own power; and this estate not so equally divided as 5000*l.* *per annum* to every individual, but to some the command of 50,000*l.* a year apiece, others not 500*l.* a year. On the other hand, you must suppose a body of above twice the number fluctuating, unfixed, in the power of their Prince every moment, at furthest not able to subsist above a few years, and possessed of not near half the estate before-mentioned; is it not too evident which of these two bodies must destroy the other, if once this should come to be really the case? The Lords are Principals, and act entirely for themselves: the Commoners are no farther Principals than as to the estates they possess themselves. As our Author has stated this matter, in order to magnify the power of the wealth of the Commons, though he is all along speaking of the aggregate body, yet he would insinuate as if they had as great command over the universal Body of the People, as the Lords have over themselves. This is as much as to say, that the four Members of the city of London have as absolute command over the estates of all the inhabitants of that great *Metropolis,* as any four Lords have over their tenants. Indeed, if the Commons had a Power of laying taxes upon the estates of all those they represent, that would be the same thing in this case, provided they had it abstractedly from the Lords. But this fallacy, which is often insinuated in this Pamphlet, has been already detected. The Commons have no more power over their fellow subjects estates than the Lords: they cannot lay any tax without their Lordships concurrence. And all that is peculiar to the Commons in this matter is, that they have hitherto been allowed to chuse what tax they judged easiest for the people: but every day's experience shews us, that, if the Lords differ in opinion from the Commons, their power is at an end. The better to illustrate this *Great Point,* as our Author properly calls it; as he has computed the value of the wealth of the body of Peers, I will take the liberty to compute the value of the wealth of the body of the Commons. Supposing them to be worth, one with another, 800*l.* *per annum* including personal estates, which I am certain is not disparaging this, or any other House of Commons that has sat in a British Parliament; the annual income of five hundred fifty-eight Commoners will amount to 446,400*l.*; which is so insignificant a sum, in proportion to the value of the property of the Lords, that I will beg leave to compute his Majesty's whole Civil List with the property of the Commons, both sums together making but one million forty-six thousand four hundred pounds; and there will still remain a balance on their Lordships' side of one hundred twenty-eight thousand six hundred pounds *per annum.* *Therefore, if it is an uncontested maxim, That Power follows property,* p. 295; here is Power, here is Property; and let the body that possesses both in such a degree be but once made so independent as is proposed, would not the Crown, would not the Commons, be absolutely under the Dominion of the Lords, according to this Author's own way of reasoning?

I am satisfied the controversy is ended here: but I will suppose my Author not to have been mistaken so very grossly, and examine his argument upon an imagination that the property of the House of Commons was ten times superior to that of Lords, whereas the property of the Lords is near three times as much as theirs; yet, even in this case, the Lords would have the advantage of them; because an united constant body of men, always acting for the same interest and grandeur, and pursuing a continued scheme, must be an over-match for so transitory a body, and made up of persons of such different views and interests as the House of Commons is. To bring an example on this head. Let us imagine the stock of the Bank of England to be of the value of one million, and the stock or cash of all the Bankers, Scriveners, Goldsmiths, and dealers in Money throughout London, to be four times or eight times that sum; is there any body who does not believe the Bank, incorporated and well compacted in all respects for its own private interest, will not have a greater Power, greater credit and authority, than all those particular Proprietors of a much larger capital, who cannot possibly be ever put into any posture, so as to act with that weight for their interest, as the Bank will do for itself in the circumstances above-mentioned? The great Power of all such fixed bodies is chiefly owing to this circumstance, that two or three persons always govern the rest; and it is as well the common interest of the society that they should be so governed, as the particular interest of the governors. In this their strength chiefly consists; and for this reason five or six hundred Lords (if any body can be so wild as to suppose the Crown will ever increase their number to such a degree) will not be so terrible to the Crown or the People, as two hundred thirty-five, or any such fixed number. For to suppose that the majority of two hundred thirty five Lords, were they so fixed, would not be entirely directed and influenced by three or four amongst them of the greatest wealth, abilities, and resolution, is as absurd and improbable to common reason and constant experience, as any thing that can be thought of.

If it be allowed then, as it certainly must be, that the weight of so great Power, and of such disproportionable Property, may by this means come into a very few hands; what havock may it not make of the dignity of the Crown, and of the liberty of the People?

Thus I have shewn the certain destructive consequences of this project, as stated by the PLEBEIAN, and even as stated by the OLD WHIG himself. I must confess, I do not believe that the Authors of this scheme were apprehensive how far it would go; but since it is now so plain, that *he who runs may read*, I hope they themselves will desist from so desperate an undertaking.

I cannot help observing, that his Majesty is treated with great indignity by the Author before me, in several passages of his pamphlet. In one place he says, "Whilst the door of the House of Lords is always open, people of overflowing fortunes may find no great difficulty in procuring an entrance." In another, he insinuates, that "there is another kind of merit besides what arises from virtuous actions, learning, and industry, that has been often rewarded with Peerage." I am satisfied his Majesty has used this prerogative, as he has done every other prerogative of the Crown, with the greatest discernment, and therefore I am willing to trust it still in his hands. The House of Lords is treated by this Author still more *en cavalier* than his Majesty. His Words are these: "If the English Commonalty should (by this Bill) gain only this single advantage, I think it a very considerable one, that it will hinder the nation from being overrun with Lords. We know, that in the sale of an estate it is no small recommendation to the buyer, that there is no Lord within so many miles of it; and the distance of such a borderer is often looked upon as an equivalent to a year's purchase. But who can be secure from such a neighbour, whilst the species is so apt to increase and multiply? I shall not insist upon paying of debts, which is looked upon as a moral duty amongst Commoners, who cannot but be sorry to see any additions to an order of men that are sheltered by privileges from the demands of their honest and industrious creditors. To which many considerations of the like nature might be added, were they not obvious to the private reflection of every reader."

I cannot very well account for it, how this Author comes to take so great a liberty as he has done here; even so far, as to endeavour to make it believed, that the Lords are sheltered from their just debts; whereas every one knows, a Lord's goods and effects are liable to the pursuit of his creditors, though his person is always protected. This Author and I differ on every account, as to what relates to this branch of the Legisla ture. They seem to me to have been for many years and to be at present, a just and honourable body. This, I think, is owing to the frame of that body, and the situation it is in. I am against altering either, lest they should become tyrannical and odious. The OLD WHIG represents them to be at present a species of such a nature as I dare not venture to repeat, but must refer to his own words; and yet contends to vest them with much greater Powers than they now have.

I have but one remark more to make upon this Author, which is indeed in a matter of the last consequence, and which cannot be thoroughly considered till the next Paper. The Author of the OLD WHIG has very truly stated the Power of the Crown, as it relates to the Legislature, in these words:

"The Crown, as a branch of the Legislature, cannot desire a greater prerogative, than that of a negative in the passing of a law: and as it ought not to influence either House in their debates, what can a good King desire more, than the power of approving or rejecting any such bill as cannot pass into a law without the Royal Assent?"

As I readily admit of all that is here advanced, That the Regal part of the Legislature is to wait for the advice of its Great Council, both Houses of Parliament, and to give its negative to what it does not approve; that doing otherwise would be influencing the debates of one or both Houses, and turning the Constitution quite upside down: as I sincerely allow a good King cannot desire any more than the approving or rejecting any Bill offered him; and as I believe from the bottom of my heart, that we never had so good a King as we have now: what credit can I give to what this Author asserts, that *his Majesty has already signified his consent on this point*, of so great consequence to himself, and to the very being of his FAITHFUL COMMONS, before he has so much as once heard their Opinion? Our Author calls this an *act of unparalleled goodness.* But what I have to say upon this subject, I shall reserve to another opportunity, if what this Author seems to be assured of should prove true.

*** On the 28th of March was advertised, "The PATRICIAN, No. II. Considerations on the PEERAGE, in answer to the PLEBEIAN, continued.

> But the wild vulgar, ever discontent,
> Their growing fears in secret murmurs vent;
> Still prone to change, though still the slaves of state,
> And sure the Monarch, whom they have, to hate,
> Madly they make new Lords." POPE'S THEB.

In an advertisement of the same date, announcing the Third Number of the PLEBEIAN, is this caution: "N. B. Whereas it is suspected by a great many people, that the PATRICIAN, said to be writ against the PLEBEIAN, is really writ by one of the same side, which is an old trick amongst Writers; the Public is hereby assured, that the Author of the PLEBEIAN has not any hand in that Paper."

†‡† "To-morrow, being the day appointed for the Call of the Honourable House of Commons, will be published, by J. Roberts, "A discourse upon Honour and Peerage. Occasioned

by the present Reports of a Bill now depending relating to the state of the House of Peers By an Elector, Peer of Scotland.

Virtus repulsæ nescia sordidæ
Intaminatis fulgit honoribus."

Hor. 3 Od. i 17.

St. James's Port, April 1, 1719.

---

# THE PLEBEIAN.

## No. III. MONDAY, MARCH 30, 1719.

### BY A MEMBER OF THE HOUSE OF COMMONS.

FARTHER CONSIDERATIONS UPON THE REPORTS RELATING TO THE PEERAGE.

THE Plebeian expected before now to have heard again from the OLD WHIG, especially as to his making good the last particular taken notice of in the Paper, Numb. II. which relates to the part he was pleased to affirm his Majesty had already taken in this affair; and for which there does not seem to be any foundation. However, as *age is apt to be slow*, the PLEBEIAN is willing to wait some time longer to be satisfied in that point. In the mean while, to shew with how much candour he proceeds in this dispute, he will not decline publishing in this paper a Speech made in a kind of a private-public* Company, for the Bill; in which all the arguments on that side the question are urged with that great strength of reason, and with all that advantage of oratory, for which the honourable person who made it is so deservedly admired.

The form in which it was sent to the PLEBEIAN is as follows:

*A SPEECH in the Long Room at the Comptroller's* †

"Optat *Ephippia* BOS." ‡—HOR. I. Ep. xiv. 43.

"MR. BLADEN—Though the worthy gentleman that spoke last has represented the Bill that occasions this meeting as destructive of all that ought to be dear to every one that values his country, yet I am not ashamed to appear for it *with all the little zeal I am master of.* According to the *way that I have the honour of thinking of this matter*, this seems to

* In a Committee of the House of Commons.

† MARTIN BLADEN, Esq. Chairman of the Committee on the Peerage Bill, was Comptroller of the Mint.

‡ "The Ox would Trappings wear." DUNCOMBE.

me to be the best Bill that ever was offered us, and therefore *I shall be for it to the last drop of my breath.* I wish any gentleman would lay his hand upon his heart, and answer me whether the making twelve Lords at once in a late reign, was not the wickedest thing that ever was heard of. And such a thing I am certain may be attempted again, if we do not shew them a *new game*, and give them *one and thirty* of our own friends, to prevent any such practice for the future. The worthy gentleman was pleased to say, That the noble Lord who was the author of that advice might in some measure be excused, if that matter is compared with what is now proposed.

That Lord says, he plainly shewed that he thought what he did was a justifiable action, because he left the door open for himself to be called to account for it, in the same manner as all other Ministers had done before him; and did not endeavour to put himself out of all reach, by fixing those persons to be his judges, who concurred with him in what he did. Sir, I must tell that worthy gentleman, that though it has often happened that wicked men have been infatuated, and slipped their opportunity; yet that should not prevent honest gentlemen from providing for their own safety upon the like occasion. In all these cases, that worthy person added, that we ought to consider *quo animo* a man acts. I have already given my judgment in another place as to those words, and I shall give the same opinion here again. The gentleman, he thinks that this is a very bad Bill; that is his *quo animo.* I think it a very good one; that is my *quo animo.* As to what he said about the Scotch Lords, that this would be invading their property, and taking away their birthright, out of a pretence of curing a public inconvenience; and that in the same way of arguing, any Parliament may as well take away the Funds; nothing being more inconvenient to the publick, than paying such great and endless taxes: I hope the gentleman will allow there is a great deal of difference between what is done by friends, and what is done by enemies. If we do take away their property, I hope there is nobody here that imagines that we do it out of ill-will; and the world must allow, that what is done is rather out of kindness to ourselves, than out of malice to them. Besides, I have been informed by a very *Honourable Gentleman, That three of them are Boys at school;* and I hope nobody can imagine at this time of day, that any of those Gentlemen, for whom I own I have the greatest esteem, would be so barbarous *as to hurt young boys, out of an aversion to their persons.* As for those of *riper years*, there are several of them *Jacobites*, as the same *Honourable Person* has assured me; and I hope no such sort of people will meet with any encouragement here. Gentlemen are pleased to dwell much upon the Scotch Nobility in this case, as if their Representatives intended to take their property from them whereas it is very plain, they intend to make a Pr—— of them and is not that the same thing to the whole nation, so long as it is all amongst their *own countrymen?* And therefore I cannot imagine how any body can be so absurd, as to look upon this as a breach of the Union: And I hope we shall hear no more of that matter.

There has been one thing often insinuated in this debate, as if some gentlemen were influenced to come into this proposal *by assurance of Peerages*, as if *they had warrants in their pockets*, and I do not know what. For my part, Sir, I act according to the best of my *understanding*, and none of those mean considerations can have any weight with me. As for all their titles and honours, *I cast them all behind my back, like chaff before the wind.* For all which reasons, I shall be heartily for the Bill."

*** "The PATRICIAN, No. III. was published, April 4, 1729.

> "We are best of all led to
> Mens principles by what they do."—HUD.

On the same day appeared, "The MODERATOR, No. I. To be continued occasionally. The Arguments for and against such a Bill as is talked of, for regulating the Peerage, fairly stated, with some Reflexions upon the whole. By a Member of Parliament, *Medio tutiffimus.* Printed for J. Roberts, Price 6*d*." This seems to have been the only Number.

"The complicated Question divided, upon the Bill now depending in Parliament, relating to Peerage, written by MR. ASGILL. Sold by J. Darby and J. Roberts, Price 6*d*."

"Remarks on a Pamphlet, intituled, The Thoughts of a Member of the Lower House. Printed for J. Roberts, Price 6*d*."

On the 11th of April, 1719, the Fourth number of the PATRICIAN was published with this note from the CATO of MR. ADDISON.

> "—While the Fathers of the Senate meet
> In close debate—
> With love of Freedom—
> I'll thunder in their ears their country's cause,
> And try to rouse up all that's British in them."

# THE OLD WHIG.

---

## No. 2. THURSDAY, APRIL 2, 1719.

### WITH REMARKS UPON THE PLEBEIAN.

"———— Eja!
Quid statis? Nolint. Atqui licet effe beatis.
Quid causæ, est meritò quin illis Jupiter ambas
Iratus buccas inflet; neque se fore posthàc
Tam facilem dicat?—HOR. 1. Sat. i. 18.

"Why stand you thus? whence springs this strange delay?
None will be bless'd, yet every mortal may.
Since Heaven, incens'd, no more will condescend
To their next suit, a gracious ear to lend."—SHARD.

THE Author of the PLEBEIAN, to shew himself a perfect master in the vocation of Pamphlet-writing, begins like a son of Grubstreet, with declaring the greatest esteem he has for himself, and the contempt he entertains for the scribblers of the age.[1] One would think, by his way of presenting it, that the unexpected appearance of his pamphlet was as great a surprize upon the world as that of the late meteor, or indeed something more terrible, if you will believe the Author's magnificent description of his own performance. The PLEBEIAN, says he, starting forth unexpectedly, they were forced like people in a surprize, or on an invasion, to march immediately any troops they had. If Ca-

[1] It is for this paragraph that Addison has been accused of saying—'whose trade it is to write pamphlets."—G

dinal Alberoni's attempt, which furnishes the allusion, succeeds no better than that of his friend the Pamphleteer, he will not have much to boast of.

Our Author, in his triumphant progress, first animadverts on a Writer, whom he says he never read, which being my own case, I shall leave that Writer to defend himself. The second he mentions, considering the strength of his arguments, and the closeness of his reasoning, deserved a little more regard from the PLEBEIAN, who, it seems, with much ado went through the performance. This would certainly have been true, had he gone through it with a design to answer it.

Having routed Baronius, and confounded Bellarmine, pass we on to the next, said the Country Curate to his admiring audience. Our Author pursues his conquests with the same satisfaction and intrepidity. In the first place he is angry with a writer for assuming the name of the OLD WHIG, who may more justly recriminate upon this Author for taking that of the PLEBEIAN, a title which he is by no means fond of retaining, if we may give credit to many shrewd guessers. But he tells the OLD WHIG, that he expected from that title no less than the utmost wrath and indignation against the House of Lords. How does this agree with the censure he passes upon him afterwards, for treating that species in such a manner as he dares not venture to repeat! I must however remind this Author of the Milk with which he nurses our Nobles, not to omit his stagnated Pool; passages of such a nature, that, in imitation of the Author, I shall dispatch them with an Horresco referens!

The Author, in the next paragraph, gives us a definition of the point in debate, viz., that it is a Jumble and a Hodge-Podge, a most clear, comprehensive, and elegant account of the matter.

The Author then continues his animosities against the Ephori of Lacedæmon; but this passage I shall wave for two reasons:

First, because it is nothing to the purpose; Secondly, because I am informed there are two or three keen disputants, who will return a proper answer to it, when they have discovered the Author.[1]

The PLEBEIAN proceeds to detect an imaginary mistake in the OLD WHIG, for having asserted that there has been as great an alteration in one branch of the Legislature, as is now proposed to be made in another. A fact immediately puts an end to a dispute, and, in the case before us, stands thus:

| | |
|---|---|
| King Henry VIII. added to the House of Commons, . | 38 Members. |
| King Edward VI., . . . | 44 |
| Queen Mary, . . . | 25 |
| Queen Elizabeth, . . . | 62 |
| King James I. . . . | 27 |

The question now is, whether the restraining the numbe the House of Commons to what it is at present, was not as g at an alteration in that branch of the Legislature, as the restric on now proposed would be to the other branch of the Legislature, should it take place in it. To which I shall add the following question: Whether the inconveniences, arising from that continual increase in the House of Commons, did not make the restraint upon it prudent and necessary; and, Whether, if the like inconveniences arise from this perpetually increasing House of Lords, it is not as necessary and as prudent to put a stop to it? As for the little towns of Watchet and Dunster, our Author can draw nothing from them to the advantage of his cause, if he can bestow labour and time enough, of which he finds it necessary to be very sparing in this argument, to peruse the printed list of

[1] This is the passage alluded to by Macaulay, p. 75, and which hardly bears him out in his position.—G.

counties and boroughs, to whom the privilege of sending Representatives to Parliament was granted or restored by the several Princes above-mentioned; and to answer the short query proposed to him at the end of it, with relation to Queen Elizabeth:

After having proposed these questions in plain terms, I come in the next place to one of the PLEBEIAN's, which is carried on in metaphor, till it ends in something that is past my understanding. But these retrenchments being now made, the question, says he, at present is, whether the Commons ought to go on stripping the Crown of every jewel, till it becomes less resplendent than the Doge of Venice's coronet, or less comfortable than the Sword-bearer's Cap of Maintenance? I shall only confront this metaphorical query with one that is adapted to men of ordinary capacities. "These retrenchments being made, whether the Commons ought to accept the offer of the Crown, to part with a prerogative that is still exorbitant and dangerous to the Community?"

But our Author's chief concern is for the poor House of Commons, whom he represents as naked and defenceless, when the Crown, by losing this prerogative, would be less able to protect them against the Power of a House of Lords. Who forbears laughing, when the Spanish Friar represents LITTLE DICKEY, under the person of Gomez, insulting the Colonel that was able to fright him out of his wits with a single frown? This Gomez, says he, flew upon him like a dragon, got him down, the Devil being strong in him, and gave him bastinado on bastinado, and buffet upon buffet, which the poor meek Colonel, being prostrate, suffered with a most Christian Patience. The improbability of the fact never fails to raise mirth in the audience; and one may venture to answer for a British House of Commons, if we may guess from its conduct hitherto, that it will scarce be either so tame or so weak, as our Author supposes

The PLEBEIAN, to turn off the force of the remark upon another paragraph, has recourse to a shift that is of great use to controversial Writers, by affirming that his Antagonist mistakes his meaning. Let the impartial Reader judge whether an answer, that proves this alteration would not be detrimental to the House of Peers, is not suited to an objection which says in so many words, that it would be detrimental to the House itself. But, says the PLEBEIAN in this his reply to the OLD WHIG, it will not be detrimental to them in point of Power, but it will be detrimental on account of those talents which ought to accompany Power, the want of which the Commons will feel in their judicature. Which is, in other words, "I do not mean when I say that it will be detrimental to the House of Peers itself, that it will be detrimental to the Peers, but that it will be detrimental to the Commons." I appeal to any man, whether the OLD WHIG ignorantly mistook the natural sense of those words, or whether the PLEBEIAN ignorantly expressed that which he now says was his meaning in those words. The PLEBEIAN having in his former paper represented, that this old standing body of Peers, without receiving numerous additions from time to time, would become corrupt and offensive like a stagnated Pool, tells us here in excuse for them, that they will be offensive to others, but not perceive it themselves. If I could suppose, with the Author, that they would ever be in this lamentable pickle, I should be of his opinion, that they ought to be sweetened by such wholesome, pure, and fresh streams as are continually passing into them.

The PLEBEIAN next objects to the OLD WHIG's calculation of the probable extinction of two Titles, taking one year with another. By the calculation generally received, says this Author, I suppose he means the list published by way of prelude to this project. Whereas the OLD WHIG could not take that list for his calculation, but formed his calculation from that list, and from the nature of the alteration which is proposed This objection will immediately vanish upon discovering the fallacy of the PLEBEIAN's argument. He supposes no greater number of extinctions would happen among the English Lords were their numbers settled at 184, than happened in that body when they were only 59, 104, 142, 153, 162, or 168. At this rate of calculating, the PLEBEIAN will be sure of gaining his point, and affirms very truly that the extinctions by a just medium amount to no more than a Peer and a half for every year. But I appeal to honest Mr. WINGATE,[a] who was never looked upon as a party-writer, whether my calculation will not appear very just, if examined by his golden rule, and other curious operations of arithmetick, which are to be met with in his works; especially when the Bill, as it evidently tends to multiply extinctions, by preventing the Peerage from running into collateral lines, or descending to females, will more than answer my computation, if I should have the misfortune to disagree with the PLEBEIAN about some very minute fraction of a Lord, that might happen in the space of 116 years. As for those contingent vacancies which may be made by the edge of the Law, our Author regards the uncertainty of them as a very uncomfortable prospect to the candidates for Patrician honours, since they may have time enough to try all their patience, if they live in hopes of such an expedient for their promotion. The ascertaining of this point is indeed what I am not equal to, and must therefore leave it to the masters of political calculation. But our Author is afraid, that if such lucky opportunities of extinction should happen, Lords may still sit with their heads on, unless a seasonable increase may be made to them in such critical junctures. This, I must confess, is to me one very great reason

a The well-known Arithmetician.

for the alteration proposed; being fully of opinion with the OLD WHIG, as expressed in the following words, "Is this inconvenience better prevented in a House of Peers on the bottom it now stands? Can any who has been a good Minister be secure, if the Crown should add a sufficient number of his enemies to those who sit in judgment upon him? Or is a bad Minister in any danger, when he may be sheltered by the addition of a sufficient number of his friends?" The PLEBEIAN's answer to this passage is highly satisfactory: In either of these cases, says he, the utmost iniquity must be supposed in the Crown, which I must confess I cannot bring myself to do, and therefore my argument remains entire. I very much approve of the Author's dutiful and submissive behaviour to the Crown, which puts one in mind of the worthy Alderman, who, upon hearing a Member of the Common Council call the Emperor Nero, a Monster of Cruelty, told him, he ought not to speak disrespectfully of a crowned head. But if the Author will only go such lengths with me, as to allow there ever has been a bad Sovereign, or not to shock him with such a supposition, that there ever has been a wicked Ministry, and that it is not utterly impossible but there may be such in times to come, my argument stands entire. God be thanked, we are now blessed with a good King, and with the prospect of such for our days, but cannot answer for those who are yet unborn, since they will still be men, and therefore liable to imperfection.

The PLEBEIAN was hard-set by the answer of the OLD WHIG to his arguments, That the Limitation of the number of the Lords would run the Constitution into an Aristocracy, and has therefore very prudently shuffled the consideration of that point under another head, where he forgets the OLD WHIG's reply to what was urged against his opinion in that case, so that he has visibly given up the point which was most material in his first PLEBEIAN.

The OLD WHIG's remark therefore still stands out against him unanswered, and plainly turns his own ill consequence upon him, by shewing there is a visible tendency to an Aristocracy as the Constitution now stands, which would be taken away by the alteration proposed. But it is ungenerous to insult a baffled adversary; I shall therefore proceed to the next particular in dispute.

The OLD WHIG affirms, that the Power of giving money and raising taxes is confined to the body of the Commons, and that all the privileges together of the Lords are not equal to that One of commanding the Purse of the community. The PLEBEIAN allows the consequence, but cavils at the position, which is a received maxim among the Commons of England, the Doctrine of the House of Commons in particular, and established by the practice of every Parliament in the memory of man. Let us now see what the PLEBEIAN affirms in contradiction to it, and by the way observe whether he personates his part well, and speaks the language of one who writes himself a Member of the House of Commons. The Author asserts, That whether a Money-bill may not originally take its rise in the House of Lords, is a point never yet clearly given up by their Lordships, if he is not very much misinformed. This point, if I am not very much misinformed, was never claimed by the House of Lords, and has not a single precedent in the practice of that body in the Legislature. He afterwards asserts that the Commons have no more power over their fellow subjects estates than the Lords. Is not the power of granting a supply, fixing the quantum of that supply, appropriating every part of it to particular uses, and settling the Ways and Means for raising it; is not this power over their fellow-subjects estates much greater than that of the Lords, who can neither add to, diminish, nor alter any one of these particulars? And if the power of the Commons extends itself to all these points, how can the Author further affirm, that all which is peculiar to the Commons in this matter is, that they have hitherto been allowed to chuse what tax they judged easiest for the people! But what shadow of reason is there for him to proceed in asserting, that every day's experience shews us, that if the Lords differ in opinion from the Commons, their Power is at an end; since, on the contrary, experience shews us, that whenever the Lords have pretended to such a power, they have always been over-ruled by the Commons! Our Author tells us, the concurrence of the Lords is as necessary to a Money-bill as to any other Bill. That is not denied; but he must allow that the Lords concurrence to a Money-bill is not of the same nature with their concurrence to any other Bill, which they may undoubtedly change, amend, and return, upon the hands of the House of Commons, for their concurrence in such amendments as the Lords shall think proper. Besides, to shew the PLEBEIAN how much the purse of the community is at the command of the Commons, let him consider the case of a vote of credit, which is transacted wholly between the Sovereign and the Lower House To this we may add, that the Sovereign himself, in his Speeches to Parliament, applies that part which relates to money to the House of Commons, distinct from that of the Lords; by which method it is plain the Crown supposes those privileges are vested in the House of Commons, to which every Member of that House has always pretended, except the present Author.

The PLEBEIAN in the next paragraph makes use of a very sure and wise method of confounding his antagonist, by putting his own sense upon a passage in that Author's pamphlet. The OLD WHIG represents how dangerous it would be to our constitution, if the Crown, which is already possessed of a certain means to over-rule one branch of the Legislature, should ever be able to influence the Elections of a House of Commons, so as to gain one to its measures; in which case, if liberty was endangered in the Lower House, it could not make a stand in the other. The PLEBEIAN perverts this meaning after the following manner; This Author, says he, assures us, that the Crown has Power enough to gain a House of Commons of what complexion it pleases; and, after puzzling himself in his own voluntary blunder, is displeased with the OLD WHIG for not proposing to cure an inconvenience which he never affirmed to be in the House of Commons, as well as that which he proves to be in the House of Lords; so that he would have had him quit the subject which he had undertaken, to speak of one which he had nothing to do with. But supposing the PLEBEIAN had rightly stated the sense of the Author, the inconvenience in the House of Lords is that which is woven into its very Constitution, and therefore at all times exposes us to its ill consequences; whereas what the PLEBEIAN suggests with regard to the House of Commons is only extrinsic, and accidental to that body, if it ever happens in it.

It is not probable that this dispute between the PLEBEIAN and the OLD WHIG will last many weeks; but, if there was time to discuss the whole point, I think it may be shown to a demonstration, that the check of the Crown upon the House of Commons, which is the Power of Dissolution, is, by infinite degrees, a weaker check than that it has in the present Constitution upon the House of Lords, which is the power of adding to it what number, at what time, and for what purpose it pleases: nay, that the power of Dissolution is also in its nature a check upon the House of Lords, as it dissolves them in a Legislative capacity, and may break the most dangerous cabals against the Crown, which are such as may be formed between the leaders of the Two Houses. These two points, if drawn out into such considerations as naturally rise from them, would fully establish the necessity of three branches in a perfect Legislature, and demonstrate that they should be so far separate and distinct from each other, as is essential to Legislative Bodies: Or, as the OLD WHIG has before explained it, "If one part of the Legislature may any ways be invested with a power to force either of the other Two to concur with it, the Legislative Power is in reality, whatever it may pretend to, divided into no more than two branches."

I have hitherto followed the PLEBEIAN in his own method, by examining, First, his replies to the objections made by the OLD WHIG; and come now to his Second general head, wherein he formally proposes to consider the argument as the OLD WHIG states it himself. And here I was not a little surprized to find, that, instead of answering the several distinct arguments urged by that Author in defence of the bill, as drawn from the nature of Government in general, from the British Constitution, from its effects on the Crown, on the House of Commons, on the whole body of the English Commonalty, and from the ill consequences it would remedy in the present Constitution; the PLEBEIAN contents himself with attacking but one single argument of his Antagonist. Till the PLEBEIAN shall have answered those other points, I shall take it for granted that he gives them up. Not to multiply words, I believe every Reader will allow me that an Author is not to be much regarded, who writes professedly in answer to a discourse which proceeds on many arguments, when he singles out that argument only which he thinks is the weakest; especially when he fails in his answer even to that single argument. A famous French Author compares the imaginary triumphs of such a kind of disputant, whom he was then dealing with, to those of CLAUDIUS, which, instead of being represented by the strong towns he had taken, and the armies he had defeated, were testified to the people of Rome, by a present of cockle shells that he had gathered up on the sea-shore.

But to come to the matter before us. The OLD WHIG, after

having considered it in several views, examines it with regard to the whole bulk of the British Commons. Under this head he has the following words: "But the great point, and which ought to carry the chief weight with us in this case, is, that the alterations now proposed will give such a mighty power to the bulk of the English Commons, as can be never counterbalanced by the body of the Nobility." Now, what the OLD WHIG here calls the Great Point with regard to the Commonalty of England, the PLEBEIAN insinuates he calls the Great Point with regard to the whole controversy, and descants upon it accordingly. Whereas it is evident the Author insists upon many points as great as this in other views of the question. The OLD WHIG affirms, that the Commonalty has infinitely more wealth than the Nobility, which was the proper consideration of this place. The PLEBEIAN returns for answer, that the Commonalty is indeed much richer than the Nobility, but that the House of Commons is not so rich; which was not the proper consideration of this place. It is impossible for a disputant to lose the cause, who is a master of such distinctions. I remember I was once present at an University Disputation, which was managed on the one side by a notable Peripatetick. The question which he defended in the negative was, Whether comets are above the moon? The Sophister, being pressed very hard by the force of demonstration, very gravely extricated himself out of it by the following distinction. Comets, said he, are two-fold, Supra-lunar and Sub-lunar. That Supra-lunar Comets are above the Moon I do allow; but that Sub-lunar Comets are above the Moon I utterly deny. And it is of this latter kind of Comets that the Question is to be understood.

The fallacy of the PLEBEIAN's answer being thus far discovered, all that he further adds in his own way of arguing will be easily confuted by unraveling the matter which he has very artificially perplexed. The OLD WHIG supposes that every Lord in the Legislature, taken one with another, may be worth 5000*l.* a year, in which, for argument's sake, every one knows his concession has been vastly too liberal. The PLEBEIAN values every Member of the House of Commons at 800*l.* per annum one with another, in which it is plain he has been exceeding scanty. Nay, many are of opinion, that upon casting up the whole sum of property that now resides in the House of Lords, it would not exceed that which is in the House of Commons. If this particular approaches to the truth, all arguments of a superior Power arising from its greater property fall to the ground of themselves, as being raised on a false foundation. To which I must further add, that if this increasing Power still continues in the Crown, the Property of the House of Peers will indisputably surmount that of the House of Commons; and that, on the contrary, if the Bill passes, it visibly tends to prevent the impoverishment of the House of Commons in point of property, and to fill it with men of such estates as in a few years will be more than a counterbalance to the House of Lords, even under this view.

But, further to shew the weakness of the PLEBEIAN's reasonings upon this head, I will allow that the House of Lords enjoy at present, and may still continue to enjoy, a greater share of property than the House of Commons. But notwithstanding this concession, to which the nature of the thing does not oblige me, it is still evident that the immense property which subsists in the bulk of the English Commons will render their Representatives more powerful than the Body of the Lords. This will plainly appear from considering the very nature of Representatives; from those junctures which can possibly give them an occasion of exerting their Power; and from matter of fact.

It is implied in the very nature of Representatives, that they are backed with the Power of those whom they represent; as the demands of a Plenipotentiary, let his persona wealth or power be as little as you please, have the same weight with them as if they were made by the Person of his principal. I will beg leave to borrow from the PLEBEIAN an example of the Bank of England, which, as he makes use of it, has no manner of analogy with the subject of the dispute. Is not the whole flock of that numerous Community under the guidance of a few Directors? And will any one say, that these Directors have no other influence on the publick, than what arises to them from the share which they personally enjoy in that stock? The Author urges that the Peers are principals, which in reality is the reason why their Power is not to be apprehended in opposition to that of the Commons: whereas, were they only Representatives of a Body immensely rich and numerous, they would, beside their own personal Property, have such a support as would make them truly formidable. The whole Commons of England are the Principals on one side, as the Lords are the Principals on the other; and which of these Principals are armed with most Power and Property?

To consider in the next place those junctures that can possibly give them an occasion of exerting their power. It is on both sides supposed to be in such cases as will affect the rights of the English Commonalty, in which case every Commoner of England is as much concerned as any of their Representatives. Thus if four London Citizens, to make the case exactly parallel, were deputed to maintain the rights of their Principals, as Citizens, who can imagine that they would not be supported by the whole Power and Property of the City, and not be too hard for any two or three great men, who had ten times their personal estates? Now as the PLEBEIAN's supposition reduces things to the last extremity, it can only take place in a rupture, which is never likely to happen. And in that case, as these two great bodies must act separately, there is no room for considering how far the Concurrence of the House of Lords is necessary in a Money-bill, which entirely takes away the Author's reasoning in page 321.

But matters of fact are the best arguments. We both agree that Power arises out of Property; and the Author himself has given an instance of the Power of the House of Commons in having been able to effect the ruin of the Monarchy and Peerage. Whence had the Commons this Power, but from being supported by their Principals?

The PLEBEIAN thinks he strengthens his point, by adding that the Lords are a fixed Body. To this I might reply, that the Principals of the House of Commons are as fixed a Body as the Lords; and therefore, however their Representatives may vary, they will continue intent, from age to age, to assert and vindicate their peculiar rights and privileges, unless we can believe that any body of men will act against those two strong motives of self-interest and self-preservation. I might further venture to say, that men of the greatest wealth and weight in the House of Commons are almost as sure of a seat there, as if it came to them by inheritance. But supposing the House of Lords never so much fixed, and so manageable by two or three great men (for which very reason additions are very often made to them, which the alteration would prevent), we have seen that their United Power, if their number is limited, can never be a match for that of the House of Commons, supposing still such a rupture as the PLEBEIAN all along imagines, in which each body is to act separately for itself.

The Author, in the remaining part of his pamphlet, appears like every Writer that is driven out of all his holds. He endeavours to set the Crown, and the whole body of Peers, upon his adversary; accuses him in effect of *Scandalum Magnatum;* nay, and gives very broad intimations that he ought to be indicted for High-Treason.

I should not have given myself, or the publick, all this trouble, had I not been so peremptorily called to it by the last PLEBEIAN. I do assure him, my silence hitherto was not the effect of old age, as it has made me slow, but to tell him the truth, as it has made me a little testy, and consequently impatient of contradiction, when I find myself in the right. I must own, however, that the writer of the PLEBEIAN has made the most of a weak cause, and do believe that a good one would shine in his hands; for which reason I shall advise him, as a friend, if he goes on in his new vocation,[1] to take care that he be as happy in the choice of his subject, as he is in the talents of a Pamphleteer

⁂ The Author of a Pamphlet, intituled, "Six Questions, stated and answered, upon which the whole force of the Arguments for and against the Peerage Bill depends, printed for J. Roberts, 1719, 8vo., sets out thus; "It is my opinion that much darkness and perplexity have been introduced into the question now in agitation, by words and things, very foreign to a matter which touches only the peculiar constitution of Government, in which we of this nation are concerned. If we strip the debate of such words as PATRICIAN and PLEBEIAN, which do not at all answer to LORDS and COMMONS joined with a KING in all Acts of Legislation: If we leave off talking of the nature of ARISTOCRACIES and DEMOCRACIES, which only amuse and distract the mind of the enquirer: If we take out of the question all allusions to the EPHORI of the *Lacedæmonians*, as distant in their condition from the state of our PEERS, as in the situation of their country; all stories of the NOBLES of *Denmark*, or of the Power of our BARONS in times of old, which has no relation to the Power of the PEERS of *Great Britain*, in the condition in which this Bill leaves them, surrounded with a World of rich and free Commoners: I say, if these and the like words and things be quite removed, and the consideration of Men confined to a few points which ought, and which must, determine the equity or iniquity, the wisdom or weakness, of the scheme now before the Parliament, we might hope that Gentlemen might, on both sides, be more clear, and less perplexed, in their sentiments than they yet seem to be."

[1] This certainly looks as if Addison had recognized his opponent.—G

# THE PLEBEIAN.

## No. IV. MONDAY, APRIL 6, 1719.

CONSIDERATIONS UPON THE REPORTS ABOUT THE PEERAGE, CONTINUED; IN PARTICULAR, WITH RELATION TO THE SCOTS NOBILITY. WITH REMARKS ON THE PATRICIAN, NO. II. AND THE OLD WHIG, NO. II. BY A MEMBER OF THE HOUSE OF COMMONS.

"——Quorum melior sententia menti.
— Pelago Danaum insidias, suspectaque dona
Præcipitare jubent."—VIRG. ÆN. II. 35.

—— The rest, of sounder mind,
The fatal present to the flames design'd,
Or to the watery deep.—DRYDEN.

THE PLEBEIAN has been obliged to object to the OLD WHIG, one of the *Infirmities* of *Age*, viz. *Slowness;* and he must now take notice of another, though he does it with great reluctance, that is, *want of Memory;* for the *old Gentleman* seems to have forgot, that at his first appearance he promised the public a particular Treatise on the subject of the *Peerage*, as it relates to *Scotland*, p. 304.

There is at present very little probability that he will be so good as his word, and therefore I shall not delay any longer publishing something that is come to my hands on that head, which in my opinion may be of use in this controversy. Indeed, I am informed, that it has already been produced in a weekly pamphlet, which very few people, I fear, ever read, called *The Honest Gentleman;* and therefore I hope at least to be excused in making it more public, and in using this worthy person as an ally in this quarrel, since I have so strong a confederacy against me. What I am speaking of, is a *Letter from a Nobleman of* Scotland *to a Gentleman of* England. When I mention a Scotish Nobleman, I would not have it understood to be one of the *Elect*, but one of the *Outcasts;* and as the case of those unfortunate persons will be, if possible, more abject and deplorable than that of the Commons of England, it is not strange that the PLEBEIAN should endeavour to do them what service he can.

THE LETTER IS AS FOLLOWS.

"Sir,

If the pleasure of doing good be indeed its own reward, you will easily excuse the trouble of this letter. Nothing is so talkative as misfortune: But they surely may be allowed to speak for themselves, who, as they find to their great surprize, have none to speak for them.

"I was born a Peer of Scotland, formerly a character of some importance, but at present (I am afraid) degenerating into so little significancy, that perhaps this is the last time there will be any reputation to me in owning it.

"Every one that is acquainted with our history sees very well how much we gained, and what we lost, by the Union. We lost our Senate and our Senators; we lost the service of many of our great men, and they seem to have lost —— I know not what. But yet it might be remembered by your free and generous nation, that when we resigned ourselves to that Union, we intended at least to have retained the rights of men and subjects, without the least suspicion of any encroachments upon us, which you have ever so bravely rejected from yourselves. And even at this Union, there were some articles agreed to, which seem to make for our country, and which it would be very proper for the party in the present design to consult; and if after that they can deliberately give us up, they merit all the reproaches that the injuries of a betrayed ruined people can extort from them. We justly call ourselves a ruined people: for if at present we are any thing short of it, what may we not expect from those, if any such there are, who shall dare to assume a Power which we never gave them; and that not to be used for our advantage, but to the injury of the nation they represent, and the Peerage of which they are part? It is certain, a principle that can at any time prevail above the Love of one's country, may engage them at some time or other in any designs, to the very extinction of it.

"Next to the pleasure that flows from the conscious innocence of an honest heart and a good meaning, the art of disguising and palliating a bad one gives the greatest, though the falsest satisfaction. Thus I have heard it has been alledged by some who have been too advantageously engaged on one side of the question, that there is a very ingenious distinction to be made between absolutely violating such and such articles, and a commodious deviation from them, for certain reasons; though a plain man would not immediately find out the real difference.

"I have read in very old books, that Justice was once the end of Power, and that the Great were such as were meritorious and useful. But if this Bill should pass, it would seem that those errors are to be exploded by this Bill; and yet many of the most ancient families among us believe, that they and their descendants are thereby to be made unhappy and uneasy to themselves, and useless to their country. They think the title of a Lord is the most insignificant part of his character; but when it is worn to adorn the merit and services of a truly great Man, it exposes Virtue in the most amiable light to universal emulation.—How irksome will it be to many a great spirit to be thought a mere Lord, to reflect on the worth of his great ancestors, and to inherit only their title; to have every talent of being useful, but the Power; to hear his fathers called good, and great, and wise, and himself his Lordship!—May we not expect that if great men should find themselves thus managed out of their birthrights, they will not easily resign themselves to a life of indolence and supineness, but still hope that some occasion or other may court them to action elsewhere? God forbid it should be against that country which shall have so injuriously rendered them supernumerary to its happiness, and which would then perhaps too late find them fatal to it.

"In such case they will, no doubt, pretend in their justification, that by having been thus divested of their birth-right, in representing themselves, or the right at least of electing their Representatives, that they apprehended they were implicitly disclaimed by the Government, and reduced to the condition of outlaws, and thereby discharged from the obligations and laws of society.

"But as the injuries, which we fear may be done us by this Bill, do not so nearly affect you, I might give several reasons, why as Englishmen you should reject it; and shew you, that at the same time that it will be the greatest discouragement to the merit of the Commonalty, it may end in equal dishonour to the Peerage.

"As to the Commonalty, it is apparent that almost every great Genius has for a long time been produced among them, and all the posts of service have been filled by such who were born Commoners, while the offices of mere favour and show have been supplied from elsewhere. The reason of this is evident. A Commoner finds a great deal of merit necessary to his character, as an *Equivalent* for the want of Quality; while the young Lord, infinitely satisfied with the adulations of his creatures and dependants, with ease believes what is their interest to tell him, and so aims no higher. But, should this Bill pass, a Commoner will have as little incitement to great actions as a Peer, and be as far below the possibility of rising, as a Lord is often above it.

"As to the Peerage, if we look into their assembly, and compare the many that sit there by right of descent, with the characters of those who were first created to those honours, and consider the modern education by which they are usually formed to their future greatness, how much looseness, flattery, and false politeness, they affect from their first entrance into life; we shall be able to form some notion of what sort of Geniuses that assembly will be composed twenty years hence, in case this Bill should pass, which is ever to be our supreme court of Judicature, but will be incapable of receiving into it even the most conspicuous merit of the age: I fancy it will very little resemble the body o ancient Barons of this Kingdom, whose actions supply such an illustrious part of our history. On the contrary, we may expect, that as they have before been voted *useless*, they will be in danger of being really so; and if that is ever the case, though now and then a family should be extinct, and thereby an obstacle to virtuous actions be removed, it will be in vain to endeavour to retrieve their Honour, by thinking to supply the extinction with a man of worth and merit, who will not be over fond of making one in so indifferent an assembly. So that this project, which pretends to do so much for the honour of the House, may prove as injurious to it, as to every one that is excluded from it.

"A Commoner should not too carelessly reply to this objection, That the more insignificant that House appears, the greater weight is in the Representatives of the people; for the Commons are the guardians of the Constitution in general, as well as the private rights of their Electors in particular: besides, it does not seem upon just reflection so expedient, that that Court, which is the *dernier resort* of Justice, should ever be filled with such Judges as they might despair or disdain to apply to for relief.

But, in fine, if public justice is as obligatory as private; if what is so injurious to our Country may be as fatal to yours; if such a Bill would be the greatest provocation to disaffection and uneasiness to a powerful body among us, and the greatest discouragement to merit both to you and us; if it would prove prejudicial to the reputation of the Peerage, though not to their power, which is worst of all, for at the same time it would lay the foundation of a most wretched Aristocracy; if the notions of Faith and Honour are not obliterated; if the most solemn engagements are any more than words; if we ought not to violate the Rights of Nations for mere private-convenience; this Bill will be rejected with the detestation with which all true Britons will treat every incroachment on the rights of mankind, or their fellow-subjects. I am, Sir, &c."

I cannot but think that what this Noble Briton has here said on the proposal for turning sixteen Scottish elective Peers into twenty-five hereditary ones, to the exclusion of all the rest of their principals, must make great impression upon every one that thoroughly considers it. I have not yet troubled the publick, throughout the whole course of this affair, with my thoughts on this point. For my part, I am so far from being of opinion that this *precarious situation* of the Scotch Peers is an *Evil* in the Body of the House of Lords that wants to be remedied, that it seems to me to be a very *fortunate circumstance, and the best remedy that can be provided for the Ill that both the Lords and Commons complain of.* Indeed, if the Lords can be satisfied with nothing less than being made *absolutely Independent*, which, as it has been plainly shewn, is entirely destroying the Constitution; I must confess this will not answer their purpose: but if it be reasonable they should be under some influence of the Crown, as the other branch of the Legislature is, and, however, may be desirous that their dignity be not debased, nor their weight diminished by the frequent additions of Peers, which the necessities of affairs may require to be made to their Body; is it not in this case a *desirable circumstance*, that the Crown can change once in three or four, or a few years more at farthest, so many of their Members, as may answer the intentions of the Government, and not add to their number? And in like manner, if the Commons are apprehensive that the frequent draughts out of their Body, to make an over-balance in the House of Peers, are detrimental to their power, in point of property, by taking so many considerable estates from them; are they to be instrumental in changing that precarious situation of so many Members of the Upper House, as leaves it in the power of the crown to make such alterations in that House, from time to time, as the Crown may think expedient without taking one Member from the Commons?

Besides, there is a reason of another nature why the Commons, in my judgment, ought to rest very well satisfied that the Crown has this Power over so many Members of the other House; because it is just the same kind of Power as the Crown has over the Commons themselves. And in some circumstances this may prove even such a check upon the Crown as the Commons may reap advantage from, and prevent the putting such sudden periods to their Being, as have been known formerly. Nay, I very much suspect, that if the proposed alteration should be made, the effect of it would be very soon felt; and if so, I beg Gentlemen would consider with themselves, what reception they may in all probability meet with from the general Body of the Commons of England, immediately after their having given such Power to the House of Peers, as no one ever ventured to mention to their ancestors. How this matter is understood in the country, we hear from all parts already; and this is indeed an *Advantage from the late Recess* on the side of those who are against the Bill.

But to return from this digression. How little soever what has been said may relish with some of those of another body, I am speaking here as a Commoner of England; as one that has no ambitious desire of *being a Lord*, but very great apprehensions of *being a Vassal*. As the House of Lords now stands, there are several members of it in the same circumstances with myself; what reason have I to consent to any thing that shall put any of them into a more independent state than I found them? Is there any one of their Lordships that would not laugh at a proposal for making any numbers of the Commons *hereditary*, who are now *all elective*, though it might be done with the same justice as to their principals? Their Lordships would all say, *That is the Constitution of the House of Commons, and there we will leave it.* And has not this been the Constitution of the House of Lords ever since the British nation was united?

It is allowed that, according to the treaties between the two kingdoms, confirmed by the most solemn Acts of Parliament, this is true. But then say they, other things were promised, without which they would never have consented to the Union. For my part, I have as bad an opinion of *oral tradition in Politicks, as in Religion;* and therefore nothing of this kind can weigh at all with me. But supposing that there is some inconvenience, in the present situation of the Peerage, to the House of Lords, that difficulties may happen in relation to the seats of some Noblemen amongst them; are not those difficulties arisen entirely from themselves? And is it not an odd compliment to the Commons, that if the Lords *feel a thorn in their feet, they should desire the Commons to take it out, to put it into their own?* Surely they will never be brought to do this; much less to endanger their utter ruin, for the convenience of another body of men.

Whilst I am writing this, the OLD WHIG, Number II. is come to my hands. I really thought he had been *departed;* and whether it be him*self*, or his *Ghost* that walks, I am not thoroughly satisfied.

The first OLD WHIG, I must confess, had stated his argument, and was going on very regularly, if he had not been disturbed in his progress; but this *second* is as inconsistent as possible. In the first paragraph of the performance before me, he treats the PLEBEIAN as a *Grub street*-writer; but in the last, and several other paragraphs, as a very *able shrewd fellow*

As to his remarks on the PLEBEIAN, Numb. II. he owns himself, "That he was very unwilling to have been concerned any farther in the dispute, and *nothing could have engaged him to have given himself or the publick any more trouble,* had he not been so peremptorily called to it by the last PLEBEIAN.

But as to what that PLEBEIAN calls upon him for, which was to make good what he had asserted in relation *to his Majesty's Concession,* he does not say one word about it. Indeed in his *Motto* he hints at it, and a *Fellow Labourer* of this Author has spoken out something more plainly on this subject. Upon the whole, it is very extraordinary. Here is at present the greatest favour or bounty, call it which you will, offered to the Commons, that ever was known, and the like it is probable will never be made to them again; and yet I do not know how it happens, they are so blind, or so perverse, that they will not see what is *so prodigiously for their good;* nay, one can hardly tell how to get them into it *by any means whatever.* The PATRICIAN says, "It is an affront of the highest nature to the Crown, and a petty kind of rebellion to refuse this offer." And the OLD WHIG seems to be of opinion, that they deserve *to have their ears boxed for it.* As to the rest of his *Motto, Nil ultra quæro Plebeius.** But whether this project was chiefly intended for the benefit of the Commons, I leave every one to judge from both these Authors, one of which plainly discovers, "That he has a prodigious concern for innocent Ministers, and trembles for what

* Horace, 2 Sat. ii. 188.
—My questions I restrain,
A mean PLEBEIAN born." DUNCOMB.

may happen to them from Kings who are yet unborn." But the PATRICIAN has two paragraphs, which I shall transcribe without any Commentary. "The general clamour, &c. as if the design of limiting the Number of Peers, and restraining the Prerogative of the Crown, was at first projected with a view of insulting the Prince of Wales, who by this proceeding will be debarred the liberty of creating Peers as his predecessors have done, is so low a reflection on the present Ministry, that I should not have regarded it, but that I find it a popular one.

"In short, we never know into whose hands the reins of Government may devolve. It therefore behoves us to secure our privileges, that we may not fall the victims of any aspiring Prince's enraged dispositions."

But to return to the OLD WHIG. I confess, I am uncapable to answer what he calls his Remarks, or his Objections. When I talked to him last, it was, as to the Commons, upon a foot as he had stated it himself, That the Crown could have a House of Commons of what complexion it pleased; which are his own words. As to the Lords, That they had a very considerable property of one million a hundred and seventy-five thousand pounds *per annum:* But now he says all that was only a *Jest.* And as to the Commons, the Crown has no power at all over them; and as for the Lords, he pleads poverty in their behalf. And he behaves in the same evasive contradictory manner, on every other point in dispute between us. But what is worst of all, he very frequently, for want of any the least shadow of an argument, has recourse to telling *old stories,* as if they were things that happened but yesterday; which, I confess, is another of the *defects of age.* And if he will not continue to be *testy,* I shall admonish him, that he has *every where* proved himself OLD but *no* where a WHIG. As to what he seems to insinuate in relation to what is said in the second PLEBEIAN concerning the *Ephori,* the PLEBEIAN can maintain it by the best authority. *Crags* is the man I have all along depended upon on this head, and he says, *they led the most abandoned dissolute lives;* and certainly he ought to know. His words are these, *Quamvis ipsi* Ephori *viverent indulgentius et dissolutius;* p. 78.

The rest of this paragraph is very mean; and this Author's menaces in this place are as vain, as his compassion in another part of his pamphlet is insolent.

I shall take notice but of one thing more in this pamphlet, which is the last paragraph, in these words:

"I must own, however, that the Writer of the PLEBEIAN has made the best of a weak cause; and do believe, that a good one would shine in his hands; for which reason I shall advise him as a friend, if he goes on in his new vocation, to take care that he be as happy in the choice of his subject, as he is in the talents of a Pamphleteer."

*Authors* in these cases are named upon *suspicion;* and if it is right as to the OLD WHIG, I leave the world to judge of *this cause* by comparison of this *performance* to his other *Writings*. And I shall say no more of what is writ in *support of Vassalage*, but end this paper, by firing every free breast with that noble exhortation of the Tragedian:

> Remember, O my Friends, the Laws, the Rights,
> The generous Plan of Power, deliver'd down
> From Age to Age by your renown'd Fore-fathers,
> (So dearly bought, the price of so much Blood.)
> O let it never perish in your hands!
> But piously transmit it to your Children.—MR. ADDISON'S Cato.

## POSTSCRIPT.

I BEG pardon for giving my Reader this irregular trouble, having omitted something of consequence in this affair. It is said, that by the Bill, which perhaps may be proposed to the Commons,* his Majesty is to have the naming of the twenty-five hereditary Scottish Peers; that they are all to be named before the next session: But that if it should happen that any of the present sixteen should not be of the number of those named by his Majesty, in such case the present temporary Peers are to remain Lords of Parliament so long as this Parliament subsists, and their hereditary successors are during that term to be withheld from what, it is probable, they may be more than a little desirous of *viz. a seat in the House of Peers*. If this is to be the case, I beg leave to ask these two questions: The first is, Whether any of those Lords, who at present are of the House of Peers, will continue to be *very easy company*, when they shall find themselves excluded at the end of this Parliament? For that some of them are to be excluded seems to be indisputable, if what is mentioned above is a right state of the case; for otherwise the sixteen might have been all declared hereditary, and his Majesty only left to add nine to the Scots, as he is six to the English.

The next question I would ask, is, Whether it is not very natural to think, that those Scottish Peers who are to be the hereditary successors of

* On Monday, April 6, 1719, the day on which the Fourth PLEBEIAN was published, the PEERAGE BILL was reported in the House of Lords, and ordered for a third reading on the 14th; but when that day arrived, a noble Lord in a very high station observed, "That the Bill had made a great noise, raised strange apprehensions; and since the design of it had been so misrepresented, and so misunderstood, that it was like to meet with great opposition in the other House, he thought it adviseable to let that matter lie still, till a more proper opportunity;" And thereupon the third reading of the said Bill was put off to that day fortnight. The Bill, which was in consequence dropt for that session, was revived in December following, when STEELE again figured away on the subject, as may be seen in page 381 and seqq. Several also of the pamphlets relating to that affair, printed during the preceding session, were revived, and new ones printed; among these were,

1. "An account of the Conduct of the Ministry with relation to the Peerage Bill, in a Letter to a Friend in the Country."
2. "Considerations on the Peerage Bill, addressed to the Whigs, by a Member of the Lower House."
3. "The Constitution explained; in relation to the Independency of the House of Lords with Reasons for strengthening that Branch of the Legislature most liable to Abuse; and an Answer to all the Objections made to the new-revived Peerage Bill."

the present elective ones, will not be very pressing to be put in possession? Should both these points be allowed, as I believe they must, and likewise that the patrons of this project do not wish for any thing so much as to be in the full enjoyment of this salutary scheme, then I will venture to affirm, that there is no one expedient to gratify the ardent desires of those gentlemen, to deliver them from the *disquietude* of those that *are in*, and from the *importunity* of those that are *to come in*, but the Dissolution of this Parliament. On the other hand; if this Bill should not be offered to the House of Commons, or, if offered, should not pass, I leave every one to judge whether the present Sixteen Scottish Peers will not be very solicitous of sitting out the remainder of the septennial term, to wear off the impressions which it is to be feared such an attempt as is talked of may have made upon the minds of their electors.

††† This day is published "The Occasional Paper, Vol. III. Numb. X. Of Genius." Printed for Em. Matthews, J. Roberts, &c. where may be had, the second edition of "The Occasional Paper, Vol. III. Numb. IX. of Plays and Masquerades." St. James's Post, March 29, 1719.

# THE LOVER.

BY MARMADUKE MYRTLE, Gent.

Phyllida amo ante alias, nam me discedere flevit.—Virg. Eclog. III. 78.

## INTRODUCTORY REMARKS.

The history of this work belongs rather to an edition of Steele than to one of Addison. For the present purpose it will be sufficient to say, that 'The Lover' forms a series of papers, beginning Thursday, Feb. 25, 1713–14, and ending with the fortieth number, Thursday, May 27, 1714. The first sketch of the character of the Lover is given in the Tatler under the name of Cynthio, and repeated in the Spectator under that of Sir Roger de Coverley. On resuming the subject Steele assumed the name of Marmaduke Myrtle, *Gent.* The whole work was dedicated, in the eulogistic style of the age, to Doctor Garth, author of the Dispensary. It was reprinted by Nichols in 1789. Addison contributed two papers, and is supposed to have had a hand in several others.—G.

# THE LOVER.

---

No. 10. THURSDAY, MARCH 18, 1714.

—— —*Magis illa placent quæ pluris emuntur.*

I HAVE lately been very much teased with the thought of Mrs. Anne Page, and the memory of those many cruelties which I suffered from that obdurate fair one. Mrs. Anne was, in a particular manner, very fond of china ware, against which I had, unfortunately, declared my aversion. I do not know but this was the first occasion of her coldness towards me, which makes me sick at the very sight of a china dish ever since. This is the best introduction I can make for my present discourse which may serve to fill up a gap, till I am more at leisure to re sume the thread of my amours.

There are no inclinations in women which more surprise me, than their passions for chalk and china. The first of these mala dies wears out in a little time; but when a woman is visited with the second, it generally takes possession of her for life. China vessels are playthings for women of all ages. An old lady of fourscore shall be as busy in cleaning an Indian Mandarin, as her great-grand-daughter is in dressing her baby.

The common way of purchasing such trifles, if I may believe my female informers, is by exchanging old suits of clothes for this brittle ware. The potters of China have, it seems, their factors at this distance, who retail out their several manufactures for cast clothes and superannuated garments. I have known an old petticoat metamorphosed into a punch-bowl, and a pair of breeches into a tea-pot. For this reason, my friend Tradewell in the city, calls his great room, that is nobly furnished out with china, his wife's wardrobe. 'In yonder corner, (says he,) are above twenty suits of clothes, and on that scrutoire above a hundred yards of furbelowed silk. You cannot imagine how many night-gowns, stays, and mantuas, went to the raising of that pyramid. The worst of it is, (says he,) a suit of clothes is not suffered to last half its time, that it may be the more vendible; so that in reality, this is but a more dexterous way of picking the husband's pocket, who is often purchasing a great vase of china, when he fancies that he is buying a fine head, or a silk gown for his wife. There is, likewise, another inconvenience in this female passion for china, namely, that it administers to them great matter of wrath and sorrow. How much anger and affliction are produced daily in the hearts of my dear country-women, by the breach of this frail furniture. Some of them pay half their servants' wages in china fragments, which their carelessness has produced. 'If thou hast a piece of earthenware, consider, (says Epictetus,) that it is a piece of earthen ware, and very easy and obnoxious to be broken: be not, therefore, so void of reason, as to be angry or grieved when this comes to pass.' In order, therefore, to exempt my fair readers from such additional and supernumerary calamities of life, I would advise them to forbear dealing in these perishable commodities, till such time as they are philosophers enough to keep their temper at the fall of a tea-pot, or a china cup. I shall further recommend to their serious consideration these three particulars: first, that all china ware is of a weak and transitory nature. Secondly, that the fashion of it is changeable: and thirdly, that it is of no use. And first of the first: the fragility of china is such as a reasonable being ought by no means to set its heart upon, though, at the same time, I am afraid I may complain with Seneca on the like occasion, that this very consideration recommends them to our choice, our luxury being grown so wanton, that this kind of treasure becomes the more valuable, the more easily we may be deprived of it, and that it receives a price from its brittleness. There is a kind of ostentation in wealth, which sets the possessors of it upon distinguishing themselves in those things where[a] it is hard for the poor to follow them. For this reason, I have often wondered that our ladies have not taken pleasure in egg-shells, especially in those which are curiously stained and streaked, and which are so very tender, that they require the nicest hand to hold without breaking them. But, as if the brittleness of this ware were not sufficient to make it costly, the very fashion of it is changeable, which brings me to my second particular.

It may chance, that a piece of china may survive all those accidents to which it is by nature liable, and last for some years if rightly situated and taken care of. To remedy, therefore, this inconvenience, it is so ordered, that the shape of it shall grow unfashionable, which makes new supplies always necessary, and furnishes employment for life to women of great and generous souls, who cannot live out of the mode. I myself remember, when there were few china vessels to be seen that held more than a dish of

[a] *Things where.* The adverb *where* includes the idea of *place*, and is, therefore, inaccurately used, when what precedes does not suggest that idea. If he had said—"Which puts the possessors of it upon striking out into those *paths*, where," the use of it had been proper.

coffee; but their size is so gradually enlarged, that there are many at present which are capable of holding half a hogshead. The fashion of the tea-cup is also greatly altered, and has run through a wonderful variety of colour, shape, and size.

But, in the last place, china ware is of no use. Who would not laugh, to see a smith's shop furnished with anvils and hammers of china? the furniture of a lady's favourite room is altogether as absurd: you see jars of a prodigious capacity, that are to hold nothing. I have seen horses, and herds of cattle, in this fine sort of porcelain, not to mention the several Chinese ladies, who, perhaps, are naturally enough represented in these frail materials.

Did our women take delight in heaping up piles of earthen platters, brown jugs, and the like useful products of our British potteries, there would be some sense in it. They might be ranged in as fine figures, and disposed of in as beautiful pieces of architecture; but there is an objection to these which cannot be overcome, namely, that they would be of some use, and might be taken down on all occasions, to be employed in the services of the family, besides that they are intolerably cheap, and most shamefully durable and lasting.

---

## No. 39. TUESDAY, MAY 25.

Nec verbum verbo curabis reddere fidus
Interpres—— HOR.

SINCE I have given public notice of my abode, I have had many visits from unfortunate fellow-sufferers who have been crossed in love as well as myself.

Will Wormwood, who is related to me by my mother's side, is one of those who often repair to me for advice. Will is a fellow of good sense, but puts it to little other use than to torment himself. He is a man of so refined an understanding, that he can set a construction upon every thing to his own disadvantage, and turn even a civility into an affront. He groans under imaginary injuries, finds himself abused by his friends, and fancies the whole world in a kind of combination against him. In short, poor Wormwood is devoured with the spleen: you may be sure a man of this humour makes a very whimsical lover. Be that as it will, he is now over head and ears in that passion, and by a very curious interpretation of his mistress's behaviour, has, in less than three months, reduced himself to a perfect skeleton. As her fortune is inferior to his, she gives him all the encouragement another man could wish, but has the mortification to find that her lover still sours upon her hands. Will is dissatisfied with her, whether she smiles or frowns upon him; and always thinks her too reserved, or too coming. A kind word, that would make another lover's heart dance for joy, pangs poor Will, and makes him lie awake all night.—As I was going on with Will Wormwood's amour, I received a present from my bookseller, which I found to be the Characters of Theophrastus, translated from the Greek into English, by Mr. Budgell.

It was with me, as I believe it will be with all who look into this translation; when I had begun to peruse it, I could not lay it by, until I had gone through the whole book; and was agreeably surprised to meet with a chapter in it, entitled, 'A discontented Temper,' which gives a livelier picture of my cousin Wormwood, than that which I was drawing for him myself. It is as follows:

## CHAP. XVII.

*A discontented Temper.*

"A discontented temper is 'a frame of mind which sets a man upon complaining without reason.' When one of his neighbours, who makes an entertainment, sends a servant to him with a plate of any thing that is nice, 'What, (says he,) your master did not think me good enough to dine with him?' He complains of his mistress, at the very time she is caressing him; and when she redoubles her kisses and endearments, 'I wish (says he,) all this came from your heart.' In a dry season, he grumbles for want of rain, and, when a shower falls, mutters to himself, 'Why could not this have come sooner?' If he happens to find a purse of money, 'Had it been a pot of gold, (says he,) it would have been worth stooping for.' He takes a great deal of pains to beat down the price of a slave; and after he has paid his money for him, 'I am sure, (says he,) thou art good for nothing, or I should not have had thee so cheap.' When a messenger comes with great joy, to acquaint him that his wife is brought to bed of a son, he answers, 'That is as much as to say, friend, I am poorer by half to-day than I was yesterday.' Though he has gained a cause, with full costs and damages, he complains that his counsel did not insist upon the most material points. If, after any misfortune has befallen him, his friends raise a voluntary contribution for him, and desire him to be merry, 'How is that possible, (says he,) when I am to pay every one of you his money again, and be obliged to you into the bargain?'"

The instances of a discontented temper, which Theophrastus has here made use of, like those which he singles out to illustrate the rest of his characters, are chosen with the greatest nicety, and full of humour. His strokes are always fine and exquisite, and though they are not sometimes violent enough to affect the imagination of a course reader, cannot but give the highest pleasure to every man of a refined taste, who has a thorough insight into human nature.

As for the translation, I have never seen any of a prose author, which has pleased me more. The gentleman who has obliged the public with it, has followed the rule which Horace has laid down for translators, by preserving every where the life and spirit of his author, without servilely copying after him word for word. This is what the French, who have most distinguished themselves by performances of this nature, so often inculcate, when they advise a translator to find out such particular elegancies in his own tongue, as bear some analogy to those he sees in the original, and to express himself by such phrases as his author would probably have made use of, had he written in the language into which he is translated. By this means, as well as by throwing in a lucky word, or a short circumstance, the meaning of Theophrastus is all along explained, and the humour very often carried to a greater height. A translator, who does not thus consider the different genius of the two languages in which he is concerned, with such parallel turns of thoughts and expression as correspond with one another in both of them, may value himself upon being a 'faithful interpreter;' but in works of wit and humour will never do justice to his author, or credit to himself.

As this is every where a judicious and a reasonable liberty, I see no chapter in Theophrastus where it has been so much indulged, and in which it was so absolutely necessary, as in the character of the Sloven. I find the translator himself, though he has taken pains to qualify it, is still apprehensive that there may be something too gross in the description. The reader will see with how much delicacy he has touched upon every particular, and cast into shades every thing that was shocking in so nauseous a figure.

## CHAP. XIX.

*A Sloven.*

"Slovenliness is 'such a neglect of a man's person, as makes him offensive to other people.' The sloven comes into company with a dirty pair of hands, and a set of long nails at the end of them, and tells you for an excuse that his father and grandfather used to do so before him. However, that he may outgo his forefathers, his fingers are covered with warts of his own raising. He is as hairy as a goat, and takes care to let you see it. His teeth and breath are perfectly well suited to one another. He lays about him at table after a very extraordinary manner, and takes in a meal at a mouthful; which he seldom disposes of without offending the company. In drinking, he generally makes more haste than good speed. When he goes into the bath, you may easily find him out by the scent of his oil, and distinguish him when he is dressed by the spots in his coat. He does not stand upon decency in conversation, but will talk smut, though a priest and his mother be in the room. He commits a blunder in the most solemn offices of devotion, and afterwards falls a laughing at it. At a concert of music he breaks in upon the performance, hums over the tune to himself, or if he thinks it long, asks the musicians 'whether they will never have done?' He always spits at random, and if he is at an entertainment, it is ten to one but it is upon the servant who stands behind him."

The foregoing translation brings to my remembrance that excellent observation of my Lord Roscommon's.

None yet have been with admiration read,
But who (besides their learning) were well-bred.

Lord Roscommon's Essay on translated Verse

If after this the reader can endure the filthy representation of the same figure exposed in its worst light, he may see how it looks in the former English version, which was published some years since, and is done from the French of Bruyere.

## NASTINESS OR SLOVENLINESS.

"Slovenliness is a lazy and beastly negligence of a man's own person, whereby he becomes so sordid, as to be offensive to those about him. You will see him come into company when he is covered all over with a leprosy and scurf, and with very long nails, and says, those distempers were hereditary; that his father and grandfather had them before him. He has ulcers in his thighs, and biles upon his hands, which he takes no care to have cured, but lets them run on till they are gone beyond remedy. His arm-pits are all hairy, and most part of his body like a wild beast. His teeth are black and rotten, which makes his breath stink so that you cannot endure him to come nigh you; he will also snuff up his nose and spit it out as he eats, and uses to speak with his mouth crammed full, and lets his victuals come out at both corners. He belches in the cup as he is drinking, and uses nasty stinking oil in the bath. He will intrude into the best company in sordid ragged clothes. If he goes with his mother to the soothsayers, he cannot then refrain from wicked and profane expressions. When he is making his oblations at the temple, he will let the dish drop out of his hand, and fall a laughing, as if he had done some brave exploit. At the finest concert of music he cannot forbear clapping his hands, and making a rude noise; will pretend to sing along with them, and fall a railing at them to leave off. Sitting at table, he spits full upon the servants who waited there."

I cannot close this paper without observing, that if gentlemen of leisure and genius would take the same pains upon some other Greek or Roman author, that has been bestowed upon this, we should no longer be abused by our booksellers, who set their hackney-writers at work for so much a sheet. The world would soon be convinced, that there is a great deal of difference between putting an author into English, and translating him.

END OF VOL. THREE.

www.ingramcontent.com/pod-product-compliance
Lightning Source LLC
LaVergne TN
LVHW010133110826
845151LV00002B/343

* 9 7 8 1 4 2 5 5 3 9 6 6 5 *